D1158025

Date Due

OCT 23 1973		
MAY 22 1974		
DEC 15 1976		
OCT 8 1977		
DEC 14 1982		
NOV 1 1992		
JAN 14 1993		

DEMCO NO. 38-298

The European Community in the 1970's

edited by

Steven Joshua Warnecke

Published for the

European Studies Committee,

Graduate Division,

City University of New York

The Praeger Special Studies program—
utilizing the most modern and efficient book
production techniques and a selective
worldwide distribution network—makes
available to the academic, government, and
business communities significant, timely
research in U.S. and international economic, social, and political development.

The European Community in the 1970's

PRAEGER SPECIAL STUDIES IN INTERNATIONAL POLITICS AND PUBLIC AFFAIRS

Praeger Publishers   New York   Washington   London

PRAEGER PUBLISHERS

111 Fourth Avenue, New York, N.Y. 10003, U.S.A.

5, Cromwell Place, London S.W.7, England

Published in the United States of America in 1972
by Praeger Publishers, Inc.

© 1972 by Praeger Publishers, Inc.

Library of Congress Catalog Card Number: 79-170277

Printed in the United States of America

To Joni

The contributors have used a number of designations when referring to the European Community. These include European Economic Community (EEC), Common Market, European Community (EC), and European Communities (EC). The, at times, interchangeable use of these terms—even in the documents of the Commission—is a reflection of the various stages through which the Community has progressed or is progressing.

For editorial purposes it was not possible to decide upon the consistent use of only one of these terms. In part the reader will be able to determine the particular meaning of any one of these designations from the context in which it is employed by the individual author. In part the following historical information will be helpful. On April 18, 1951, the treaty establishing the European Coal and Steel Community (ECSC) was signed in Paris. On March 25, 1957, the Rome Treaties were signed. The first one established the European Economic Community, which is also referred to as the Common Market in the treaties. The second treaty established the European Atomic Energy Community (Euratom) parallel to the EEC. In this book the singular refers to the first and the plural to both treaties. The ECSC, the EEC, and Euratom were legally and institutionally separate. Although the three Communities continue to remain legally separate, since July 1, 1967, they have shared a single set of institutions: the Commission, the Council of Ministers, the European Parliament, and the Court of Justice. The merger of the executives on that date was the first step toward efforts to draft a single Community treaty to replace the Paris and the two Rome Treaties. Consequently the designations mentioned above either refer to specific stages in the Community's development (e.g., EEC to the Common Market under the Rome Treaties, EC to a shortening of the term EEC in order to not limit the Community to economic affairs alone, and European Communities to the intention to merge the three existing treaties) or are used to refer to the entire period of the Community's existence since 1957 without distinguishing among the various stages in European Community development.

INTRODUCTION

Steven J. Warnecke

In rapid succession recent events have demonstrated that the postwar era of Soviet-United States preponderance in world politics has passed as new centers of power and new relationships among nations have emerged. For the United States the events which have reflected these changes include the failure in Vietnam, the expulsion of Nationalist China from and the admission of Communist China to the United Nations, the OPEC negotiations, the expropriation of American business holdings in Chile and Peru, as well as the independence of the members of the European Community during the current international monetary crisis.

From one perspective these changes in U.S. power and influence are relative and not absolute, since the United States is still economically and militarily the single strongest power in international politics. However, the fact that this is a relative decline does not decrease the concern in Washington that the United States at the moment is politically unable to focus and apply its power in pursuing its foreign policy goals in an increasingly complex world. If the implications of this relative decline are examined more closely they involve more than an inability to focus power to pursue specific goals. They involve the most basic questions of foreign policy ranging from the nature of the goals to be pursued to the legitimation of foreign policy itself.

In the West European case particularly the signs of competitive independence are, to say the least, disconcerting and confusing, because the manifestations of independence are the direct result of U.S. postwar policies which were designed to create a reliable, durable, and broadly based alliance through the reconstruction of Europe, the establishment of NATO, and the formation of the European Economic Community. Ironically, the identity of interests in military, trade, and financial matters which was assumed in the late 1940's has given way to fears of competition, trade wars, major differences in reforming the international monetary system, and differences in respect to collective military security. In part, the current divergence of interests is not ironic, since this development could have been foreseen to some extent when policies were first devised. However, the potential divergences were ignored or overlooked as a result of the geopolitical and geoeconomic considerations that brought Europe and America together in the late 1940's and early 1950's. The collective Western response to the Russians far outweighed and overshadowed considerations of the long-range potential effects of the economic relationships which were being established at that time. In addition, the United States was both prepared and able to make economic concessions in order to implement its foreign policy. Thus the current frictions are not only the result of European economic independence but also the result of changes in the domestic U.S. economy and the U.S. balance of payments which have greatly reduced America's ability to finance its foreign policy as well as its allies readiness to accept the methods which the United States has used until the present.

The reasons for the divergences in interests are not only economic. They also involve the simultaneous erosion of the moral, political, and strategic consensus upon which postwar U.S. policies were based. This consensus justified American leadership of and hegemony over the anti-Communist bloc, the acceptance of this role by the Europeans and the legitimation of a worldwide network of alliances and periodic interventions in the internal affairs of other countries. It is the latter area particularly which has most seriously called into question the right of the United States to present itself as the defender of Western political values as well as demonstrating the bankruptcy of the moralistic anti-Communism upon which so many aspects of American foreign policy have been founded. The Cuban missile crisis, the Vietnam War, and bilateral arms control talks between the United States and the U.S.S.R. have also contributed to a European lack of confidence in the identity of security interests between a power with global commitments and a group of nations oriented primarily toward Europe. The divergence in this area was reflected in the Brezhnev-Pompidou discussions in Paris in late October, 1971, which led to French-Soviet support for a European Security Conference.

It is obviously necessary for us to rethink and reformulate our foreign policies as well as the basis for the legitimacy of such policies. In any such reformulation Western Europe will continue to play a decisive role. This is not only a result of the numerous ties American policy-makers forged between the United States and Europe in the late 1940's, but also because they clearly perceived the importance and relevance of Europe and America to each other. But for many reasons the reformulation of policies will be very difficult. Psychologically, the United States is entering a new phase in its international relations with which it is not quite yet prepared to deal. In the postwar era we acted from a position of great strength and predominance. In a multipolar or "pentagonal" world as Andrew Pierre describes it in his article, the United States must adjust to its new role and position in a more complex international scene with many more players and many more centers of power depending upon which issues are salient. In this pentagonal world, the United States will be confronted with states and blocs which are simultaneously attempting to construct new geopolitical and geoeconomic basis for their international policies. In the case of the European Community there is a lack of clarity about where our interests are, which policies we should pursue, and what internal developments we should support within the enlarged Community. The unintended long-range implications of our original policies have come back to haunt us, particularly as our own redefinition of our interests are perceived by leaders of the European Community as being disruptive to their vital interests. One major indication of this conflict was mentioned by former French Premier Couve de Murville in a speech presented in New York City on October 29, 1971. He observed that the current international monetary crisis is undermining the solidarity of the EC* at a time when the Common Market is grappling with the problem of adding Great Britain as a new member. American policies were specifically divisive in respect to the EC efforts to establish a monetary union.

Stated simply the articles in this book are about the future relationship between Europe and the United States. But—in the 1970's—which Europe? The political, economic, and military frameworks within which European cooperation have taken place have not been identicial with one another either organizationally or in respect to their political goals and orientations. Economically the nations of Europe have been organized into the European Free Trade Association (EFTA) and the European Economic Community (EEC). Militarily they are members of the North Atlantic Treaty Organization with its effort to create an "Atlantic Community" which includes America. Strategically, this last point indicates the difficulty of separating a European sense of their interests from those of the United States', although in this area the geopolitical identity of Europe has been further complicated by the proposed security conference, the SALT talks, and *Ostpolitik*.

However, in recent years the problem of Europe's identity has become somewhat less complex. The Atlantic Idea and NATO have

---

*See "Editor's Note," page vii, for the Editor's explanation of the use of "EC" in this book.

reached their peaks and are now in decline as the political framework for Europe. European interest in the Soviet proposal for a security conference as well as efforts to assert a more independent role through the European Community are manifestations of these changes occurring in Europe's military alliance with the United States. The division of Europe into two economic blocs, EFTA and the EC, is now rapidly changing as the principal members of the former become members of the latter. In fact, the bloc which increasingly predominates in influence and power is the European Community. This predominance will be greater after the admission of Great Britain, Ireland, Norway, and Denmark to full membership in the EC. However, the EC has not yet superceded either its constituent member states or the remaining nonmember states in Europe by becoming the political representative of the entire area through the force of an independent legal, political, military, and financial identity.

In spite of the many achievements of the EC, the current period involving the enlargement of the EC is both enticing and anxiety provoking. It is enticing insofar as it provides the intimation of the possibility for greater political unity in Western Europe, even of the possibility for creating a United States of Europe. It is anxiety provoking insofar as the European supranational Federalists fear that their goals are potentially threatened by the enlargement of the EC from six to ten members. Although not all European political leaders share the goals of the Federalists, most thoughtful Europeans are concerned about the future framework of European cooperation. It has only been through the way stations of the Marshall Plan, the OEEC, NATO, and finally the European Economic Community that the individual European states were able to begin to reverse the decline in influence and power of Western Europe in world affairs. This was done in close cooperation with the United States. However, the identity of interests which made this cooperation possible has changed substantially. As François Duchêne wrote in the October, 1971, issue of *Foreign Affairs*, in light of these changes Europe will have to find a military identity for itself within the NATO framework. In addition, the Europeans will have to be prepared to deal with another major change in the international environment. With a relative shift away from quasi-military confrontations of the Cold War to the civilian and political processes characterizing the increasing interdependence of industrial societies, the Europeans will have to assert their political, economic, and technological identity if they want some degree of independence from the United States and the Soviet bloc.

Whatever confusion may exist about the political framework for future European cooperation as well as about the viability of the

European Community as this framework, Ambassador J. Robert Schaetzel, United States Representative to the European Communities, observed concisely in testimony before the Foreign Economic Subcommittee of the House Foreign Affairs Committee on July 20, 1971, that:

> The academicians, the theologians, the romantics, the pragmatists and the businessmen all can agree on one proposition: There is a European Community which has survived a series of hard tests and crisis—it exists; this Community will be enlarged and will include ten member states by 1973.

Although the Soviet Union has only begrudging begun to admit the existence of the EC, the Chinese Communists have, for political reasons, been much more enthusiastic about the EC. Peking has expressed approval of Western European integration on the ground that it is weakening the "imperialistic" forces of both the United States and the Soviet Union. Thus the European Community is gradually emerging as an important factor in world politics.

What the existence of the EC means can be seen from a few facts and figures. From 1958 to 1970 the gross national product of the member countries increased from $159 billion to $500 billion. The per capita GNP increased from $965 to $2,500. If Britain, Ireland, Norway, and Denmark become members, the EEC of Ten will have a population of about 260 million people (U.S., 210 million; U.S.S.R., 250 million) and a GNP of $600 billion. By 1980 it will have a trillion dollar economy. After the enlargement it will be responsible for more than 40 percent of world trade.

In an increasingly complex international system, the European Community not only presents other nations with a new trading partner. It presents them with a new ally through whom they can diversify their foreign political contacts as well as reduce their dependence on the United States. These changes and developments have been reflected in the various agreements the EC has negotiated or is negotiating with other nations. The Yaoundé Convention affiliates eighteen former European African colonies and Madagascar with the EC in a preferential trade and aid agreement. The Arusha Convention links Nigeria, Kenya, Uganda, and Tanzania in a somewhat similar agreement to Brussels. There are associative agreements with Greece and Turkey not to mention the trade talks with Japan and the remaining EFTA members which are going on now. Moreover, talks are to begin soon with Latin American countries on the basis of the Buenos Aires declaration. In terms of aid, as Uwe Kitzinger points out, the EC and its member states now give $5.3 billion or 1.2 percent of their GNP to the rest of the world. In 1969, the Ten gave $6.3 billion in comparison to the United States which gave $4.6 billion or .5 percent of its GNP. Finally, during the summer of 1971, the EC unilaterally created better trade conditions for ninety-one underdeveloped nations by making available generalized preferences without waiting for other advanced countries to make similar concessions.

In an address on March 26, 1971, before the American Bar Association meeting in Chicago Professor Ralf Dahrendorf, the member of the EC Commission responsible for external relations, described these developments as the basis for "the evolution of a mature partnership" between the United States and the EC. The effects of this new role were first demonstrated for the United States by the negotiating front of the EC in the Kennedy Rounds. The current European positions since the May, 1971, monetary crisis and President Nixon's announcement of the new economic policy are further manifestations of the relative shift in economic and political power between the United States and the EC. In fact, the President's Trade Commission Report (The Williams Commission) issued on September 14, 1971, speaks of the United States operating in a "radically" changed environment from the one we knew before World War II. It believes that it is "imperative" for the United States to "bring its international trade and investment policies into line with the new realities."

In order to explore the implications the consolidation and impending expansion of the European Community have for the United States, a multinational conference was held at the Graduate Division of the City University of New York on October 8-9, 1971. It was sponsored by the Graduate Division's European Studies Committee and was entitled, "The Future of Relations Between the United States and a Uniting Europe: Rivalry or Cooperation." The papers which were presented examined the following questions. In respect to domestic European affairs will the enlargement of the EC provide a new impetus for cooperation among the member states? Can the enlarged EC maintain its unity? How will the EC composed of ten nations function? In regard to exterior matters what attitude should the EC take toward the United States and the Third World? What policies should it pursue in international trade and monetary matters? What policies should the United States pursue toward a uniting Europe? In addition, in order to adequately cover the range of issues, other contributions were requested from European and American specialists, though these were not presented at that conference. Finally, the collection was designed to place the examination of regional efforts at cooperation and integration in a more complex and dynamic political and historical framework than is currently used in American political science. This is reflected particularly in the various articles in this volume which discuss the great extent to which domestic European political and economic integration is interrelated with and dependent on the successful co-ordination of the member states' foreign policies and on a favorable international environment for these policies. This is an area which is also inadequately dealt with in the functionalist approach to the integration process.

The first section of this book deals with the internal political and economic structure of the EC. Both the article on the political structure "The European Community After British Entry: Federation or Con-federation?" and Uwe Kitzinger's article on the political economy of the enlarged Community present complementary analytical perspectives which critically assess the relevance and viability of the Federalist approach for dealing with European political and economic problems. While both articles strongly affirm the necessity for strengthening economic and political cooperation, they find a lack of a clear and binding image of what the domestic institutions and goals of the enlarged EC should be. This problem is particularly evident when the notion is examined that the EC is simply the nation-state writ large. Which state is meant is not clear since there are a wide range to choose from among the member nations. Moreover, is this analogy of EC institutions to those of the nation-state a valid one? By placing more emphasis than in the Federal approach on the continued existence of the nation-state, the authors suggest it may be premature to speak of a confederal or federal framework as the model for European develop-ment. It may be possible to conceive of an evolution in which functional integration is paralleled by political diversity. Such a pos-sibility seems to be supported by the problematic nature of the functionalist "spill over theory" which is examined in both articles. Furthermore, the political dynamics of a EC of ten member states may intensify factors already present in the current EC of six states that impede further movement toward supranationalism. Although the increasing interest among European leaders in a summit conference to decide upon future EC policy after British entry is not treated specifically, the discussions of the Davignon formula and the Davignon Committee in the Pierre and Jaquet articles are relevant to under-standing many of the aspects and problems of the framework in which such a conference would be held. In addition, the examination of the "Wieland Europa" newspaper articles in the first contribution to this book suggests the inference that the use of a summit type forum in light of the dynamics of the EC analyzed in the first of these articles could potentially lead to a revival of some elements of the Fouchet Plan. Heinz Hartmann's article is a case study of the efforts to create a

European labor-management policy. He addresses himself to the question of whether it will be possible to standardize labor-management relations in Europe to the point at which companies in different countries can merge without significant upheaval in the relationships between employers and employees. In order to examine this question, he deals with changes in union structure and forms of participation as well as with working class ideologies and aspirations in the member states. Institutionally, he focuses on the German form of comanagement as one possible framework for a "harmonized" labor-management policy in the EC. By placing this problem in a dynamic political and social context rather than concentrating on its technical and legal aspects he reaches important conclusions concerning the difficulties as well as the opportunities for establishing new forms of cooperation. The first section concludes with excerpts from the De Wolff Report on the EC Medium Term Economic Policy. The excerpts are included as an introduction to the prospects and difficulties in respect to coordinating national economic policies and priorities.

The second section of this volume examines the various aspects of the current economic difficulties between the United States. William Diebold's contribution presents an excellent and relevant analysis of these complex problems. He examines the original reasons for American support for European unification, the ways in which this support was given and the conditions which were attached to it as well as the specific features of integration with which the United States has been primarily concerned. By placing this constellation in an historical framework he demonstrates how American policy toward Europe has changed, and how the evolution of this policy has contributed to many of the economic tensions between the United States and the EC today. He concludes that the first task of diplomacy is to keep the inevitable disputes under control. The next task is to devise a framework through which change can occur. The construction of such a framework will not be easy, since as his article demonstrates it must take into account the relative change in America's world economic and political position while not dividing and consequently weakening Europe on such issues as the proposed monetary union. Unfortunately, the task is all the more difficult since neither we nor the Europeans have a clear and viable policy toward the political and economic structure of the EC.

Ralf Dahrendorf's article should be entitled "The Possibilities and Limits of a European Communities Foreign Economic Policy," since such policy is at present the principal area in which the EC can be active in world affairs. In spite of this qualification the article not only reveals the emergence of the EC in world commercial and financial relations but also the efforts of that member of the Commission responsible for exterior relations to define such a role for the Community. Of particular interest is his discussion of the Davignon Committee as a potential framework for decision-making in the enlarged EC. Harald Malmgren's contribution significantly raises bilateral U.S.-EC trade disputes to a global framework by defining the solution for these disputes in terms of their general economic and political effects. He emphasizes that there are essentially two options for the EC and the United States. One is to allow the emergence of bloc orientations in the global economy. The other is based upon a conception that economic nationalism and regionalism are politically divisive and that international rules and procedures are necessary to minimize conflicts between the major powers. Such a system would not only be beneficial for the major powers, it is crucial to the less strong nations. However, the separation of economic and political questions in the European Community as a result of its institutional structure permits it to operate without taking into account these broader considerations. In the case study for this section, Christopher Wright observes that there has been little effort in Europe to develop an authoritative overview on a multinational or transnational basis for technology policy. Among the problems which he explores are the difficulties in selecting projects, formulating investment policies, planning for larger markets, and developing plans for enlightened social control of new technologies. He includes important discussions on the conditions under which advanced technologies can be developed and the types of markets for which planning must take place as well as the extent to which technologies will lead to cooperation and common decision-making structures. This latter point is of particular importance since it involves an examination of the functionalist assumption about technical cooperation leading to joint political structures.

The last section of the book deals with the major foreign policy issues not only between the EC and the United States but also between Europe in the broader sense and the United States. Andrew Pierre's article presents a comprehensive evaluation and assessment of the relationship of U.S. global interests to our European responsibilities and obligations. By placing his analysis in what he describes as the emerging "pentagonal" framework of international relations he examines from this new perspective the development of multilateral diplomacy in the 1970's. He writes that American global responsibilities for an accommodation with the Soviet Union will lead to American efforts to reduce some of its security responsibilities in Europe during the 1970's. If Europe is to be prepared to deal with this problem it must develop additional and revived institutions based upon a European sense of security identity. However, both its foreign political and military policies will be more regional than global. Both he and Louis Jaquet agree that Europe will still be our most important ally, but the divergences and convergences in the two articles reveal the extent to which the interests upon which past cooperation have been based are being examined and redefined. In addition, Jaquet's article brings out clearly how the creation of the European Community was a result of the foreign policies of six countries and how, to a great extent, the continued evolution of the EC is a foreign policy question for the Six. He also provides an examination of the Davignon Report and the Davignon Committee not only in terms of the viability of the latter, but also in respect to how such a committee designed for foreign policy coordination will contribute to or detract from efforts to consolidated European cooperation around the European Community framework. Gordon Adams' case study on the efforts of the EC to devise a common African foreign policy is a highly relevant companion piece to that section of the Jaquet article on foreign policy coordination. He describes the different economic and political interests of the Six in Africa and analyzes how these differences impeded the formulation of a common Community policy. He concludes that if a common policy is likely to be the case on any issues, national interests will naturally have to coincide. He feels, however, that it is difficult to attain such a consensus, and, in any case, such a consensus is precarious and easily disturbed by external forces. Consequently, the addition of new member states may not only make the process but also the substance of foreign policy coordination more complex and difficult. This will have significant ramifications for the future of the EC as the current efforts to establish simultaneously a European monetary union and define an external international monetary policy demonstrate.

In conclusion the editor would like to express his appreciation to the contributors not only for their valuable articles but also for their willingness to coordinate their efforts with one another to produce a balanced and comprehensive volume. He owes his thanks to them for patiently suffering his inquiries, memos, and long letters, as well as the documents and newspaper clippings he sent to them. The editor and contributors to this volume are grateful to the Ford Foundation whose support made their collective effort possible. Appreciation is also due to the members of the City University of New York's Graduate Division Faculty Seminar on European Community Studies who participated at our monthly meetings where many of these ideas were discussed, as well as to the Chairman of the European Studies Committee, Professor Feliks Gross for his interest and generous assistance.

Finally, the editor is particularly grateful to two Europeans whose efforts to encourage European and American cooperation are known to their friends: Mr. Franco Ciarnelli and Dr. Philipp Schmidt-Schlegel.

CONTENTS

EUROPE
OF THE TEN
IN THE 1970's

THE EUROPEAN COMMUNITY
AFTER BRITISH ENTRY:
FEDERATION
OR CONFEDERATION?

Steven J. Warnecke

After years of stalemate and crisis the movement toward European political unification seemed to receive a new impulse as a result of the Hague Conference of December, 1969. In a joint communique the leaders of the six member nations stated that they were meeting "to reaffirm their belief in the political objectives which give the Community its meaning and purport, [and announced] their determination to carry their undertaking through to the end and their confidence in the final success of their efforts." The French, who under De Gaulle had blocked new initiatives designed to expand the powers of the Community's institutions, provided the conference with a concise, enticing, and ambiguous political formula: Achèvement, Approfondissement, Élargissement—Completion, Deepening, Enlargement. By the end of the conference—nine days before the EC twelve-year transition period was to end and much to the surprise of observers—the foreign ministers of the Six made a series of important decisions for implementing the goals espoused by the political leaders and heads of state. In order to make immediate progress beyond the institutional immobilism which had prevented completion of the EC within the framework of the Rome Treaty, the foreign ministers reached agreements concerning the permanent arrangements for the financing of the the Common Agricultural Policy, providing the Community with its own financial resources from 1978, and strengthening the European Parliament's budgetary powers. In respect to the deepening of the Community the political leaders instructed their foreign ministers to study the best way to achieve progress in political unification within the context of Community enlargement. This was to be based on their determination to develop monetary cooperation on the foundation of harmonized economic policies and their commitment to "rapid progress" toward economic union. Shortly thereafter, the Davignon and Werner Committees were established to draft plans on these long-range economic and political goals. Both issued plans in 1970, the former for foreign policy cooperation and the latter for monetary union. Finally, the Hague Conference cleared the way for serious negotiations with Great Britain, Ireland, Norway, and Denmark to enlarge the EC.

Professor Ralf Dahrendorf, the member of the Commission of the European Communities responsible for external relations, commented on these developments in an address before the American Bar Association meeting in Chicago on March 26, 1971. He said that "if we continue along this road but a little further, we shall have reached the point of no return of the <u>political</u> association of European states."

DIVERGENT APPROACHES TO UNIFICATION

In spite of these considerable successes there is great confusion about the continued institutional development of the European Community. The conflicts concerning these institutions are not a result of the impending enlargement, but simply an intensification of difficulties which have existed since the EC was established. In fact, these difficulties were inherent in the evocative French formula for the Hague Conference. However, the formula hid them by neatly skirting the divisive political question of supranational federalism and governmental confederalism by not referring to any specific institutional structure.

After nearly fifteen years these models with their diverging perspectives on the nation-state and national sovereignty are still the principal plans that divide the supporters of European cooperation. Confederalism has been most clearly identified with General De Gaulle and the Fouchet Plan, while Federalism has been most closely associated with such supranationalists as Jean Monnet, Altiero Spinelli, and Walter Hallstein. The Confederalists believe that the nation-state is the only unit that can provide the political basis for European cooperation. Consequently, they are not prepared to transfer sovereignty in vital areas to a European government. Instead they prefer the European Community to be an intergovernmental framework through which national cooperation takes place. Therefore, they have emphasized the importance of the Council of Ministers as the representative of the States rather than the Commission as the potential European supranational executive. This position is advanced, however, with the qualification "at present," thus not entirely foreclosing developments beyond a confederal framework. The Federalists accept the continued existence of the nation-state but only as a subordinate unit within a supranational federal framework. They envision major changes in both the powers and role of the nation-state as it voluntarily and gradually transfers sovereignty in several key areas to an independent European government. Such a European government will receive its legitimation from and base its independence upon a directly elected European Parliament.)

While the confederal approach does little to alter the basic powers and prerogatives of the nation-state, the federal approach is more complicated since its goals are more ambitious. Consequently, two processes have been elaborated for attaining a supranational federal framework: the functionalist administrative approach most closely identified with Monnet and the "political" federalist approach identified with individuals such as Spinelli. The Functionalists, instead of making a frontal assault on the nation-state, have developed a more indirect, rationalistic, legalistic method for an ad hoc process of regional integration. This method is based on the policy that segmental cooperation and "integration" in a sufficiently large number of specific areas would inevitably "spill over" toward and precipitate the crystallization of more complete and comprehensive forms of political and economic union. The model for this method is the European Coal and Steel Community. The Confederalists have criticized this method as being apolitical and technocratic. Federalists such as Spinelli have maintained that it is too slow and too vulnerable since it leaves the political future of the Community too much at the mercy of the nation-states. The best means for attaining the Federalist goals is to create a political Europe first on the basis of a mass political movement. Therefore, the directly elected European Parliament becomes a key element in plans to establish a supranational European government. Since sovereignty still resides in the hands of the nation-state the method of the European Community has been closer to the Monnet approach.

The Federalist and Functionalist plans have been of major importance for providing the political goals and procedural guidelines for the formulation of cooperative policies within the boundaries of the Rome Treaty. However, the conflict between the political antipodes of Federalism and Confederalism have been apparent at every juncture in the efforts to establish and develop the EC. As a result of these unresolved tensions the EC, which was finally established by the Rome Treaties as well as the formal and informal institutions that have emerged on the basis of the treaty are the confusing and unsystematic mixture of international, regional, and national components. They defy description according to the standard categories of either international cooperation or national political organization and have lead to two widely diverging interpretations—which contain strong normative elements—about the EC and its future.

The Federalists, borne forward by a great faith that there is or can be a relatively unilinear movement from the nation-state to a supranational Europe, see the EC as an evolving political system which is in part superceding, in part modifying, the sovereignty of the nation-state. The Rome Treaty, which is the "constitution" of the emerging political system, has modeled the European institutions very closely to those of the nation-state parliaments, executives, and high courts. It imposes deadlines for steps toward integration and gives the EC authority to make laws and sign treaties in specific areas with third countries without the need for ratification by member state parliaments. Within this emerging political system the Federalists focus on the Commission as the government *in spe*. The existence of the Council of Ministers and the Permanent Representatives, both representatives of the nation-states; the problem of unanimous voting in the Council of Ministers; and the lack of real European political parties are seen as remnants of national sovereignty which will disappear in time if the political will is present for making such changes. In addition, the May monetary crisis, the establishment of the Davignon Committee, and British entry are interpreted insofar as they detract from or contribute to the supranational aspirations of the Federalists.

From the Confederalist perspective, the Federalists are moralists who emphasize the ideal without devoting sufficient attention to what is or what can be realistically constructed on the basis of what does exist. They feel it is misleading to assert that a European "community" composed of nation-states is analogous to a national community with an historical identity composed of regions. Such an analogy leads to the effort to construct European institutions in the image of national institutions. President Pompidou restating the Gaullist position said in an interview on BBC television on May 17, 1971: "There is no European nation. There are British and French and German and Italian nations. So I do not believe that a purely technical and administrative power can impose itself on the various states and the various nations. . . ." In other words institutions without the force of historical legitimacy behind them could not be adequate substitutes at this time to discharge the domestic and external responsibilities of the national governments.) Thus the Confederalists emphasize the Council of Ministers and the Permanent Representatives rather than the Commission as the key institutions of the EC) In addition, the French opposition to further institutional development along supranational lines has been reflected in the Fouchet Plan as well as the number of executive functions delegated to committees independent of the Commission. Moreover, although there is cooperation in a wide range of economic matters, foreign policy and military affairs still remain principally the domain of the nation-states. In fact, the entire history of the establishment and elaboration of EC institutions is the history of high diplomacy among the member states. Thus when the Commission is permitted to represent the EC it is on the basis of multilateral diplomatic compromises among the six governments. In addition, the Six continue to pursue "independent" foreign policies, although efforts are now underway as a result of the Davignon Report to coordinate these policies. However, the institutional form of the Davignon Committee and its responsibilities are one manifestation of the policy to prevent the shift of important sovereign responsibilities from the nation-states to the Commission. The Commission has attempted to circumvent these tactics through the process of "engrenage": of coopting national civil servants and interest groups into the decision-making process of the EC. However, this has not been an effective policy. The result has been the failure to develop a political infrastructure for a supranational community.

IMPLICATIONS OF BRITISH ENTRY

As was to be expected the Hague Conference and the British negotiations have triggered intense controversy and political maneuvering concerning the future political structure of the EC. Each group has projected its particular hopes into the implications of British entry for the Community. At first the Federalist cause seemed to gain most from the Hague Conference after years of being held at bay by General De Gaulle. This was particularly true after the Council of Ministers accepted a modified Werner Plan which outlined a gradual movement toward supranational institutions in the monetary and economic union. However, a series of events has demonstrated once again the extreme vulnerability of the Federalist movement as a result of its dependence on the nation-states and national groups. Aside from the May monetary crisis which demonstrated the extent to which European cooperation and integration are intermeshed with international problems, the principal event was the reintroduction of the confederal idea by President Pompidou at his press conference on January 21, 1971, four days before the Franco-German talks. In retrospect it was the announcement of the political price both Germany and Great Britain would have to pay for French acceptance of British entry into the European Community. In his May 17, 1971 interview on BBC television before his historic meeting with Prime Minister Heath, President Pompidou repeated his position in much greater detail. Consequently, it was not surprising when Heath and Pompidou issued a joint communique on May 21 at the end of their meeting stating: "With regard to the organization and evolution of the Community the talks revealed that their views were completely identical." What this identity of views means is expressed very clearly in the British White Paper issued in July.

> The Community is no federation of provinces or countries. It constitutes a Community of great and established nations, each with its own personality and tradition. The practical working of the Community accordingly reflects the reality that sovereign Governments are represented round the table. On a question where a Government considers that vital national interests are involved, it is established that the decisions should be unanimous. . . . There is no question of any erosion of essential national sovereignty; what is proposed is a sharing and an enlargement of individual national sovereignty in the general interest.

The British position did not represent a capitulation to the French design for the European Community. As De Gaulle had realized the British on the basis of their history and tradition would be much more likely to support a confederal rather than a federal organization for the European Community. In addition, at the Franco-German talks in January, 1971, Chancellor Brandt had indicated that the German government would be taking a much more "pragmatic" approach to the establishment of a supranational Community than the past policy of the Federal Republic had indicated. In fact, there are some signs that a strong supranational European Community may not be entirely in the economic interests of Germany. Moreover, this new tact away from supranationality is apparently reenforced by the fact that in spite of the present political framework of the EC the Six member nations have been able to operate within the institutions of the EC to their own mutual economic advantage without having to transfer sovereignty to Brussels.

A somewhat different manifestation of the vulnerability of the Federalist Movement is exemplified by the General Resolution of the Eighth Congress of the Socialist Parties of the EC countries held in Brussels from June 28 to June 30, 1971. The Congress rejected any form of confederation and reaffirmed its conviction that the integration process "must be continued through the economic and monetary union to its ultimate completion in a federal United States of Europe." It foresaw that not only these goals but "the cause of democratic socialism will be greatly enlarged by British membership in the EC." These resolutions are ironic given the extremely defensive, nationalistic positions of former Prime Minister Harold Wilson and the Trades Union Congress.

THE ROLE OF THE COMMISSION

The apparent success of the French initiative to revive the confederal approach to European unity has caused great concern at the Commission in Brussels as well as among its Federalist supporters. However, the Commission's efforts to defend itself against this strategy by presenting optimistic interpretations of the implications of British entry for the EC institutions in terms of its own federalist aspirations are not convincing. First of all the failure of the Community to create a supranational structure probably made British opinion more favorable to entry than might otherwise have been. In addition, the appeals to the traditional federal goals and to moral suasion as contained in such restatements of the original position by Professor Hallstein in *Der Unvollendete Bundesstaat* no longer seem to have the same usefulness and relevance they had during the years of the EC. Not only have serious doubts been raised about the realism of the Federalists' position in respect to their understanding of the nation-state but criticisms have been expressed about their legalistic approach to political psychology and political sociology in their efforts to create the political infrastructure for a supranational Community. This problem has emerged most clearly when agreements reached by national elites on highly defined technical issues are examined in respect to the extent to which they actually have or can have those psychological and institutional implications necessary for establishing a political union. Furthermore, the waning fortunes of the Federalists are a result of the failure of the Commission to sufficiently strengthen itself by shifting powers from the nation-states to Brussels. The concomitant "decline" in the influence and power of the Commission during the 1960's has also weakened the Federalist Movement. British entry, as many suspected who fought against the enlargement of the Community, appears also to be making a contribution to the weakening of the supranational goals of the Federalists. This may not only be a result of the conscious choice of a confederal policy, but the inevitable outcome of an association of ten sovereign states. Finally, as Altiero Spinelli, the member of the Commission responsible for industrial and structural policy, indicated in a speech before the Chambers of Commerce of the Community in Rotterdam on June 11, 1971, the various plans for strengthening the EC are too vague. Stated more strongly, there appears to be a lack of a clear, generally accepted official vision for the future of the European Community.

Although he indicated his continued support for the establishment of a European government independent of the member states' governments with real decision-making powers and its own administration, Spinelli, very significantly, expressed doubts about the role the Commission would play. He even suggested that the present task of the Commission is to examine "precisely what is meant by 'create a European government' independently of whether the Commission itself will be this European government or not, what prerogatives are to be transferred from the individual States to the central institutions and what powers the European Parliament should possess."

In anticipation of British entry and in opposition to the Gaullist position, ad hoc efforts have been made to shore up the Commission and the Federalist hopes attached to its survival by developing strategies based on moral and legal interpretations of the various treaties and agreements concerning the EC structure and goals. In an interview for the Southwest German Radio Network, Joseph Luns, former Foreign Minister of the Netherlands, observed that the Community cannot continue to make all decisions subject to unanimous vote. It would be necessary sooner or later to move toward decision-making by majority voting. Wilhelm Haferkampf, a member of the present EC Commission writing in *Europäische Gemeinschaft* stated that the "engagement phase" with England, which was to last until the association treaty goes into effect on January 1, 1973, should be shortened by one year. This would prevent unnecessary delays in the internal construction of the EC. Spinelli during a symposium in London on July 13, 1971, on external relations of the enlarged EC warned against the danger of losing momentum since it would lead to the loss of the opportunity to create a supranational Europe because national policies would diverge again. These are basically technical and legal moves based on moral imperatives. Such tactics amount neither to a policy nor to an effective political defense of what has been attained, since they continue to operate within the framework of the Federalist Movement. What is needed is a "realistic" analysis of why the Federalist ideals have not been translated into practice. This analysis must go beyond the claim that only political will has been lacking.

Oddly enough, the most extreme analysis of the weaknesses of the present Community has been attributed to a member of the Commission. This analysis, which caused severe internal conflicts within the Commission and the European Parliament after it was published, appeared in the July 9th and 16th issues of the Hamburg weekly *Die Zeit*. Writing under the pseudonym of Wieland Europa, the author claimed that the treaties upon which considerable developments were possible are now exhausted. Supranationality did not evolve and, in fact, the fiction of a European government free from national control was only bearable for the member nations as long as there was little to do on the Community level. As European affairs have become more important for the member states, the states have withdrawn responsibility from the Commission and placed it elsewhere. Thus as Europe is more important the Commission looses its importance. Consequently, a new basis for political cooperation is necessary and is contained in Article 15 of the final communique issued at the Hague Conference. In this article the foreign ministers were charged with the responsibility of determining the best way to make progress toward political union within an enlarged Community. The Davignon Report, which dealt with this problem, has created an intergovernmental formula which is international rather than supranational. It allows the foreign ministers to go beyond the treaty without having to resort to tortuous interpretations. Although created for cooperation in foreign affairs, it is directly applicable to the European Community. Thus in place of the formula of "supranationality" which has increasingly been a brake to further European cooperation, the author proposed a new formula, the common exercise of sovereignty of the European nations (. . . gemeinsamen Ausübung der Souveraenität der Europäischen Nationen). The major difficulty with this reformulation, which the author himself recognized, is that unlike the supranational formula for cooperation, which is morally, if not implicitly legally binding, the intergovernmental formula is considerably more vague in this respect.

Unfortunately, rather than meet this interpretation head on, the Commission apparently is continuing to work within a legalistic framework. The tasks alluded to by Spinelli in Rotterdam were finally embodied in a new committee established by the Commission on June 30. The mandate of the committee was prepared by four members of the Commission—Raymond Barre, Sicco Mansholt, Wilhelm Haferkampf, and Altiero Spinelli. The committee is composed of fourteen independent political figures from member and candidate countries with a special knowledge of constitutional law. The mandate has charged the committee members to explore the possibilities for widening the powers of the European Parliament in conjunction with the gradual widening of the Community's power as well as to examine the gradual transfer of national responsibilities to the Community in order to arm the EC with an effective institutional system The committee should pay particular attention to the relationship between the strengthening of the European Parliament's powers and its direct election by universal suffrage. Finally, the committee should direct its work by the institutional implications of the transition from the first to the second phase of the economic and monetary union.

(In order to understand the potential implications of British entry for the EC institutions as well as to evaluate the accuracy of the Confederalist approach and the viability of the Federalist plan, it is necessary to move beyond the obvious manifestations of power politics and the description of strategies and events. Thus such questions as the reasons for the continued existence of the nation-state and the failure until now to construct a political infrastructure cannot be circumvented by accepting the assertion that only the absence of political will or diplomatic impasses stand in the way of shifting sovereignty from the national capitols to Brussels. This must also include an examination of the extent to which the terms of the French formula—completion, deepening, and enlargement—are compatible or incompatible, as well as the extent to which the EC can be more effective in political and economic affairs than the nation-state.

Unfortunately, the moralistic idealism of the Federalists and the technocratic orientation of the Functionalists have clouded the discussion of the constellation of external and internal conditions which have contributed to and supported regional cooperation. In addition, both approaches have led to a misunderstanding and misinterpretation of the role and reasons for the continued existence of the nation-state as well as the direction in which cooperation has been evolving and the causes of the present stalemate and confusion about further developments. Moreover, as a result of the effect of recent events on the viability of the Federalist plan, it is not entirely clear whether Professor Dahrendorf's statement that the EC has almost crossed "the point of no return of the political association of European states" can be interpreted optimistically for the supranationalists.

In order to briefly examine these questions the dynamics of a Community composed of nation-states will be analyzed particularly in respect to the proposed monetary and economic union.

THE DYNAMICS OF NATION-STATES IN A REGIONAL COMMUNITY

The Federalists have asserted since 1945 that the nation-state was no longer the adequate or legitimate basis for political organization. After the failure to establish the European Defense Community, efforts to establish a European political community were limited to economic matters. Under these circumstances only that part of the Federalist argument was used which asserted that the nation-state is undesirable because it prevents the establishment of a continental market which would lead to a pooling and more rational and efficient use of resources. Such a continental market would cause the Gross National Product of the Community to grow more rapidly, contribute to the general welfare and strengthen the competitive position of a European Community in world trade. What was necessary was to create the legal, institutional, and technical framework for such a market.

Consequently in the Treaty of Rome each member state obligated itself to coordinate economic policy and to pursue the gradual approximation of economies. Such convergence and compatability in the common interest seemed desirable because of the increasing interdependence of the economies and the necessity for the effective defense of common interests in international monetary and trade matters. This leads logically to shared institutions. Thus, in February, 1971, the Six formally launched a three-stage plan for a complete economic and monetary union by the end of 1980. The first stage runs from January 1, 1971, to December 31, 1973. By the end of the last phase there could be a common reserve, fixed exchange rates, and a single currency for the entire Community. During the first stage the Six are supposed to narrow the exchange rate margins between their currencies, set up a $2 billion medium term reserve pool to support member states suffering from fundamental balance-of-payments difficulties, coordinate short and medium term economic and budgetary policy, hold regular meetings of their finance ministers and central bank governors, gradually adopt a joint position on international monetary questions and step up harmonization of taxes. For the functionalists with their "spill over theory" the monetary union is the logical step beyond sectoral integration toward a full-fledged European political economy. Although in its initial stages this plan is a technical agreement among national elites, in turn, it is supposed to lead to significant restructuring of the behavior of parties, interest groups, and governments. The next "logical" step in the creation of a European political economy is the Medium Term Economic Policy, since a monetary union is not possible without price stability and coordinated rates of growth. In addition, the medium term economic policy will not only contribute to the more rational use of resources through monetary, fiscal, regional, structural, and investment policies, but these policies will also contribute to the convergence in standards of living through the EC. Such policies are to be the basis for social stability in and the political acceptability of the EC.

Both plans are fascinating insofar as they attempt to deal with the EC as though it were or could be one political economy. The De Wolff Report of March, 1971, on the Medium Term Economic Policy not unexpectedly indicates that the major difficulty in establishing the political union necessary for a European political economy is that decision-making is still principally the responsibility of the nation-states. As long as sovereignty remains on the national level, the other difficulties facing a successful medium term policy such as the weakness of Community institutions, the inadequate harmonization of economic and social goals of the member states and the lack of coordination of the macroeconomic instruments of the member states will continue.

The Federalist efforts to construct an economic and political community have a logic in terms of their own assumptions. Once these assumptions are examined there appear to be major difficulties. The first difficulty is that the model the Federalists and Functionalists use for understanding the EC and the integration process is not sufficiently political or historical. It is based almost entirely on legal and technical approaches to the solution of problems defined exclusively in economic terms. Political problems arising from questions of class, region, religion, nationality, and political philosophy are either transformed or reduced in magnitude by being redefined in terms of "efficiency" from the viewpoint of production, organization, decision-making, invest-ment, and distribution. One example is the legally and technically correct assumption that in a currency union balance-of-payment problems of member countries would be transformed into regional problems. Such ideas suggest the possibility of a continental political community. However, as long as national communication patterns and national governments and administrations exist such efforts to trans-pose political problems into an apparently "nonnational" key are false. These problems would only emerge in a different or modified form.

The second major difficulty arises from the assumption that the problems of coordinating macro- and microeconomic policy in a continental market composed of nation-states is analogous to dealing with similar policies on the national level. It assumes that a system exists or can be created through which to exert control, that techniques of analysis and prediction are available and that decisions can be reached, enforced, and accepted. If the political economies of the member states are examined what is most striking are the struggles for the establishment of priorities and how they often conflict with notions of "efficiency," the difficulty of accurate forecasting, the range of possible interpretations and policies based on available statistical indicators, and the weaknesses of existing institutions for translating policies into practice. In addition, inadequate or ineffective policies often lead to domestic crises and bring down governments. In an age where interest representation is extremely focused and intense and there is a revolution of rising expectations tied to the GNP, the margin of error in domestic economic policy is considerably decreased. In order to maintain the viability and legitimacy of national political institutions, complex arrangements are made to deal with conflicts arising between regions, classes, parties, and professions. Global changes become more difficult because of the inevitable reaction. Consequently, as long as a European political economy has as many problems as indicated in the De Wolff Report, the speculative risk of shifting sovereignty to a supranational Community is still too great for the nation-state.

The third major difficulty arises from another assumption of the Federalists and Functionalists: the analogy, which is increasingly under attack, that the European supranational Community is the nation-state writ large. This is reflected in their institutional model for a federal Europe which is based on idealized notions of national institutions and practices. Thus national constitutionalism, national pluralism, and national parliamentary life are transposed to the European level as though the change from one level to the other were one of kind and not of quality. This is not to say that intensified and expanded European cooperation is not desirable. But it is wrong to think of such cooperation in the EC in political and economic terms which until now have only been applicable to the nation-state. The Commission is neither a cabinet nor an national executive. The problem of representation is not resolved by resorting to a legal fiction about a European electorate, the technique of direct elections, and the construction of a parliamentary body. What the nation-state provides and the European Community cannot provide is the discipline of a legitimate system to deal with the antagonisms and centrifugal forces inherent in any political community. When De Gaulle referred to the force of history and tradition he, in part, meant the role both history and tradition play in making a system acceptable and durable in more than utilitarian terms. Although the glorified nation-state of the nineteenth century and early twentieth century with its integral nationalism that created a sense of community has passed, it has been replaced by a no less tenacious form: the welfare state bound to the growth of the gross national product. The stability of such political units is predicated upon guaranteeing the comparative and competitive advantage of its citizens in relation to one another as well as in relation to other nations. Thus the absence of a viable supranational European infrastructure for superceding or augmenting the nation-state as well as the feeling that one is not in the offing reinforces hesitations about how effectively national interests would be protected if the risk were taken of shifting power to Brussels. The reaction of former Prime Minister Harold Wilson and the Trades Union Congress are important symptoms of this problem because they shed light upon the minimum conditions for national allegience to and acceptance of a supranational Community: to maintain what one has and to ensure that this will both continue and increase. To argue that mutual advantage is increased through supranationality is once again to avoid an important question: the relationship of increasing demands on the part of groups which are also increasingly articulate about their demands to the resources available to meet these demands. The European level is not yet prepared to deal with mediating among and fulfilling these diverse demands. If it tries to define them in economic terms without taking questions of nationality into account, it will be trying to control centrifugal forces with which it is not prepared to deal. These doubts about the potential implications for national stability and welfare of the establishment of a supranational Community are the most serious stumbling block in the way of the Federalists. Oddly enough, what has made the EC at all viable is the nation-state as an intermediary. Furthermore, the national system will become all the more important in ensuring domestic stability and welfare if the first stage of the monetary union is undertaken.

Thus, the German position concerning the monetary union clearly reflects these difficulties. It questions how member states can be expected to renounce control over their own economic and monetary goals and interests, when there is insufficient clarity and agreement concerning the structure and goals of the future final form of the Community's political system. The German position rests ultimately on the assertion of the necessity of parallelism in the following areas for the establishment of the economic and monetary union:

1. parallelism between progress toward convergence of national economies and increasing obligation to a EC monetary policy;

2. parallelism between the increasing obligation to follow an EC monetary policy and the transferal of economic sovereignty to the Community level;

3. parallelism between the construction of Community powers and the corresponding construction of Community institutions which can function.

In effect, the German and French position, as outlined by General De Gaulle and President Pompidou, are very close, even though they start from opposite premises. Put in other than institutional and legal terms, could a transitional plan for a shift of sovereignty be coordinated with the necessary psychological shift of allegience?

As long as a European political system does not exist, the continued existence of the nation-state is not only ensured but necessary. In addition, if a further implication of the Confederalist position is accepted that a supranational Europe might weaken each state economically and politically, then the Community collectively and each state individually would be militarily vulnerable. The Federalists, if they have dealt with the security question at all, have related it to the establishment of the as yet nonexistent European government. A European government would be responsible for European security. But both in security questions as well as in political and economic matters the Federalists' Europe survives or falls on the extent to which there is or can be a durable and extensive identity of interests among the member states which would encourage them to transfer sovereignty to a European government. Not only is such an identity of interests among nation-states in a supranational Community at present a theoretical question because of the inevitable divergences in military and foreign policies which arise, but as long as the nation-state continues to exist, even if it is reduced to the fiction of a region, with its borders intact, its political and economic systems still functioning, and its population with some sense of identity remaining, there will be diverging interests as a result of differences in economic, political, and military power. The disruptive element of power in a Community composed of nation-states has been submerged behind the apolitical and ahistorical legal and technical fictions of the supranationalists. As long as the EC cannot replace the nation-state, the element of power based on competitive advantage, modified balance of power politics, aspirations to political leadership of the Community, and differences of interest will play a vital role.

These manifestations of national interest are the other side of De Gaulle's understanding of the nation-state as an historical community. What has bound the Six together until now is not just the sense that they had common economic interests which could best be protected in an economic community. For Germany, the EC was also the road back to international legitimacy and away from the trauma of national sovereignty. For the Italians it is one of the ways out of hopeless internal political morass. For the Federalists it has been a way to escape power politics based on the nation-state. The French have seen the EC as an instrument through which to magnify their national sovereignty and maintain a relative equality of power between itself and its neighbors. For the British the EC has finally become the most appropriate bloc through which to stop the decline of British power and prestige. To a certain extent these have been compatible motives and goals in the past, but will they continue to be in the future? Now, for instance, German policy appears increasingly unpredictable and too independent to the French. This change in Germany's stance in regard to the EC is an inevitable result of the degree of self-denial it imposed upon its own foreign policy after 1945. As the author of the two articles in *Die Zeit* observed: Those who want to prevent the return of nationalism into the EC would be well advised to defend carefully national interests within the EC framework.

If these forces are taken into account, then the relative revival of the nation-state after 1945 as reflected in the French veto of the European Defense Community, the British refusal to join the EC, or the German floating of the mark in May, 1971, will be interpreted correctly. Such actions will not be rejected moralistically as being traditionalistic and anachronistic. As long as there are no structures to replace the nation-state and sufficiently durable and extensive interests to support such supranational structures, the nation-state will continue its traditional role of protecting and maintaining the national community for which it is responsible. As Giscard d'Estaing said at a press conference held in Brussels on March 26, 1969:

> In the world in which we now live, our countries are best able to exercise their sovereignty and safeguard the modern form of their independence within the framework of European institutions. The countries of Europe acting alone and isolated in international affairs do not have the dimensions necessary for independence.

In other words under the conditions described above the central struggle since 1945 for the European nations has been the conflict between their efforts to maintain some autonomy while finding means through which to deal with their dependence on and interdependence with other nations. Under these circumstances the unique and daring nature of the European Community emerges because the task of changing centuries of independent history has been enormously difficult. The European Community is complex because the problems are complex. Efforts to ride roughshod over these tensions and historical forces by forcing the nation-state to legislate itself out of existence because of the theoretical desirability of establishing a supranational government may intensify the centrifugal forces already inherent in the EC. The Federalists consistently run the danger because of their legal technocratic approach to Europe of underestimating the historical and political forces within the nation-state with which any supranational Community must deal.

There is no doubt that the political leaders of the EC will continue their efforts to find mutually acceptable institutional forms as the basis for further cooperation. The EC has been too successful as a framework within which agreements based on common advantage can and have been achieved. However the efforts to devise such institutional forms will have the greatest chance for success if the tensions between autonomy and dependence and convergence and divergence of nation-state interests are kept in mind. Consequently, such plans will have to stop treating the Community within the political framework designed for understanding the nation-state. The centrifugal forces in international organizations and nation-states are not entirely the same nor are the social, political, and psychological relations to international or regional organizations and nation-states entirely analogous to one another. The approach to the role of organizations and institutions, the nature and context of the enforceability of political decisions, the problems of legitimacy and stability and the quality of representation and responsiveness are qualitatively different in nation-states and regional communities. The French position concerning these problems has, unfortunately, in many instances been unjustly criticized. Thus plans for the future will have to grapple with the problems of identifying more clearly and sharply national and European interests and finding common denominators for bringing these two sets of interest together. Such efforts must avoid the dissonances between the nation-state and supranationalism which will make national leaders resistant to more intensified forms of cooperation as well as avoid the centrifugal forces inherent in a weak confederal structure.

It is obvious that the future structure of the EC will determine not only the degree of political and economic cohesion in the Community but also how effectively and how quickly the EC can speak with a united voice in world affairs and how quickly it can make and enforce internal decisions in conjunction with its exterior and interior goals. However, the EC is now entering a period fraught with uncertainties about its institutional development. The uncertainties are so extensive, involving intra-European and international problems, that at present it is extremely difficult to even devise an adequate much less a potentially successful policy. During this period the EC must absorb four states into its existing framework. While the Community can look back proudly on such accomplishments as the customs unions and Kennedy Rounds, the "completion" of the EC was done within the context of treaties which have left open the long-range structure of the Community. Consequently, the EC which has emerged is without an adequate focus of authority or responsibility, with a diffusion of leadership and unclear institutional structure. As long as the central structure remains relatively weak and so long as the EC does not have a binding military, financial, and foreign policy "identity," it is open to sudden disrupting intrusions of foreign policy matters and destabilizing tactics from inside the Community. The years of Gaullist opposition, the current stalemate in the first stage of the monetary union, the malaise surrounding the role of the Commission, and the delays which will inevitably result from British entry have contributed to or will contribute to the political vulnerability of the EC. In addition, SALT, NATO, the proposed European Security Conference, and *Ostpolitik* introduce the danger of centrifugal foreign policies and divisive pressures into the EC. Finally, although enlargement of the EC has been a goal of the Commission it has been brought about by "high" diplomacy of the member states. This has demonstrated once again as has already been mentioned the extent to which the Commission is not only dependent on the individual member states but the extent to which the continued existence of this high diplomacy weakens the Commission's potential leadership role in the EC of six or ten. Moreover, since this recent manifestation of high diplomacy was combined with the French confederal approach to the institutions of the Community, it is uncertain what the EC can do to counteract the forces in a confederal approach which might contribute to a relative weakening of the present institutions.

THE CHANGED NATURE OF THE ENLARGED COMMUNITY

Within the context of these problems the addition of four new member states will change the nature of the EC. The Commission's hope that enlargement of the EC would strengthen the Community in a supranational direction may not be borne out in practice, since this is not simply a numerical addition of new members to an ongoing concern, but a qualitative change in the nature of the EC. It will throw into sharper relief that this is a unique association composed of unique political units: nation-states. It will raise the geographical and psychological question of what constitutes Europe, since the dynamic of enlargement means changes in the EC's borders. The larger the land area covered by the EC, the greater the danger that the political allegiance of the individual European will be weaker and more diffuse. It will mean an increase in the vital interests which must be protected and consequently voted upon unanimously in the Council of Ministers. Even when questions of vital interests are not involved, the diversity of interests, which already seem too varied in a Community of six, will now become more difficult to manage. The Community method of finding a least common denominator for formulating policy may even become more watered down with ten nations than it has been with six. Finally, the historical halo which surrounded the initial years of the Community and seemed to provide a compelling basis for political allegience has all but disappeared. The EC which is entering the 1970's has become a bureaucratic affair deeply emersed in very technical problems. It does not have the "romantic" image which could evoke the political emotions necessary to expand the Commission's political role in a direction consonant with a supranational federal framework. The enlarged Community will probably intensify the technical nature of the EC.

As far as the compatibility of enlargement and deepening are concerned, for many, deepening, particularly in supranational and democratic terms, was already difficult for six states and should have been completed, if at all, before enlargement. But deepening most likely would have worked against enlargement by having presented potential new members with arrangements that were too far-going for sovereign states to accept. The enlargement, however, is not the cause of these difficulties in the way of supranational and democratic aspirations, but simply one more obstacle. From the beginning Europe has been the work of technical elites without democratic participation. In fact, democratic participation most likely would have been a major obstacle to reaching agreements. In addition, the Community which has been constructed has the tendency to repeat in a more intensified form what happens on the national level: the drift of major decision-making powers to executive bodies. The Medium Term Economic Policy as well as the plans for a monetary union have strong dirigist elements which conflict with the high degree of voluntarism upon which these policies not only are, but must be, based. Certainly, the modern tendency of power to gravitate to executive bodies will only be underscored in a Community of ten nation-states. Moreover, the necessity for making swift decisions implies that too extensive a right to participate is a potentially disrupting factor. It is already difficult to envision how a Commission or Council of Ministers representing ten nations will be able to function efficiently in order to meet its responsibilities for trade and financial matters. Moreover, the fact that there will be an even greater awareness of national interests in the enlarged Community probably means that governments, and particularly foreign ministers, do not want to leave the fate of their nations' "vital interests" in the hands of a European Parliament. The issues are too complex and will grow more complex in the enlarged EC.

Under these conditions efforts to continue to deal with the EC through Federalist legal and constitutional concepts and institutions will be increasingly inappropriate. Neither the power relationships and problems within a Community of nation-states nor the effort to redefine national interests in terms of a federal framework will fit neatly and comfortably into these categories. Unfortunately, during this transition period, as a result of the various trends already discussed which have left the EC vulnerable, a vacuum may emerge in which the old concepts upon which association and cooperation were based are no longer binding and new concepts concerning the future basis for political and economic cooperation have not taken their place. Such a development is all the more serious since the confederal idea in conjunction with the expansion of the EC appears to be on the ascendancy. This ascendancy is reflected in the decline of the supranational formula and the growing interest in the new formula of the "common exercise of the sovereignty of European nations."

While the supranational formula and the difficulties of establishing a European political system have been major obstacles in dealing with the institutional dispersion of authority and responsibility as well as expanding the jurisdiction of EC institutions, both the ideal of supranationality and the Commission have had important symbolic and practical functions. They have been the unique elements which have provided the necessary legitimation and institutional framework for creating a counterbalance against the centrifugal forces inherent in an association of nation-states. If, however, the "realities" of the existence of the nation-state are given the degree of recognition accorded them in the new formula and the supranational formula is abandoned or further undermined, there may be no institutions, movements, or moral and legal ideals to effectively represent what can be defined as a European interest against the individual member states of the EC. Then the centrifugal forces inherent in a Community of ten nations may lead to weaker forms of cooperation and less ambitious goals then envisioned in the Treaties of Rome. On the other hand, it may be necessary to accept some elements of the new formula if the EC is to move beyond its present immobilism. This means making more allowances for the continued existence of the nation-state during the reformulation of the goals and institutions of the EC. Such a policy will not simply be a tactical move but the delayed recognition that as long as an adequate institutional framework and policies for a European political system have not yet been found, the nation-state will continue to be the basis for the Community. In this case two major questions must be answered concerning the EC framework for cooperation. If the EC is to remain something more than an association of states will it be possible to perpetuate, modify, or find a substitute for the supranational ideal? Second, will this ideal be coupled to the Commission, whether in its present form or in a revised form, to provide the EC with the focus and counterweight necessary to balance the centrifugal forces in an EC composed of ten members. There seems to be no immediate and obvious way to deal with the conflicting goals and trends within the EC. However, it is possible, on the basis of the preceding analyses to examine some of the suggestions which have been made.

ANALYSIS OF PROPOSALS FOR REFORM

The author of the *Die Zeit* articles has illuminated at least part of the problem of institutional development through his efforts to consistently apply the new formula to the EC. According to him the intergovernmental formula would permit the foreign ministers meeting in the Council of Ministers to confer once again as foreign ministers rather than have to operate within the highly restrictive framework of the current supranational formula. In other words, rather than have to work within the fiction of being delegates to a quasi-supranational Community in the process of development, they could meet as the representatives of sovereign states. Under these circumstances nothing could be excluded from their agenda, as has been done previously, because it was not considered by a member state to be within the legal boundaries of the Rome Treaties. He maintains that such a change would not imply a weakening, but, to the contrary, a strengthening of the Community institutions and EC cooperation, since it would create one of the conditions necessary for a stronger and more direct and realistic engagement for EC affairs than the supranational formula could. This would be reflected in the increased extent to which, as Stanley Hoffman observed, the foreign ministers would be able to distinguish among agenda items that involved incipient interest group politics, the domestic politics of the EC, and continuing issues of traditional interstate politics.

The problems in the way of a monetary and economic union, for instance, would be clearer if these distinctions were made. It would then be easier to realistically assess the issues of competitive advantage often hidden behind the "apolitical" technical discussions of such a union as well as to bring out more sharply which policies and institutions would be required for ensuring an "equitable" distribution of resources among classes, regions, professions, and nations. In addition, the institutional framework as well as the distribution of powers among the nation-states and the EC would be devised on the basis of an understanding of the political, economic, and social dynamics of a Community composed of ten states.

In terms of the dispersion of authority, the author of *Die Zeit* articles believes that even if the EC members continue to represent their interests in a variety of forms such as the Council of Ministers, the Davignon Committee, the Monetary Committee, or other committees and bodies dealing with military and financial matters, the membership in these organs would be similar or overlap and the formula under which they would operate would be uniform. Such congruence in membership and legal authority should potentially contribute to the reduction of the dispersion of authority and responsibility in the EC. Simultaneously, since the Council of Ministers would continue to be the key EC institution, the EC would be able to operate without antagonizing the nation-state by concentrating what national governments feel is too much authority in the hands of a supranational Commission. Moreover, by maintaining the Council of Ministers as the principal institution of the EC an adequate and appropriate forum would be available for dealing with the inevitable manifestations of potentially disruptive national interest with which the EC will have to contend in the coming years. In this situation if the supranational formula and majority voting were applied in the Council of Ministers, nations which could not go along with decisions taken would resort to the policy of the empty chair. In a more intergovernmental framework, nations which could not agree with certain decisions would not have to face the stigma of undermining a supranational Community.

While the new formula does have many advantages, particularly in regard to the extent it takes into account the complexities of the EC, its major weakness is that it does not provide the same quasi-legal, moral impulse for cooperation that the supranational Federalist formula and the existence of the Commission have done until now. If its logic were followed, it would be difficult to ensure an adequate role for the Commission. It is precisely at this point that the lack of political will to which the Federalists have often referred becomes relevant. In spite of the institutional difficulties outlined, the leaders of the ten member states do have a choice to opt for a framework in which there is or is not a counterweight to the nation-states. Such political will would be most visible in their treatment of the Commission.

At present the Commission has the following important functions. It is responsible for administering the ongoing affairs of the EC and for developing proposals on its own initiative and on the basis of political decisions taken by the Council of Ministers. In addition, it represents and watches over, as guardian of the Rome Treaties, what has already been achieved. It is essential that it continue to be responsible for these functions because the Council of Ministers must be faced with a distinctive representative of a European interest. Without this built-in lobby for "Europe" on the Community level, the pressure for European cooperation would most likely diminish. Such a split in the responsibilities and authority of the Commission and the Council of Ministers in the near future might profit the EC, if both organs would force each other to define their positions more clearly than has been done until now. This should open the way for a more serious discussion of the viable forms for political cooperation in the enlarged Community. Such a discussion would have to include the problems of the waning of the original European ideal, particularly in its Federalist form, as well as the rethinking of the goals of the Community.

In the long run these responsibilities will not be enough to ensure the Commission an adequate role and powers to act as a counterbalance to the nation-states and as a focus for "Europe." This will not only result from the redistribution of power in the enlarged EC but from the inherent conflict between the intergovernmental and supranational approaches. Consequently, it might be of vital importance to make a significant institutional innovation such as establishing the cabinet-level post of European Minister in order to strengthen the Commission and the framework for intra-European cooperation. The nature of such a post and its potential relationship to the Commission, Council of Ministers, and European Parliament are at the moment difficult theoretical questions. However, the suggestion is of sufficient interest that it is worth mentioning. The Commission might best secure its own role through its relationship to such European Ministers rather than through its efforts to displace the nation-state by expanding its authority through the development of a political infrastructure modeled after that upon which the national governments base their authority and legitimacy. This kind of political and social integration and harmonization on a European level does not seem either possible or probable at the present time. Direct elections of a European Parliament as the catalyst for such an infrastructure would very soon prove to be a Pyrrhic victory for the supranationalists. Not only will Europe Number Two be no less capable of evoking the political emotions and political loyalties necessary for supranational institutions than Europe Number One, but such a political base for the Commission might undermine its role because of the political forces such an infrastructure would focus on Brussels. The Commission has been separated from the sources of political power enjoyed by national governments not only by the "lack of political will" among national leaders but because it has not been able to adequately demonstrate the feasibility of a European political system. While these factors have been sources of its weaknesses, they have also been sources of its strength. Although it has competed with national governments for political influence and power, the Commission has not had to see its initiatives tied to governing directly the entire Community or individual nation-states. The nation-states have served as intermediaries, and this has permitted the Commission to define an institutional role for itself without the concomitant erosion of its authority and power through the continued exercise of political responsibility. Moreover, if it could assume the full range of powers and responsibilities of a national government with a direct link to the electorate it would open itself to dangerous confrontations. The Commission has not established a legitimacy for itself which would permit it to survive such confrontations, nor could it establish such a legitimacy by suddenly becoming a European executive. Any such efforts will be all the more risky in the enlarged Community.

If the role of the Commission is somewhat less than that of a government, the role of the European Parliament should also continue to be somewhat less than that of a national parliament. However, a European Community composed of ten constitutional democracies needs an organ which embodies the moral and representative qualities of a parliament. Efforts to reconstruct the European Parliament in the direction of a full parliamentary body in a supranational system must be deferred not only until this institutional form is thought through again but until the dynamics of the enlarged EC become clear. Most likely, the European Parliament will remain for some time an indirectly elected body with qualified representative functions. Its symbolic importance, like that of the Commission, will be to attempt to prevent the drift of a "confederal" Europe toward a weaker regional alliance by serving as a forum for emphasizing those interests the ten member states and their citizens have in common. In addition, in spite of the indirect election of its members, it can still serve the function of providing some further legitimation for the Community to the national electorates. If, however, efforts are made to use legal and technical devices for turning the European Parliament into a supranational body in order to "strengthen" the enlarged EC, the devices will probably have opposite results. For example, the attempt to increase participation of a "European" electorate in EC affairs through democratic fictions and voting procedures would have more apparent, than real, results. If more intense forms of participation are desired in the enlarged Community, they would best be attained through decentralization and the augmentation of national participatory patterns at the regional level. In respect to parliamentary control of the executive, this will still best be realized in the first instance on the national level. The parliaments of the ten member states should establish European Affairs Committees which are designed to be counterparts to the concentration of responsibilities and authority for European affairs in the hands of national foreign ministers, cabinets, and even eventually European Ministers. The European Parliament, at this stage, will be a consultative assembly, with modest budgetary powers, for coordinating those matters at the European level in which the European Affairs Committees on the national level feel coordination is both possible and necessary.

CONCLUSIONS

If the preceding suggestions are tentative and incomplete, it is because the dynamics of the EC, especially on the threshold of enlargement, are complex and unclear. In the immediate future, the confederal approach will probably most strongly influence policy-making in the enlarged EC. It is vital during the period leading up to full membership for Great Britain, Ireland, Norway, and Denmark on January 1, 1973, that some firm actions be taken in regard to the institutional structure of the Community. If such actions are not taken many avenues now open to the EC may be closed as a result of international trade, financial, and military decisions taken elsewhere. However, adequate decisions can only be made once the supranational fiction upon which notions of integration have been based is modified. This will open up lines of inquiry concerning more practical forms of cooperation. Finally, institutional changes must be coordinated and made in conjunction with policy decisions concerning the exterior and interior affairs of the EC. Otherwise, structural modifications will remain empty forms without the specific contents necessary to make them effective and operative. The formulation of such policies will be very difficult not only because of the range of issues, the number of member states and the interrelations between European policy and international politics. It will also be difficult because such policies must be approached, as was previously indicated, as simultaneously being interest group politics, domestic European politics and traditional interstate affairs. The dividing line among these issues and perspectives is very thin and shifting. However, the future success of the EC depends on the extent that it can define a large area as being strictly the domestic concern of Europe. If this is possible, then it might be possible to provide the Commission with a larger role as well as establish European Ministers. Among the substantive fields in which such definition seems possible are the "approximation" of national economic structures and the coordination of economic policies as well as regional and intra-Community employment policy. Such policies, even on the basis of an intergovernmental formula, can be framed and administered in such a way as to create greater cohesiveness in the enlarged Community while establishing a realistic European political infrastructure.

2

PROBLEMS
OF A
EUROPEAN POLITICAL
ECONOMY

Uwe Kitzinger

There was once a Latin American dictator who, after some years, issued a proclamation that he had found his country ungovernable and resigned to live in Switzerland. In Britain some time ago—in the halcyon days when both major parties were declared champions of entry into the European Economic Community—one Labor Minister confessed, "You cannot plan only for one country." The Labor Chancellor of the Exchequer, who has now reverted to an anti-EEC stance, claimed to have learned from his time in office: "My experience over the last two and a half years has led me to the conclusion more and more that to a very large extent nations are not free at the moment to make their own decisions. . . ." On the Conservative side skepticism as to the possibility of not socialism but economic salvation in one country was of somewhat longer standing. Where Hugh Gaitskell had argued in 1962 that anything that the EEC could do for Britain, Britain could do on her own by pulling herself up by her own bootstraps, Harold Macmillan had coined the phrase of the "bracing cold shower" needed by the British economy from competition within the EEC. As the 1960's evolved, bringing with them one economic defeat after another, increasingly for Britain the EEC became a nostrum that would impose from the outside what the British political system itself was not strong enough to achieve within. In a sense, accession to the Common Market today thus represents a deliberate abdication of British government— abdication in favor of a more remote, less responsible, less responsive, and therefore tougher system required now that Britain on her own terms has been proved to be ungovernable.

The political dangers with which entry into the EEC in that spirit is pregnant are formidable. In the late 1970's we must, in Britain in any case, anticipate and guard against a wave of xenophobia as the second generation of colored immigrants reaches the labor and marriage markets in the expectation of full equality against the background of Anglo-Saxon color consciousness. It will be at much the same time that competition from better paid, more highly capitalized continental labor will appear in the form of unrestricted imports of continental automobiles and other consumer durables, engineering products, and so on. Third, an economic government consisting mainly of foreigners and sitting on the continent will be imposing a heavy financial burden, higher prices, and all sorts of changes in rules and regulations on the British worker, taxpayer, consumer, and citizen. However much "they" in Brussels may try to soften the impact of the second, and however well they may try to manipulate, camouflage, and compensate for the third factor, a nationalist backlash seems almost inevitable.

To anticipate and guard against such a psychological reaction is an internal British social and political concern. But to understand the nature of the process to which Britain is being subjected—and much the same may hold good in the Irish and Norwegian cases—is vital for the EEC itself. I make no excuse therefore for this parochially British introduction. The British case is, after all, only an extreme, more abrupt example of what the EEC will represent as soon as it develops from being a customs union with an agricultural policy—in accordance with its logical and declared ambition—to a monetary and economic union.

ECONOMIC AIMS

By its nature a mere customs union should by itself have constituted such external discipline. In the case of coal, the European Coal and Steel Community (ECSC) did indeed hasten the closure of some Belgian mines. But for the rest, the EEC was fortunate in that it was installing its internal free trading system at a time of general expansion, of fast-growing national products, fast-rising wages, and only moderate inflation thanks to high capital investment. Britain has had a low rate of investment right through the postwar period, only slowly growing real wages, and latterly a very high rate of inflation. It will depend on the monetary arrangements between the Six and Britain's exchange rate with them how hard continental competition will hit Britain in this situation.

But, in any case, on the continent, too, if the rate of growth of world liquidity slows down, if moderate deflation becomes the general trend in the world economy, if wages do not rise, investment is cut back, and the rate of real economic growth slows to the minimal levels experienced for example in the Federal Republic of Germany in 1968-69, the effects of international competition, instead of merely "biting" on potential investment and redirecting it into areas of greater competitive advantage, may start to hit existing production lines and people's actual jobs. In other words, it is not simply the accession of "the sick man of Europe." It is also in any case the possibility of a change in the world economic climate that will reinforce the case for progress beyond the customs union toward the economic union concept.

Those of us who twelve or fifteen years ago hailed the European Economic Community as a forward-looking concept were of course right—at the time. But time has passed since then. The Community has, if anything, gone back on its original concept in institutional mechanisms and hung back behind its program in almost everything but the customs union and agricultural policy. The customs union was completed well ahead of time, has worked smoothly within the EEC, and has contributed markedly also to the general lowering of tariff protection between industrial countries. The farm policy, on the other hand, has been more problematic.

The Ministers have been spending 70 percent of their time and the Community has been spending 95 percent of its money on that one industry which now contributes only some 6 percent to the gross Community product. It is also the industry due for further decisive contraction from the 25 percent of the labor force in 1958 via the present 15 percent or less to something under 10 percent by 1980. It has, of course, been a social rather than an economic policy, a humanitarian exercise in easing out over-age uneconomic farmers by paying them uneconomic prices for surplus products, without keeping them in a state of prosperity that might encourage their sons to follow in their fathers' footsteps. Political pressures have at times meant that the farmers have done better, even on these criteria, than they should have. Inflation coupled with prices that were kept constant for three years has moderated this trend. General rises in world food prices have also served to reduce the extravagance of the policy. It must be remembered, however, that insofar as national subsidies still constitute a multiple of Community support for agriculture, that Community policy is at once more excusable and also an addition to the economic extravagance. But overall the Community's policy may indeed be described as being in that sense a backward-looking one.

And yet there are considerations of a broader economic kind that underlie the farmers' ideology which the strictly GNP-oriented economists (by whose criteria the Anglo-Saxons tend to judge the common agricultural policy) have overlooked. Writing this a thousand miles from reference books and statistics in a fishing and wine-growing village of the Languedoc, one is acutely aware not only of the in many respects fine balance between the credit and the debit side of the ledger of industrial growth, but also of the social benefit of continued agricultural production beyond the money value of its food output. As living standards rise, as leisure, environmental amenities, and travel come to be valued more highly than the latest model car or the second transistor radio, the "park-keeper" functions of agriculture and its contribution to the mental and physical health of a community may come to be recognized beyond the farmers' lobby. To include the output of oxygen and similar amenities in the efficiency calculus of farm policy may of course mean shifts of resources out of pesticides into wildlife afforestation, and so forth, within the agricultural sector. But that is another set of problems of which the second Mansholt plan is partially aware. All of these points, of course, are as relevant to American and British, as to EEC, agricultural policy. It has been estimated that without the battery of different support programs deployed in these three areas, close to 40 percent of the agricultural production would fold up in each of them.

A European political economy, to put the point more generally, will have the need—and from the diversity of the economic habits and ideologies that go into it, it may also have the opportunity—to have much conscious thought devoted to its optimal rate of growth. "Growth in what?" is a perfectly fair and relevant—indeed the essential preliminary—issue. Growth in total or growth in per capita incomes? If the latter, what are the consequences for population policy? There are wide variations in the social policies of different member states, with France in particular encouraging an increase in its birthrate through allowances and rebates of generous proportions. How much economic growth, in fact, is required merely to finance the investments needed for population expansion? And would zero population growth, after a lag, allow zero growth in a suitably defined economic indicator?

What, moreover, is a suitable economic indicator? Gross national product measures both the price of the cigarette and the training and services of the lung surgeon who is required to cope with the consequences, both the output of the chemical factory and the public expenditure to try to offset its polluting by-products on our environment. Japanese policy makers, having witnessed the appalling social cost of a 10 to 15 percent rate of growth in GNP, are coming to operate in terms of net social value. Europe may be at half the level of GNP per capita of the United States, it may be at less than half the growth rate in GNP of Japan, but questions of this kind are not for that reason any the less relevant.

Part of the "instinctive" opposition to Common Market entry in Britain, Norway, and Ireland is precisely the fear of being caught in a rat race in which too much of the present is sacrificed to the future, too much leisure sacrificed to physical objects, too many "civilized" patterns of behavior to the shibboleth of efficiency. On the other hand moderate growth in gross national product in Britain could easily conceal an actual decline in net social value as increasing density of inhabitants, traffic congestion, demands on hospitals by an aging adult population, demands on schools by swelling numbers of younger cohorts, erosion of natural recreational facilities, and generalized obsolescence of social infrastructure capital imply the need to run faster just to stand still.

As in the case of population growth, so in that of social value one has to ask questions not merely as to actual levels, but as to the effects of changes, and of changes in rate of change, on the polity at large. Can a society sustain a sense of declining real satisfaction of wants without souring up politically, industrially, socially, and perhaps in spite of itself spinning into a vicious spiral leading to increasing internal disruption? If so, "rat race" may be essential just to stop the rats if not physically at least by "inner emigration" from leaving the slowly sinking ship. Or is it the extra pressure that would break the camel's back—the "bracing cold shower" in fact giving the patient pneumonia? A great deal will depend not merely on the objective economic situation and challenge, but on the language in wich it is perceived, on the symbolism and atmosphere of social leadership from the local to the Community level.

EXTERNAL OBJECTIVES

In all this, so far, we have considered only the internal objectives of a European political economy. In fact of course, just as the Community of Six was from birth confronted with its external role almost before it had time to grapple with its internal tasks, so an enlarged Community is confronted with the "foreign policy" implications of its formation even before enlargement has taken place. The Kennedy Round was the result of the 1961-63 threat of British accession. The Nixon measures of August, 1971, though primarily no doubt directed at Japan, came at the end of a long period of deep irritation with EEC agricultural protectionism, a shorter period of disappointment at European failure to revalue, and under the shadow of an enlargement of this trading bloc on the other side of the Atlantic aggravating effective discrimination against American business. And so Mr. Barber's flight to Brussels in August became symptomatic of the Community of Ten, even before it was finally decided upon, having to face up to its external role in the world monetary system. The fact that it failed to be able to concert its actions is proof of another side of the story, to which I shall revert.

What has not at all been consciously decided upon in this sphere is the kind of role that the enlarged Community is in fact to play vis-à-vis the United States. One may guess that the Kennedy Grand Design of partnership between two equal and coordinate pillars of the Alliance is an offer that has lapsed for lack of European response and as a result of changed external circumstances, heightened internal preoccupations, and a different political mood about their world role in the United States. The Gaullist concept, or some of its variations, must be considered even more obsolete or futuristic. The notion of a Europe from the Atlantic to the Urals defending traditional continental values against the cultural barbarians beyond the seas and exercising special missionary activity through the diaspora of Quebec seems merely fanciful, unless the Soviet Union were, one distant day, to grow so jealous of the Washington-Peking axis forged by Richard Nixon as to wish to consolidate the landmass of Eurasia against the Pacific seaboard powers. Neither economically nor politically does there seem much prospect of a relationship with Eastern Europe that is closer than, or even symmetrical to, that with the United States.

The possibility of a Europe from which the United States appears to be withdrawing, envisaged half as a hope and half as a contingency against which to guard, is perhaps rather less distant. The United States balance of payments and the level of its foreign exchange and gold reserves, insofar as gold still has relevance, will no doubt hasten the diminution in American Troop expenditure in Europe. Though how far that will affect the military efficiency and political significance of the American presence is another matter. Perhaps rather more marked may be the effect of monetary problems on the level of new United States investment in Europe, together with any effects that realigned or more freely fluctuating rates of exchange may have on the level and type of U.S. exports to and imports from Western Europe.

It is of course too early to foretell the passing of "the American challenge" in its variously understood forms. This involves American business borrowing in Europe to buy up European firms and make them into mere ancillaries and distributors of American high-technology products, or of European firms falling behind American ones in technological achievement and thereby losing their brightest manpower. It also involves European government and business and armed forces all being dependent for their sophisticated equipment on United States sources of supply and therefore vulnerable to the threat, exercised after all against Gaullist France, of being denied available equipment they require. The facts, insofar as they can be reliably estimated, appear to be an increase in direct U.S. investment in the EEC of Six from under $2 billion in 1958 to around $13 billion in 1970. By 1968 U.S. subsidiaries will be selling $14 billion in products—two and one-half times the value of U.S. exports to the Community—and repatriating in 1970 some $1 billion in profits. EEC direct investment in the U.S.A., by comparison, appears to have been about $3.5 billion in 1970.

It may of course be that this "American challenge" will now change in the emphasis of its manifestation. But whether it does or not the fact remains that the Community of Six failed to formulate any technology policy worthy of the name, either in response to any of the interpretations of the American challenge, or even, regardless of external factors, to exploit the potential complementarities between its technologican growth-points. How far must Europe go in duplicating advances made elsewhere in order to feel and be "independent?" To what extent must she do this to retain and challenge her own technical personnel and thus safeguard her biological stock of talent from erosion to the laboratories and beaches of California? To what extent must she do this for the sake of the commercial spin-off and in order not to have her growth slowed down absolutely by problems of a relative technical time-lag? To what extent, on the contrary—as with Japan, which has simply not gone into certain fields such as airliner construction at all—should she have a selective policy buying in foreign technology available in some fields the better to concentrate, partly with foreign tools on technology in certain other fields? The thinking, let alone the decision-making, on this aspect of Europe's foreign economic relations seems far behind the need for a coherent policy. But this is a subject which will be discussed later in a purely internal European context.

Similar considerations apply to the stance which an enlarged Community will take toward the developing world. On the one hand it is certainly worth noting, and not generally realized, to how large an extent even the present Community of Six already contributes to the trade and aid of the less-developed countries (LDC) beyond Europe. In 1969 the total public and private flow of financial resources to these countries from the United States came to $4.6 billion. That from the Six came to $5.3 billion. Taking the Ten together their financial contributions came to $6.3 billion. Similarly, in the case of exports from the LDCs, those to the United States amounted in 1970 to $10.4 billion, those to the Six $16.1 billion, and those to the Ten $22.3 billion. Over the past decade, in other words, even the present Community has overtaken the United States as the most important trade-and-aid partner to the developing world. In 1971 aid may have risen above that of the Six alone. But recent measures suggest that if total aid from the developed world is not to be cut, Western Europe and Japan will have to step up their efforts even further to make up for the reductions President Nixon has announced in U.S. aid flows.

In terms of gross national product, the flow of financial resources from the Community at well over 1 percent is already more than twice as important as that from the United States of 5 percent of GNP. Yet at the moment only about one-twentieth of that is channeled through the Community agencies of the European Development Fund and the Bank. The rest is uncoordinated national and private flow. It may well be that from the recipient countries' point of view there are major advantages in a lack of coordination between countries of origin. Certainly this is not meant as a plea for a European political economy to become an aid monolith that would prevent one donor being played against another and might inhibit experimentation in forms of aid and investment. Given the perplexity of all the major aid agencies as to the most effective development policy to pursue, it is also no reproach to the West Europeans that they seem to lack any coherent trade and aid philosophy or program. But the search for it is an unavoidable task, perhaps the one by which in the eyes of future historians, the Community will in the long run be most critically judged. It is one on which, with the exception of two somewhat restricted areas, Western Europe has not really begun to work. Moreover in certain domains, sugar being one of them, the implications of domestic agricultural policies on less-developed countries seem actually to be a negation of the Community's declared aims.

The two regions in which starts have been made are the Associates under Part IV of the Treaty—the overseas associated countries and overseas territories—and the Mediterranean basin, several of whose states are associated under Article 238 while others have special trade agreements. Part IV of the Treaty will be transformed in scope by the accession of ten or twelve more African states and the Carribean Commonwealth countries, raising the populations included from about 80 million people to about 190 million. The Yaoundé system is an attempt at combining financial with technical aid, public with private investment, and all these trading opportunities and special assistance to help find outlets for produce overseas. Clearly, however, it is too small a program to make a decisive difference to any but small regions within the Associated states.

The second area in which the Community has been fumbling toward a policy—or been pushed into stumbling into a series of measures now being rationalized into a policy—is the shore of the Mediterranean from Israel to Spain. Only in the case of Turkey, now that the association agreement with Greece has, for political reasons, been put into cold storage, is there any attempt to coordinate aid with trade. For the rest, it is a problem of not discriminating against one country in favor of another that was able to get an agreement earlier. All this must be done without depriving the Italians and the Associates of too many of their advantages. One need not be surprised that the fruit growers of Florida feel discriminated against, and that the United States could use the scarcely veiled defiance of GATT by the EEC as an offsetting factor for its own 10 percent import surcharge. The Wilson government's surcharge of 1964 is after all an even better analogy.

Taken together, however, the African association and the Mediterranean preferences raise a more fundamental question than the observance or avoidance of an international instrument drafted between the industrialized nations of the world twenty-odd years ago. As the Alliance for Progress sets up or consecrates a special North-South relationship in the Western hemisphere, so the Associations have set up special North-South relations between Europe and Africa. Of course, U.S. aid and trade is also vitally important in Asia, and of course Britain, Germany, and some other European countries are also involved in aiding and in trading with Asia. However, the parts of Asia on which each concentrates are by no means congruent. A European political economy will have to ask itself whether this kind of splitting up of the world longitudinally into spheres of influence is in the long run the most useful type of arrangement, as it may well be, or whether the dangers inherent in it (and of which the United States appears to be conscious in Latin America) outweigh the advantages. It is also not surprising that some Asians wonder if they will some day become relatively neglected between these two special North-South relationships. They point to their own vastly greater numbers, and ask if they are really to be left to Russia, China, and Japan, whatever the future constellation of these three powers with the United States may turn out to be.

ECONOMIC AND INDUSTRIAL STRATEGIES

If both internal and external objectives are ill-defined—in some ways thanks to the acceleration of general change, indeed almost incapable of any but the most generalized definition—there are also senses in which a certain skepticism as to the powers of implementing any objectives put limits on the extent to which a definition is seriously sought. Nevertheless a good many of the strategic problems are of the "if we had some ham, we could make some ham and eggs, if we had the eggs" variety. The problems of an economic strategy for the EEC have been hashed over for so long, that it is only in the context of the enlargement that one dare take another bite at this *cramba repetita*. What "eggs" are in fact added by the accession of Britain and the others and how much more urgent has a new mix of policies become?

To take up the question first in more general terms of political economy, one must confess that it is difficult to be precise in assessing the impact on a Community of six continental states of the entry into it of two islands and two peninsulae to the north of it with their maritime traditions and their, at least at times in their history, more puritan motivations. Sociologists have barely begun to explore the present behavior patterns and attitudes to time and punctuality, work-hours, work-intensity and work-involvement, money, status, competitiveness, and cooperative behavior among peer groups and within hierarchical organizations. This also includes value-systems competing with industrial efficiency at any particular moment and level, and value-systems functional to it. And little is known of how fast changes in social and industrial structure force the adaptation of goals and behavior, and of the magnitude of successful change required for the "bracing cold shower" effect—both where the existing member countries and where the candidate countries are concerned. Nor is it simply a one dimensional problem of a challenge that is "not too little, not too much, but just right." Each of the countries involved has complex stratifications of different behavior patterns and attitudes overlying each other, differentiated regionally, occupationally, socially, and in all sorts of other ways. There can be no attempt here at unification or, to use the famous term of the Val Duchesse negotiations for the Rome Treaty, "harmonization." Only more or less inspired guesses can be made as to what sort of quasi-chemical rather than quasi-mechanical reactions may result.

Yet this kind of speculation is not simply one of academic curiosity. It has very concrete application down to the kinds of regulations that have to be issued in Brussels. There has been a fair amount of discussion of the impact of Roman-type codified law on the British system, or rather on the English system, as the Scottish is closer to the continental already. No doubt the practice of English lawyers will to some extent affect that of the Community. The Court will presumably have an English judge before long. But politeness has inhibited almost any discussion of varying fiscal moralities, which may well require tacit recognition in the application of common tax laws. It would be interesting to know how far this is already a problem in which, for instance, Italian traditions have clashed with German traditions. Finally, the major shift from direct (and therefore on the whole socially progressive), to indirect (and on the whole socially regressive) taxation implied for some of the candidates by entry is after all not least due to collecting problems in "far off countries of which they know little." Clearly again there are differences of political style ranging from rhetoric to negotiating tactics, from the relative concepts of "civil servants" and "politicians" to the administrative practices via permanent department heads or via private offices. It has been a recurring argument in British debate over the past ten years that British civil servants are both too stupid and, perhaps therefore, too honest to make the most of the bear garden procedures of Brussels, Luxembourg, and Strasbourg.

To some extent, by dint of working together and living closer to each other in terms of all kinds of social transactions over the past twelve to twenty years (the Schuman Plan is after all now twenty-one years old), the Six have made progress in mutual adaptation. The candidates' problem of coming fresh into an organization that has had a fairly intense life of its own for so long may have been eased by the lengthy learning process of ten years' fluctuating negotiations from outside and by a certain anticipatory adaptation on the part of sections of the business community since 1961. There has also been an increase in cultural, academic, political, and industrial contact between candidates and members quite apart from the upsurge in trade. Nevertheless this sort of communication may have to be sharply intensified. The much more acute contiguity with the Community into which entry will throw the candidates—with much less of a transition period than the present members had, considering the crystilization of patterns without the candidates—could otherwise result in lack of mutual comprehension and a backlash reaction (even perhaps among the present members) that could be embarrassing all round.

Yet even here there are no clear-cut guidelines to tell us how much suspicion is bred of ignorance. On the other hand what dose of familiarity may breed contempt? It would be worth looking at the experience of past forms of deliberately stimulated contacts from the thousands of officials annually involved in OECD committees to *au pair* girls, from reciprocal television broadcasts to veterans' visits to battlefields to learn from them any lesson that can be derived as to positive harm, mere failure, and success. How are national stereotypes and attitudes affected in different circumstances at different levels of interaction? The Franco-German treaty of 1963 would be a good case study in point.

Let us now turn to the question of the challenge of enlargement in terms of economic geography. Again, it once more raises in a more acute form problems which were already inherent in the political economy of the Six. Each of the new member states will be geographically remote. Moreover, except in the case of Denmark, each will be inaccessible by ordinary land transport from the industrial heartlands of the Community in Northern France, Belgium, Holland, and North-West Germany. Each of them, except Denmark, is already affected internally by serious regional maldistribution of economic activity. This is very likely to be accentuated by entry into an area of free trade and movement of factors of production in which their remoter regions become even more eccentric to the main poles of activity.

The results of enlargement will therefore be to accentuate the need for the Community, for the first time in its history, to take serious positive measures on nonagricultural problems of various kinds. So far all its main measures outside the farming sector have been of a negative character. When the treaty was first signed transport policy was put on a par with agricultural policy. It has since sadly dropped behind. But of course transport policy, however, effective it were made, is not enough. No one would believe that a mere Channel tunnel or anything of that type would be sufficient to overcome the geographical disadvantages of the United Kingdom, Norway, and Eire.

It remains obvious that no one who can serve the enlarged Community, 75 percent of whose purchasing power is on the continent with the remainder scattered between Norway and the British Isles, would, other things being equal, choose either Norway or Ireland or Britain to set up shop. Southern Italy's development has been problematic in spite of comparatively low wage levels. Other things must therefore be made unequal if a problem of geometry is not to turn into a national economic and Community political disaster. This means that from concentrating their attention on decaying agricultural regions to the extent they have in the past, the Community institutions will have to come to grips with the problems of decaying, and of mushrooming, industrial regions as well. Particularly if there is to be freedom of capital movement (and all the more so—a problem to which we shall revert—if exchange rate variations of the periphery against the center were ruled out by some form of monetary union), regional policy must move into the very center of the Community's concerns.

It is in any case now incumbent on the Community, not only for reasons of regional policy or merely to take into account its external objectives discussed above, to formulate a positive industrial policy. Its industrial weight in the world after enlargement can be stated simply in terms of the few figures provided in the following table:

	Some Leading Indicators — 1969			
	EEC	U.S.A.	U.S.S.R.	Japan
Steel Production (million metric tons)	137	128	110	82
Motor Vehicle Production (million)	11	10	1	5
Primary Energy Production (m.m. tons coal equivalent)	506	2020	1050	76
Imports ($ billion)	50	36	n.a.	15
Merchant Fleet (million tons)	77	19	n.a.	27
Industry as Contributor to GDP (%)	46	37	n.a.	39
GNP ($ billion)	564	948	490	167
Population	256	210	250	102

At the time the Spaak Report was written, outside of agriculture there were few domains in which the philosophy of laissez-faire did not—to the bulk of those preparing the treaty—seem at least for the moment to be fairly adequate for the EEC. Planning consciously for positive public interference at the Community level was scarcely envisioned in the treaties outside transport and sections of energy policy. In the energy field the West Europeans were, and as the above table shows, still are lagging behind some of their competitors. But coal had already been preempted by the ECSC and nuclear energy was hived off as requiring distinctive treatment by the separate Atomic Energy Community. The harmonization of factors affecting competition and the prevention of harmful restrictive practices seemed about the sum of what was required over and above the elimination of trading obstacles. As in so much else the legal instruments enshrined what were accepted to be the requirements of an age that already lay a little way back rather than the needs of the problems about to become the most acute. The ECSC was set up to maximize coal and steel production. Within a few years it had to be stood on its head to try the far more difficult task of leading an orderly retreat of coal in the face of other energy sources, notably oil. In addition, Euratom was effectively stymied by the French. It had little more practical success than ELDO (The European Launcher Development Organization) and ESRO (The European Space Research Organization) whose existence is all but forgotten except by the connoisseurs of functionalist experiments.

As a result, what cooperation there has been in technology policy has been not of a Community but of an intergovernmental, one shot, and oligolateral type: e.g., the abortive Franco-German tank—the Jaguar, the Airbus, and Concorde. In technical and financial terms, such cooperation has not been overly successful, and in any case it has been scant. The problems underlying it are various. The need to balance advantages on each project separately between countries leads to needless complications and suboptimal allocation of tasks. Both in their turn push up costs. Bilateral or oligolateral allocations of funds subject to unilateral national cutbacks and cut-offs overhang such projects with an aura of dicyness from the start. Lack of commitment to it by nonparticipant European states (as in the Airbus case) reduces the *chasse guardée* market on which the viability of the project depends. Lack of a common civil and military purchasing agency that would "Buy European" up to a certain point and bargain about technical ingredients where it buys from outside Europe leaves the fragmented European industries at a disadvantage on the market as well as on the development side.

The answer suggests itself, though it is obviously not in turn without problems of the most diverse kinds, from the negative statement of affairs. A wider technological community would have far more and more diverse projects available between which to strike a long-term balance of national advantage along technical rather than short-term political criteria. A Community policy in technology could then attempt to devise a truly European strategy of research and development by public, semipublic, existing, and new private entrepreneurial ventures on the supply side. Moreover, wherever possible, this would have to be matched by a common public procurement policy (from hospital and national insurance offices to public oil companies and air forces), to give effectiveness on the demand side to whatever the policy might be. It could be to "Buy American" in certain fields, to "Buy Japanese" in certain others, and to "Buy European" or even buy from Southern Italy, Northern Norway, or from the development regions of the British Isles. Later it might even include Malta, Senegal, or Jamaica. In any case buying would be based up to a certain margin on the best guestimate of long-run external economies to the Community of following any one of these policies or a combination of them.

It follows from some of the other considerations advanced concerning economic objectives that transport, energy, regional, industrial, and technology policy would remain qualified by a common environment policy. At first blush the problems of pollution may appear to be separate ones, of particular sources of nuisance in restricted areas suitable for piecemeal action. But quite apart from the absurdity of cleaning up, for instance, the Rhine through national action, the extra costs involved in, e.g., dealing with chemical works in any one area through any one national legislation become very much easier to impose if all competitors within the Community are simultaneously obligated to conform to analogous standards.

Perhaps this last of possibilities sounds as though it were a utopian set of platitudes. How can one have common military procurement without a common strategy which requires the same type of tactical weapons? For example, one Anglo-French aircraft project set out to combine fast climbs for interception from Lorraine airfields with long-range strafing operations East of Suez. How can one have a powerful regional policy without far greater political solidarity between countries? Just as the common agricultural policy was a method of "milking" the Germans for the benefit of French farmers, so a regional and industrial policy could boil down to milking the Germans for the benefit of Ulster and Scotland. How can one have ham and eggs unless one has both the ham and the eggs?

It is one of my contentions, however, that the accession of these particular four new members reenforces simultaneously the urgency and the incentives for much faster progress outside the agricultural field and also particularly in the field of industry and technology. It involves a dowry which makes common high technology industrial advance rather less difficult. EEC technology had little chance without the United Kingdom. With it in computers, in sections of the airframe industry, in nuclear equipment, in the rationalization of motor and other engineering industries, there is far greater scope. This is possible provided that the instruments for the purpose are forged, that vastly greater sums are made available for long-term Community commitments in which national compromise is struck not over every detail but only in the sum of all the parts. In other words such progress is possible, provided that the institutions of the Community are tightened up, strengthened, and given a new dynamic not for "political" reasons but for concrete operational and technical reasons.

MONETARY UNION

At the Hague Conference in December, 1969, apart from a general blessing to the idea of enlarging the Community, particular emphasis was given to one possible way of strengthening the EEC: by setting up a monetary union by the year 1980. The Werner Report has spelled out some of the implication, largely within the Euclidean system of fixed world exchange rates under the International Monetary Fund (IMF). As a first step the Six decided on a narrowing of the 1 percent band around the parity notified to the IMF within which market fluctuations are, or were allowed, to take place by central banks. In the long run, as the Germans correctly pointed out, a common monetary unit implies common decisions on fiscal and monetary policy insofar as they affect demand management in the Common Market as a whole. But since the French were not prepared to accept the logical corollaries of such union, the Germans were prepared only to accept a probationary five-year first stage to begin in the summer of 1971 with narrower fluctuations.

The irony of the situation began in May, 1971. Overwhelmed by a sudden influx of dollars, Germany proposed that since European currencies appeared overvalued in relation to the dollar a new policy was necessary. This was particularly true since both the common farm policy with its fixed intra-Community prices and the agreed first step to a monetary union means that the EEC currencies should stick closely together. Therefore, the Germans proposed that all curriencies should float together against the dollar. The French, in particular, rejected this plan. Thereupon the Germans and the Dutch began to float their currencies by themselves. This went as high as 8 percent above their notified parities and included not only a float against the dollar, but also against the lira, and the French and Belgian francs as well. This occurred just a few weeks before the exchange rate variations, according to Community agreement, were to be narrowed to 0.75 percent. In mid-August, the Six once more failed to reach agreement in even more monetarily dramatic circumstances when the dollar itself had joined the deutschemark and the guilder in "floating" against gold. The French were determined, at least as far as commercial transactions were concerned, to keep their gold parity fixed. However, they were prepared for nontrading transactions to institute a "controlled float."

This is not the place to discuss the future of the world monetary system, though the role which an enlarged Community with six seats on the Committee of Ten must play in any such reform is clearly of the first rank. Whether on a world scale the external adjustments that become cumulatively unavoidable as a result of internal divergences are made by either more or less controlled "free" market prices every business day, or by market prices fluctuating within a certain margin along "crawling pegs," or by market prices within very narrow "fixed" bands suddenly altered sharply by devlauations or revaluations overnight, is a far wider question than that of a European political economy. The plan for a European monetary union by 1980, particularly in the light of the accession of new members to the EEC, does however raise many of the same questions and in a no less acute form.

The Werner Plan foresees immutable exchange rates between the EEC countries to be consummated in a single currency in the way that the Scottish and English and Belgian and Luxembourg currencies have become unified or even more so if a single currency becomes acceptable without discount throughout the EEC as a single dollar is throughout the fifty United States. Now there is a respectable body of economic theory concerned with the advantages and disadvantages of a customs union or a free trade area both in static and, laterally to some extent, also in dynamic terms. But one looks in vain in the literature for the economic as distinct from the psychological and political arguments, in favor of a monetary union between areas whose psychological, political, social, and economic conditions remain substantially differentiated.[1] Moreover, respectable economic historians believe that southern Italy suffered greatly from monetary union within northern Italy. One may argue about the effects of monetary union on the Southern states in the United States and crucifixion on the cross of gold. And Scotland and Ireland might have had a different history but for monetary union. No one who was at the Hague has yet suggested that monetary union was pushed into this prime place in the final communique—or pulled out of his hat on the second (not the first) day of the conference by President Pompidou—as the result of profound economic cogitations.

Assuming the invariable rates of exchange have been acceptably set at the beginning (it would be making major assumptions to use the word "correctly"), the key problem is that of differential rates of inflation. It is a problem which after a period of relative quiescence has over the last two or three years made itself felt again with renewed salience. The Six managed from 1958 until 1968 to keep their exchange rates relatively stable. A French devaluation by 17.5 percent in December, 1958, on the eve of the first tariff cuts, and a German and Dutch revaluation in 1961 by 4.7 percent were the only variations in parities. In 1969 there were both the French revaluation by 12.5

percent and the German and Dutch revaluations after the first brief "float" occurred. The cumulative divergence in price levels and balance-of-payments positions was becoming too large to be ignored.

In the 1960-68 period the annual rate of change in consumer prices, not necessarily the most relevant index but at least a very salient one, varied within the Community by between 2.5 and 4 percent per annum. On the other hand, in the twelve months to the spring of 1971, the rate of increase was as low as 3.7 percent in Belgium but as high as 6.6 percent in the Netherlands. Among the candidate countries the figure was 8.8 percent in the United Kingdom and 10 percent in Ireland. Simple arithmetic shows that a differential of 1.5 percent compounded over eight or ten years must lead to a sizable discrepancy. The events of 1969 with their relative shift in value from the franc to the Deutschemark of about 20 percent confirm what small cumulative differentials can necessitate major exchange rate adaptations. When the differentials are as large as they have become between Belgium's under 4 percent and the United Kingdom's nearly 9 percent in price rises in twelve months extrapolation of these trends immediately points to major problems about the whole concept of a monetary union.

The latest adaptation of David Ricardo's theory of international trade shows that production patterns between countries takes place according to comparative advantage. Between areas of the same monetary region, however, where above all there are downward rigidities in the price of the factors of production, adaptation of production patterns will take place according to absolute advantage. If it is cheaper to produce both cars and chemicals in Milan than in Naples, or in Birmingham than in Belfast, or in Holland than in Britain, then both cars and chemicals, other things being equal, will be produced in a monetary union wherever they are cheapest to produce. Thus, in the preceding example Holland would bloom while Britain becomes a depressed area. The corollary of monetary union in such a case must be the massive transfer of resources through regional and industrial policies from one country to another. This is a deliberate highly visible policy that presupposes enormous political good will (analogous to that of Germany for France during the formative period of the EEC) or leverage (analogous to France in the Gaullist period) and very wide powers and a very large budget, indeed, for the Community institutions.

One may ask whether the time until 1980 is not sufficient for the basic governing differential rates of inflation to be harmonized. Clearly some of the factors will be ironed out in any case by competition within the customs union. However, freedom from customs' duties would of course be achieved for the new members only two years before the present deadline for monetary union. But there are other factors that are not modified too easily. The expectations of the population at large may not adapt as fast as necessary. At the moment there may just be no overlap at all between the maximum rate of inflation tolerable to the German electorate without serious political ructions and the minimum rate that will keep other economies growing or even just steady. The organization, ideology objectives, and tactics of trade unions in different countries vary as sharply as, indeed probably more so, than the private expectations and investment behavior of management and capital. This is a problem that will by no means be overcome, in the medium and smaller scale enterprise at any rate, even by the unification of European capital markets and free right of establishment. Of course to some extent it has been part of the "dialectic of intensity" of Monnet-type Community building to put the cart deliberately before the horse and make the horse catch up. But some carts are just so large they threaten, unless one is very careful, to run over the poor horse.

Obviously it follows from the whole concept of an economic Community that unilateral rogue elephant policies in exchange rate matters cannot be allowed. When France and Italy go one way and Germany and Holland the other it may not be easy to tell which is the rogue elephant. But that only makes matters worse. Of course monetary policy and exchange rates become a vital matter of Community concern. A devaluation may be far more protectionist than any new tariff imposition, and a period of wage restraint can act the same way. But to deduce that there, therefore, must be monetary union eliminating all possibility of exchange rate variations between areas within the Community is to leap to an unjustified conclusion. Certainly by renouncing the possibility of revaluing or devaluing the nation-states are abandoning a vital aspect of sovereignty. But by establishing a monetary union they are not transferring it to the Community. They are simply throwing it away. Monetary union means that the Community itself is abandoning a major potential instrument of its own monetary, economic, regional, and industrial policies: the possibility of balancing regional disparities by exchange rate policy. That rules must made about common decision-making on exchange rates is one thing. But that no differentiation within the Community should be possible by the most traditionally liberal of all instruments is a very different matter. In view of the geographically eccentric and in parts regionally depressed character of at least three of the applicants, the arguments about monetary union—already dubious within a Community of six—will now, particularly after the events of the summer of 1971, need to be sharpened up a great deal.

INSTITUTIONAL REQUIREMENTS

Almost everything said in this paper so far about whether a monetary union is or is not implemented has institutional implications. The mere increase in the number of states which are members, the particular characteristics of the present candidate countries, the extra weight in the world which their accession will carry in its wake, the need in any case even for a Community of six to turn increasingly to positive action beyond the farm sector all have a variety of important implications. At the very least they imply far greater willingness by the nation-states to implement the spirit of the treaty and let the institutions work as they were intended or beyond what was intended. They even imply embarking on actual reform of the institutional practices, though not necessarily apart from the adaptations of the treaty texts required by enlargement.

Constitutionally, the treaties for key policy decisions remain based on the qualified majority vote in the Council of Ministers on proposals submitted by the Commission. The reality of constitutional practice has always respected what were generally recognized to be the vital interests of any nation-state. The Commission was in any case there to see that no coalition of interest could override minority interests *per se,* but only, if at all, as a by product of the elaboration of a Community policy. That means in the interests of the Community as a whole. The national sacrifices entailed on one side or another were softened in Community practice by the concept of a package deal obtained by the deliberate constitutional device of a crisis against a deadline. These package deals consisted of the demand for national sacrifices from several or all participants in different fields but simultaneously.

This crisis mechanism escalated in 1965 when the Commission gambled on a package deal. In fact, it was not such a deal between nation-states at all but one between the Commission itself and France. It is not surprising that President De Gaulle, as a result of his entire conception of nation-states as ultimate political realities and his contempt for Community institutions, rejected the bargain of vastly more powers for the Commission in return for an agricultural policy profitable to his farmers. Yet after the French elections in which the farmers showed their displeasure, the Six reached the misnamed Luxembourg Compromise of January, 1966. This was a formula of agreement to disagree. The other five recognized that France believed that "when very important issues are at stake, the discussion must be continued until unanimous agreement is reached." In other words each state has the right to declare some issue as being very important to itself, and, therefore, irresolvable by qualified majority vote. On a minimalist interpretation perhaps the Luxembourg formula merely formalized political realities as they stood before the 1965-66 crisis. These were realities already being shifted by the deliberately somewhat ostentatious brinkmanship of the French government. Nevertheless, this express formulation by removing an area of deterrent uncertainty may itself have further shifted constitutional practice.

The problem now poses itself in the form of a dilemma. On the one hand, it was expressly and openly part of the deal reached between the British Prime Minister and the French President in May, 1971, that the Treaty of Rome must be handled along the lines of the French interpretation (or misinterpretation) with due respect for the vital interests of each member state. One may perhaps disregard the question of principle as to how far a single candidate country could legitimately make such a bilateral agreement on the meaning of a treaty to which it was not yet a party. This is all the more complex since the signatory of the treaty with whom it reached agreement had avowed itself by the Luxembourg formula isolated on this particular point from all the remaining parties to the treaty. Tactically, both in terms of domestic opinion and in terms of diplomatic requirements, one can argue that there may not have been much else the Prime Minister could have done. Clearly, the other five states as they had shown earlier in their reactions to the "Soames affair" were anxious that the British should come to terms with the French in one way or another. But on the other hand what matters now, and it is a problem of desperate urgency, is how the Community will be run in a period when its tasks will have become substantially larger and in many ways more pressing both at home and in its world role. National interests will have become more variegated and potentially much more opposed to each other, yet they are implicitly recognized as being subject to protection by ten possible vetoes.

It is my belief that whatever the present intentions of the British government or the present attitudes in British public and popular opinion, over the next few years circumstances may well make the British adopt, or wish they had adopted from the beginning, a rather more "supranational" stance. Her geographically eccentric position, her past neglect of social infrastructure, her low rate of capital investment, her problems of cost inflation, the precariousness of her balance of payments and the low level of her foreign exchange reserves compared with her liquid liabilities make it in Britain's interest to enlarge the scope of Community action. This includes an enlargement of the Community budget, the strengthening of its executive, and a streamlining of its decision-making machinery. In an EEC the relatively weak must benefit from the assistance of the more advanced. In product per head Britain will come about seventh or eighth in the EEC or Ten. It is obviously in her interest for the EEC to become as much of a Community as possible with large reallocative functions and an efficient output of policy and implementation of decision.

Yet one can hardly wait for such a conversion on the part of the British before any changes are made in the practice of the Council of Ministers to adapt it to the complications of a Community of Ten. The price to pay for everyone to learn the dangers of, for instance, subjecting all decisions to an Irish or Danish veto, might be too great. The further the EEC proceeds toward integration beyond the agricultural sphere, the more decisions will have to be made and the more urgently will they have to be made. Such decisions will be made in circumstances where delay or absence of decision constitutes in effect the adoption of certain alternatives and the rejection of certain others by default of conscious positive Community action. Nowhere is this more clear than in the monetary domain. Much the same holds good in the EEC's external relations where opportunities cannot be put into cold storage and circumstances are undergoing constant change. Thought must, therefore, be given to the forms of procedure to be adopted from January 1, 1973, on.

Among the suggestions put forward to obtain more decisive action on Commission proposals requiring a qualified majority vote perhaps the following is the most feasible. The member states should at least bind themselves not to abstain from voting in cases where the Commission feels that a decision one way or the other must be made. It then becomes necessary for a state either to declare its vital interests threatened and thereby to warn off the others explicitly, or else to vote and if necessary submit to the results of that vote. This is preferable to operating in the ambiguity of delay and indecision. It must again be recalled that such qualified majority voting takes place only on proposals of the Commission. The Commission is there specifically to seek Community solutions and to prevent the formulation of policies simply suited to interest constellations of the member states.

There is also an older proposal which was revived by the French President early in 1971. He suggested that each government should appoint a Minister of European Affairs to represent it at the Council. The idea has certain virtues. The Council deals with very many matters that are not foreign but traditionally domestic policy. Indeed, perhaps the major part of its business is of that kind. A Minister of European Affairs could thus not simply act as coordinator of home departments involved in problems of a European dimension (and most home departments seem to have a good many of these problems now), but also take these problems out of the surroundings of traditional diplomacy as represented by foreign offices. This would mark the fact that relations within Europe are not foreign policy but the domestic concern of a Community. Where the external relations of the Community are concerned, naturally the foreign offices would be involved at least as much as the agricultural ministeries are concerned in the EEC's agricultural problems. Several countries have gone some way along the road, including Britain, though Mr. Rippon remains a minister at the Foreign Office. But there are clearly problems of coordination either way, and it may not be wise to impose uniform solutions on all ten member states.

But there is also a structural problem, or rather several interconnected structural problems, in the case of the Commission. These are areas in which the agreement of Members do seem a matter of priority. These again are problems which would have arisen in any case as the EEC has to turn to positive action beyond farm policy and as the external demands made on it as highlighted in the summer of 1971 become more pressing. Enlargement will quantitatively and qualitatively accentuate them. Simply to increase the Commission back to a size of fourteen members seems likely merely to make it more unwieldly. The wider cultural and political gamut of the constituencies from which Commission members will in effect be dispatched to Brussels will tend to aggravate the difficulties of collegiate decision-making and collective cabinet responsibility. This will occur without by any means ensuring that the main subjects which need competent attention at the Commission level can in fact be looked after by a Commission member competent in them. So here again enlargement should be made an opportunity to re-think what would have to be re-thought in any case.

Perhaps the requirements of cohesive policy formation in the conditions of the later 1970's can best be met by changes in the method of appointment of the Commission which would not entail any change in the Treaties of Rome. If agreement could first be reached informally by the Council on a Commission President and this prospective President could then be consulted—or preferably exercise his own informal initiative in the selection of his colleagues to be appointed by the Council—then a truly collegiate Commission could emerge. This would include a coverage of the range of subjects along coherent lines on which they all are agreed from the outset. Indeed it is constitutionally not easy to make sense of the European Parliament's right to dismiss the Commission only in a body unless it is in fact a politically integrated team rather than a miscellaneous collection of individuals meeting as a by-product of national balancing acts and having to put up with each other for their periods of office. One does not have to stress the long-term political effects of such an approach to the formation of the Commission as an embryonic European cabinet-type executive and policy initiator. What does have to be stressed are the internal and external economic, social, and political implications of not moving toward a much more coherent and dynamic European Community. Unless it now equips itself and makes concrete decisions on how to act as a government with immediate duties to its own 250 million people and with a cardinal share in world tasks far beyond its own continent, it may find itself paralyzed and by its very weight in the world incurring a heavy responsibility for failing the rest of humanity. As far as Britain is concerned were she to abdicate the instruments of government she does have and to merge within a wider unit with bigger and more diverse problems still, there would then be no way out of her impasse. It would be to go from being difficult to govern to entering moderate chaos—like committing suicide for fear of death.

NOTE

1. See, however, the more recently published article by J. M. Fleming "On Exchange Rate Unification," *Economic Journal*, (September, 1971); and *Integration Through Monetary Union?*, Institut für Weltwirtschaft an der Universität Kiel, J. C. B. Mohr, 1971.

3

INDUSTRIAL
RELATIONS
AND THE
EUROPEAN COMMUNITY

Heinz Hartmann

Everybody is dissatisfied with the sagging tempo of European economic integration. I am not going to predict more rapid advances in the future. On the contrary, in looking at some apparent obstacles, we have identified only the top of the iceberg. Some recent developments on the European social scene allow us to infer that economic integration will be slowed down even more than in the past. In particular, recent stirrings of class conflict, the development of a new working class, and increased insecurity on the part of the trade unions are turning into handicaps for the establishment of a European economic community.

In developing my point, I propose to start by looking at industrial relations patterns in EEC countries. Will it be possible to standardize labor-management relations in Europe—to the point where companies in different countries may merge without significant upheaval in the relationships between employers and employees? Plans have been developed by the EEC for a uniform system of industrial relations. But precisely at the point, when first steps are taken by organized labor and management in the direction of a uniform scheme, such incipient cooperation is disturbed by a revival of class antagonisms and similarly adverse events.

Class conflict, of course, is nothing new to the European scene and there have been intermittent outbursts in all of the countries concerned. Even where the traditional class structure has broken down the ideologies of social strife have been perpetuated. Apart from the

Communists, many West European trade unions have refused to abandon their class-conscious view of employer-employee relationships. More recently, their intransigence is reinforced and, in fact, rivaled by the militancy of worker groups outside of organized labor.

In order to concentrate attention on industrial relations, class conflict, and economic integration it is necessary to leave out some highly worthwhile but time-consuming subjects. For one, it is not possible to go into the question of why present labor-management relations have come to be as different as they are. Second, official efforts at raising the "property status" of employees which often is considered the alternate route toward securing and improving their social standing will not be discussed. Third, countries now outside the EEC, such as Yugoslavia, which for reasons of current policy or analytical model-building might offer extremely useful information, will not be included.

On the other hand, disproportionate attention will be devoted to the case of West Germany because current planning for employee representation and participation in a European corporation, i.e., a firm operating on a standardized system of industrial relations, is strongly oriented toward the rules which regulate labor-management relations in West German industries.

CONSULTATION, CODETERMINATION, CONTROL IN PRIVATE ENTERPRISE

There are many ways in which to characterize industrial relations. For reasons which will become more apparent later, I prefer to use categories which classify systems of industrial relations by the degree of formal representation of employees.

At the outset, for systematic reasons, a distinction should be made between three levels of employee participation: 1. influence over decisions on the job, 2. participation at the company level, and 3. employee representation at the industrial or national level. In the free market economies, employee participation is most common at the level of the individual firm. There are some few exceptions in which representation is to be found at the national level. Surprisingly, employees rarely enjoy institutionalized rights to participation on the job. As one German source points out, none of the West European countries shows any significant evidence of joint decision-making on the job, on the basis of law or private contract.[1]

Concerning the company level, a set of descriptive categories is presented by George Strauss and Eliezer Rosenstein.[2] In their terminology, minor degrees of representative participation are subsumed in the joint consultation model. This model applies where management makes the final decisions but workers' representatives are permitted to be heard. There is a general indication by management here that it will take into account workers' interests. But there is no formal way in which workers can suspend or redress managerial decisions. The joint consultation model extends over a fairly wide range of participation. At one extreme, it implies nothing more than relationshiops of information. In this case, workers at least have a claim to information. At the other extreme, joint consultation approaches highly cooperative relationships. Management consults with labor so that eventual decisions are the outcome of joint deliberations—even if there is no formal system of joint decision-making.

The second model implies just that: In the joint decision-making model, workers, representatives, and management are jointly represented on a decision-making body. Labor representatives here are privileged to vote. But with this model, too, we have to examine the range of applicability. Specifically, employee influence on the shape and content of decisions depends on the composition of the decision-making body. Where employees are in a minority, management may get away with decisions which in fact are unilateral. Where the composition of such bodies is more balanced, employee influence can be considerable. The latter extreme, however, is fairly rare, as far as the market economies are concerned, such a full-fledged system of comanagement exists only in the German coal and steel industries. It may be for this reason that a literal translation of the German term for this system of joint decision-making: *Mitbestimmung,* codetermination, is used for this model.

Following Strauss and Rosenstein, "finally, we have the workers control model whereby final authority rests in the elected representatives of the work force. In theory, these representatives make policy and employ management to carry it out." There are other conceptions of workers control, some of which are not as demanding as the definition just quoted. According to a Belgian analyst of the trade union movement in his country, the tendency toward workers "control" aims at preserving the maximum of independence and autonomy for the trade union.[3]

Interpretations occasionally vary within one source. Another noted Belgian author, Ernst Mandel, in referring to workers' control sometimes implies veto powers for workers' representatives. At other times, he refers to the occupation of company premises by workers as practiced in recent strikes in France and Italy. Obviously, this third model also covers quite varied cases of employee influence.[4]

INSTITUTIONS OF EMPLOYEE PARTICIPATION IN EEC COUNTRIES[5]

Legal arrangements for employee participation in France, Italy, Holland, Belgium, Luxemburg, and West Germany are highly diverse. On top of this diversity, we often note a discrepancy between *de jure* and *de facto* situations. What is more, the institutions of participation are in a state of flux and unless one follows changes from month to month, even current information is likely to become obsolete. Fortunately, we do not have to exhaust the intricacies of participation legislation here. But, for reasons which were indicated, the situation in the Federal Republic of Germany warrants special attention.

In Western Germany, contrary to the United States, trade unions are not organized on the company level. Organizationally and operationally, they are focused on the level of the industry where they set wages in collective bargaining with employer associations. This particular structure and activity at times has been called a source of weakness for these trade unions. Since they only set floors for wages and working conditions, an active works council in conjunction with employee members on the supervisory board frequently can improve on the agreements concluded by the trade unions and thereby acquire invidious standing. Since West German trade unions are also not very active ideologically they tend to occupy a position on the periphery of industry relations rather than in the center.

In the other EEC countries where the institutionalization of consultation and codetermination have lagged by comparison, trade unions tend to play a much more important role. In the absence of strong works councils, let alone labor directors or significant entrenchment in supervisory boards, the organizations of labor tend to exercise influence well into the individual plant. Besides, many of the trade unions in these other EEC countries subscribe to militant class ideologies. Thus they make their presence felt all the more. This is not to deny, of course, that their ideological preoccupations also lead to organizational rifts which drain some of their strength.

In Western Germany, the mainstay of employee participation lies in the works council. This council which is representative of blue- and white-collar workers is organizationally independent from the trade unions even if most council members as a rule are trade union members.

The council enters into joint consultation with management on a number of issues. In the area of personnel, the powers of a German works council in many instances informally border on joint decision-making. The distribution tends to be the reverse in the supervisory board which roughly corresponds to the board of directors in an American firm. Employees occupy one-third of the seats in this company organ. Formally, they are included in the supervisory board for joint decision-making. Because of their minority status, however, their influence in fact remains at the level of joint consultation.

To the extent that industrial relations in the Federal Republic of Germany have drawn the attention of outsiders, their interest has concentrated mostly on the novelty of codetermination. Codetermination or comanagement was introduced to the German coal, iron, and steel industries twenty years ago. The Codetermination Law of 1951 gave new powers to the works councils of old. It also stipulated that half of the seats on the supervisory boards in these industries should be allocated to employee representatives. Under the chairmanship of one neutral, not party to either management or labor, employee representatives genuinely influence managerial decisions. From the vantage point of this board, labor members are in a position to extend their influence well into the executive ranks below this apex of the company hierarchy.

A third major provision of the Codetermination Law provides for the inclusion of a labor director on the executive committee. The labor director, often considered the symbol of "comanagement German style," is a full-fledged member of the committee, that is, his responsibility and privileges are not limited to his prime function of personnel administration but extend to general management. The labor director is appointed by the supervisory board from a trade union slate which, as a rule, is argued out between representatives of the employees of a specific company and representatives of the national trade union.

In France, works councils as a rule enjoy no more than the right to joint consultation. It is true that in nationalized industries, employees are empowered to occupy one-third of all seats in the supervisory board (conseil d'administration or conseil de surveillance). As we noted for West Germany, employee representatives have not been able to make much out of such a minority position. The ultimate reasons for this failure in France may be different from those in Germany. The fact remains that what looks like an important institutional advance in fact does not amount to significant social influence.

There are other instances to show that the discrepancy between *de jure* and *de facto* situations in France is especially large. Concerning information, for example, legislation in France stipulates that the works council may have access to all bookkeeping data in a corporation. Or, works councils have been given the right to express their opinion on increases in prices. In spite of such specific and far-reaching concessions, however, employee participation in France in effect has long lagged behind such formal rights.

In Belgium and Holland, the institutions of employee participation are not very widely developed. As in France, the head of the firm at the same time acts as chairman of the works council. In Belgium, he in fact may nominate delegates of his own to the works council as long as their number does not exceed the number of employee representatives in the works council. In the Netherlands, management faces nothing more than the general obligation to acquaint works council members with the economic situation of the firm.

The rate of progress in institutionalized participation has been slowest in Italy. Even though the Italian constitution explicitly concedes the right to employees to participate in management, Italy has been slow to develop those features of industrial relations which in other EEC countries have long been taken for granted. It was only in the 1950's and 1960's, that contracts were concluded between trade unions and employer associations to establish works councils in a number of firms.

If there were more space available, we would have to look into other questions concerning the institutions of participation. To what extent, for example, are the legal institutions backed by public opinion, by a general desire on the part of the respective population to see employee participation regulated and promoted. In the case of Western Germany, for instance, we know that in 1970, 70 percent of all informants in a survey of West German citizens above eighteen years of age endorsed joint consultation and codetermination as they now exist in their country. The degree of approval naturally was higher among workers (82 percent). But even among professional and managerial personnel, about half of all informants voted in favor of the current regulations.[6] Such popular consensus casts an important light on the staying powers of the existing pattern and on the potential for growth in participation.

PLANNING FOR CODETERMINATION IN A EUROPEAN CORPORATION

It is obvious that this heterogeneity of national solutions to industrial relations problems provides obstacles to the unification of

European economies. Notably, this diversity impedes the free mobility of labor and of firms between nations. It is a handicap in the establishment and management of foreign subsidiaries and it interferes with the merger of companies within the confines of the European economic community. In addition, there have been indications of fear that the retention of diversity in industrial relations systems among EEC countries will lead to an exodus of firms into those nations which maintain the least stringent, the most conservative forms of employee participation. These fears will never prove justified to the extent that they are now voiced. But there is no doubt that different levels in social privileges and responsibilities will exercise a somewhat similar effect to that of different levels in wages and other material benefits.

In the interest of standardization of industrial relations, the Commission of the EEC has given thought to a constitution for a European corporation which because of its generally accepted and uniform arrangement of labor-management relationships could easily shift its headquarters between EEC countries, establish subsidiaries across national boundaries, and enter into mergers with similarly constituted companies. The Commission has asked a Dutch expert, Peter Sanders, and a French lawyer, Gérard Lyon-Caen, to prepare drafts for such a generalized system. In the meantime, especially the ideas of Professor Lyon-Caen have received wide circulation and drawn comments from both employer associations and organized labor.

In their intentions, the two drafts move in different directions. The suggestions by Sanders more or less imply a retention of the status quo in the respective countries. Existing institutions of consultation and codetermination are to be maintained. But there is to be no export of advances in some countries into other countries which are presently satisfied with comparatively low degrees of employee participation. Furthermore, Sanders limits himself to discussing participation in select bodies of the company hierarchy. He practically excludes from his consideration employee consideration at the level of the works council and employee representation by the trade unions.

By way of contrast, Lyon-Caen in his draft pays attention to a wider range of forms of participation. His suggestion is that different patterns of industrial relations be evaluated regarding their consequences for labor and management, and that top executives in a European corporation should jointly deliberate with the trade unions concerned which, of a number of equivalent patterns of employee representation, should be adopted. Lyon-Caen tries to identify three combinations of industrial relations arrangements which might be considered alternatives in the choice open to a European corporation. On top of his own selection, he is open to suggestions from outside as long as the newly proposed alternative proves functionally equivalent to the three patterns singled out so far.

There is no doubt that the recommendations by Lyon-Caen are more progressive than those by Sanders. Lyon-Caen, it is true, also is willing to accept national industrial relations traditions—to a point. The various patterns outlined by Lyon-Caen are expressive of different national styles and preferences. On the other hand, he goes beyond Sanders in several ways: 1. He modifies existing patterns so that he arrives at fairly equivalent solutions; 2. the overall level of employee participation in the three patterns now offered for choice is approaching the German model of comanagement or codetermination; and 3. he explicitly takes into account trade union interest in shaping industrial relations systems by asking that the final choice be argued out in joint discussions between management and organized labor.

In recognition of the opportunities and dangers arising from the emergence of blueprints for a European corporation, trade union experts and sympathizers have begun to ask for the formation of a European trade union organization which could serve as an effective partner in negotiations at the EEC level. As is to be expected, such developments are motivated not only by cooperative intents but are supported also by defensive motivations: organized labor wants to stand ready to meet any new challenges on a European scale. In the meantime, such insights and demands have led to a concerted organizational effort on various fronts. The new trend of union organization is spearheaded by the representatives of the metalworkers in EEC countries. Building on a European Metal Committee established in 1963 as a clearing agency for trade union information, the European metalworkers unions have entered upon several projects of European cooperation and upon the formation of a European "supertrade union."

For example, individual projects of cooperation were launched in multinational companies with subsidiaries in more than one of the EEC countries. Thus, metalworkers' representatives from five countries in the Community combined to negotiate with Philips management in Holland. Executives of the metalworkers' unions in various subsidiaries of the Ford Motor Company in West Germany, Great Britain, and Belgium met to discuss their joint interests vis-à-vis management. A second incentive for trade union cooperation in Europe has been sheer correspondence in production lines between such major European employers as Fiat in Italy and Citroen in France or Sabca in Belgium Fokker in Holland, Dassault in France. Third, trade unions have responded to organizational cooperation on the part of different firms in the EEC. Thus the merger of Fokker in the Netherlands and VFW, a

German aircraft company, led to new linkages between the respective Dutch and German trade unions. But mere technical cooperation between select European firms also proved a stimulant to cooperation on the union side. The joint efforts of the British Aircraft Corporation and Sud Aviation in France in building the "Concorde" or between German and French firms in developing a European airbus led to increased communication and interaction between British, French, and German trade unions.

Meanwhile, the European metalworkers' unions have been presented with a suggestion by the German unit to establish a European metalworkers' federation before the end of 1971. The author of this proposal, highly respected among European union officers, was careful to point out that he does not have in mind a general fusion of national unions. But he said the time was ripe to develop a program of action to which all unions in Western Europe could subscribe. In particular, he asked the Brussels Commission to make sure that the rights of employees and their trade unions would not be depressed below their current achievements. From the context, it seemed obvious that he had in mind the full application of the German codetermination model to a European corporation.[7]

Another vanguard in the drive toward the establishment of a united union front within the EEC is to be found among the organizations of the chemical workers in Europe. As early as in 1968, most trade unions in this particular branch of industry who participated in a conference at Frankfurt, West Germany, showed some inclination to accept the German pattern of codetermination as their objective in a European solution to industrial relations problems.

The appeal of codetermination as practiced in the Federal Republic of Germany and reflected both in European trade union programs and in EEC planning for a European corporation may well be traced to the comparative success of the German model. While the effects of codetermination still cannot be assessed in terms of dollars and cents, there is widespread agreement in West Germany that comanagement of this type has not interfered with industrial efficiency, that authority relationships have been improved, that overall relationships between employers and employees have developed in a mutually satisfactory manner.[8]

The very trade unions which strongly insist on comanagement take pride in the claim that German trade unions, in comparison to the organizations of labor in other industrial nations of the West, since 1945 have least disturbed economic development by strikes or other measures of industrial conflict. In between 1962 and 1966, for instance, workdays lost per one thousand persons in Western Germany amounted to 2; in Belgium, 16; in France, 23; in the United States, 55; in Italy, 139. This record is advanced by trade unions themselves as evidence of the workability and efficiency of the codetermination pattern.[9]

Even in times of crisis, comanagement is said to work. When mass unemployment and plant shutdowns threatened industrial peace in 1967, trade union executives in the codetermination industries claimed credit for upholding social stability. As the president of the mineworkers union maintained in 1968, there would have been killings and other violence if, during the times of crisis of the German coal industry, codetermination had been missing from this industry. It was only because of the comanagement system, he said, that the union officers were able to channel and drain off the emergent radicalism.[10]

There is a temptation at this point to draw certain conclusions from our materials. If discussions at the European Commission revolve around a projected industrial relations scheme which fairly closely approaches the codetermination pattern; if the European trade unions are accepting comanagement as their common objective and are allying themselves as partners for negotiations; if the codetermination institutions have worked reasonably well in West Germany then a standardization of the industrial relations systems in Europe and the economic integration of which it is part may not be hopeless or in fact imminent. Such a conclusion, however, would ignore criticisms of codetermination in which the positive relationships between joint decision-making and worker integration into the social system of the firm are thrown open to doubt.

TRADE UNIONS AND SPONTANEOUS ACTION

One of the most cogent reasons for skepticism vis-à-vis codetermination and the trade unions backing this system lies in the fact that Western Europe including Western Germany in the past two years has seen a rash of labor-management conflicts which either slipped out from under union control or originated outside the formal labor-management system to begin with. It is true that trade union influence has increased in some ways recently. In France, for example, the December reforms following the May revolts of 1968 explicitly did away with the former exclusion of trade unions from the individual firm. Inasmuch as such exclusion had been named responsible for the frequent failures of labor-management relations in France, the improvement in trade union standing seemed to signal a major advance. On the other hand, the very revolts of May, 1968, had shown that the French trade unions, including the powerful CGT, were unable for a time to control their members—let alone unorganized workers; that the overall allegiance of the rank and file left much to be desired for the union leadership; and that the activities, or more precisely the inactivities, of the union apparatus frequently provoked bitter criticisms from a militant membership.

It is not exaggerating facts to say that worker unrest in France in May and June of 1968 clearly had revolutionary overtones. This violent opposition against the prevailing social system which involved the occupation of factories such as Renault or Sud Aviation was not encouraged to any significant extent by the trade unions but promoted by individual workers and small worker groups who were acting "spontaneously" on their own. This independent, rebellious movement gained added significance from the fact that it was not a downtrodden proletariate which rose from dumb suffering but rather the highly qualified segment of the labor force in such companies which took the lead in attacking the system.

Another spontaneous revolt which received less publicity occurred less than one year later in the Fiat works of Turin, Italy. The scope of this uprising, to be sure, was considerably smaller. Still, this case also is instructive because it shows not only that there are bitter antagonisms between workers and union bureaucrats but also demonstrates how workers can react constructively.[11] The drawn-out strike at Fiat originated in a comparatively minor incident. On April 12, 1969, Fiat management decided to transfer a labor agitator among its employees from one job to another. In immediate protest, thousands of Fiat workers went on strike. As this strike became more organized, a rival system of worker representation emerged. Apart from the "departmental delegates" (delegati di linea) who enjoyed the confidence of the trade unions, there suddenly appeared "group delegates" (delegati di squadra) who operated outside the trade union system, supported by their immediate work groups. The group delegates abruptly asked for full-fledged codetermination in questions of concern to Fiat workers. During the following months strike after strike occurred in the company. As time went on, the alienation between the official representation apparatus and spontaneously acting groups of workers gained in momentum. Workers openly denounced the trade unions and the Communist Party which they claimed had resigned themselves to working within the system. The radicalism of worker demands increased. As posters on the barricades within the company announced: "What we want is: All." By means of leaflets and daily bulletins which were prepared by the workers themselves (*Lotta Continua, Potere*

Operaio, etc.), the independent struggle of workers was given voice and system. They interpreted the Fiat strikes as a decisive step toward the autonomous organization of the Italian working class.

Labor dissatisfaction at Fiat took on ever new degrees of militancy and finally spread into the community. Workers organized parades of protest inside the factory and destroyed new cars and manufacturing equipment. They demonstrated in city streets, refused to pay rent for their living quarters and fares for public transportation. Finally, they achieved a new peak of escalation by turning against their own trade unions. Decrying the departmental delegates drawn from trade union slates, they proclaimed: "All of us are delegates." They in fact denounced the official delegates as being enemies of the worker. Unions and the Communist Party of Italy were denounced for using workers as figures on a political chessboard on which they tried to conclude their own self-centered deals. They asserted that the workers' objectives of establishing an autonomous organization of labor could only be achieved outside and against the trade unions.

Between 1967 and 1970, West Germany also saw an unprece-dented number of spontaneous strikes. Until 1968, such activities mostly were of a defensive character. Typical of such defensive actions were demonstrations against the shutdown of mines in the Ruhr area. Up to this point, the German trade unions had managed to retain some degree of control over worker demonstrations. Then came the notori-ous September strikes of 1969. To use a literal translation of a German expression, they taught the unions to be afraid. Wildcat strikes erupted in a large number of companies. The first of these started in one of the largest German steel mills. When management did not immediately respond to spontaneous wage demands, close to 300,000 workers went on strike—and increased their demands by 50 percent. Within one day, management completely gave in. Two weeks later, wildcat strikes had spread to another sixty-eight companies and the total workdays lost was well above half-million. In most cases, the workers were able to achieve their objectives.

The September strikes lacked the militancy which was character-istic of the French and Italian strikes. While strikes and demonstrations occasionally involved a show of black and red flags, German workers as a rule abstained from radicalism. On the other hand, the September strikes involved a similar alienation between trade union organizations and individual workers as had been apparent in these other countries. It is true that a good many of these strikes were organized and promoted by trade union members or lower officials. But the formal trade union leadership tended to frown on these strikes. Union officers watched with a certain awe and tried to regain influence over worker demands and activities. On the other side of the fence, workers openly showed disappointment over the sedate role of the trade unions. At the same time, they were more definitely oriented toward economic rather than political goals. This may be explained in part by the fact that the government and local authorities shied away from confrontations with the workers.

In September, 1970, the Federal Republic of Germany witnessed another round of wildcat strikes. The problem continues to be unsettling to the organized part of the labor movement since unions have a real fear of loosing their well established influence over a long docile membership.

These developments tend to show that in the standardization of industrial relations systems and in the reliance on trade unions for partnership in such an effort, an important new variable has intervened in the form of spontaneously acting workers and groups of workers. Whether their demands be purely economic or oriented toward autonomy even in the political sense, they tend to suspend existing rules or to initiate new ones. The dynamics introduced by this new variable put into perspective the formal patterns which preoccupy so much of the thinking of trade unions, employer associations, and academic experts about the design of industrial relations systems. What good, one might ask, are official negotiations over arrangements such as offered by Lyon-Caen, if significantly large groups of workers refuse to be bound by any limited choice.

THE DEVELOPMENT OF A NEW WORKING CLASS

Much attention has been given during recent years to the fact that some of the spontaneous strike activities were spearheaded by highly qualified workers, i.e., workers with a high degree of formal education or specialized training. In fact, some of the most radical actions were traceable to this sector of the labor force. Such attention coincided with the recognition that highly qualified manpower represents an ever increasing percentage of the total of persons employed in industry. On the Marxist side, the awareness of these facts and trends is supplemented by the notion that this new variant of the social intelligentsia: subprofessionals, technicians, highly skilled workers in the conventional sense cannot identify ideologically with management but rather enter into solidarity with other segments of labor.

It was the French author, Serge Mallet, who in his article on la nouvelle classe ouvriere identified this particular category of employees as "a new working class."[12] The members of this class—in the description of Serge Mallet—are characterized by their occupational focus on the *creation intelectuelle,* that is, on research, on management, on control. These workers are fairly close in their occupational status to management. In fact, they are much concerned with leadership. But according to Mallet, this new class is very much aware of its employee status and actively interested in defending itself against its employers. In this struggle, the "new working class [is] conscious of its importance and its strength and anxious to see its [rights and] responsibilities for the running of the undertaking brought on a par with those [it has] for the operation of the [production] processes."[13] According to the source just quoted, the French crisis in May and June of 1968, during which demands of this nature were much more vocal in the sectors using advanced technology than in others, has confirmed Mallets' theory. In the opinion of Ernst Mandel, the growing contrast between technological developments and the inhumanity of formal and personal constraints in the company organization is felt most keenly by those employees who graduated from higher levels of education or specialized training. The higher the occupational qualifications of the employee, the more transparent this contrast—and the more explosive. In the case of a fully automated industry, the contradiction between authoritarian or quasi-authoritarian structures of work and, on the other hand, the individual's capacity for self-determination if he is highly educated will become extreme. So Mandel leads us to expect that to an ever increasing degree, the initiative in protest will shift to the members of the new working class.[14]

Anticipations like those by Ernst Mandel have not gone unchallenged. The very fact that highly qualified workers were able to regain some of their work autonomy may center their attention on their work task rather than the relationship to the company hierarchy. Experts are predisposed to value problem-solving to begin with. Now, the less they are drawn into heirarchial conflicts over the degree of autonomy on the job, the more they are likely to loose themselves in tackling their particular task. Doubts concerning the leadership potential or, more modestly speaking, the conflict potential of highly qualified labor also are encouraged by the fact of their middle class origin. In combination with their incipient or explicit professionalism, this middle class background—often of the petite bourgeois variety—is expected to encourage political conservatism or apathy.[15]

To the extent that such fears are warranted, the new working class may not be much of a class at all. On the contrary, the highly qualified members of the labor force rather than sharing a general and possibly militant class consciousness may have to be viewed as self-centered and task-oriented specialists. This is not to say that they would be incapable of defending their interests against an exploitative management. Instead of joining in with their brothers-in-fate, however, they would rely on individual actions and isolated protest. This picture appears to be the very opposite of that described for the spontaneously acting workers or groups of workers. While the activities of the latter are dominated by a spirit of unadulterated collectivism and aboriginal socialism, there is good reason to suspect that the supposed new working class tends to be individualistic in its approach to the work assignment and problems of social superiority and subordination.

Certainly, the highly qualified segment of labor played a much less conspicuous role in the September strikes of 1969 in Western Germany compared to the role which Mallet and others attest to it in the May-June unrest in France in 1968. New empirical tests seem to be called for to check Mallet's thesis.

The relevance of such trends for the standardization of industrial relations in the context of the EEC should be apparent. If highly qualified workers come to acquire a class consciousness of their own and if they will actively engage in the defense of their collective interests, the trade unions of today will soon be forced into a major reorganization—even if there be some solidarity on their part with the less qualified part of the labor force. The form and content of the union programs vis-à-vis management will have to be reshaped, new organizations will arise, new alliances and rivalries between labor organizations will come into being. In this case, we obviously cannot build European unification on the basis of currently existing organizations. Rather, the trade unions now offering themselves as partners in EEC-wide negotiations for new organizational constructs are themselves in for major organizational upheavals.

If, on the other hand, the supposed new working class turns out to be nothing more than a conglomerate of self-centered specialists, then their individualism may well render absurd the present limitation of industrial relations patterns as it is suggested in the Lyon-Caen proposal or other drafts. Just like the growing alienation between trade unions and spontaneously acting workers, the ascendancy of highly qualified labor in this case will contribute to the multiplication of industrial relations arrangements—and the slowdown of European unification.

ECONOMIC PROSPERITY AND CLASS CONFLICT

In a situation where organized labor offers scant promises of stable partnership and developments outside of the trade unions are equally discouraging, some proponents of economic unity and growth continue to put their faith into a positive relationship between material prosperity and social integration. In other words, they believe that a prosperous economy will commit its beneficiaries to the maintenance and promotion of the established system. Altogether apart from trade union activities, workers are expected to draw lessons from rising incomes and improved consumption—lessons which would lead them to accept the prevailing socio-economic order and to desist from class conflict. In such an atmosphere of conformity and adaptation, the relationships between employees and employers would offer few serious problems and hardly interfere with the unification of European economies.

Contrary to such expectations, however, empirical studies have shown little evidence of the projected effects. Studies in Great Britain and West Germany do document that workers in recent years are financially better off than previously. But they also indicate that there is very little adaptation on the part of the workers to the life styles of the middle class. Rather, two cultures continue to exist separate from each other: a working class culture and a middle class culture. In spite of the material advantages which they gain through employment, workers do not identify with the company or the economy as objects of positive valuation. Their consumption patterns in many ways remain traditional. There are very few crossovers in their contacts to adjacent social strata. And their political loyalties remain the same as those which were always characteristic of the working class.[16]

There are differences of opinion among analysts about the more limited changes which one might observe within these contexts. On the one hand, British authors maintain that workers are loosing the attitudes of worker solidarity and collectivism and that, instead, an "instrumental" orientation is spreading among the affluent workers.[17] They now conceive of their own labor as means for the achievement of their own goals. Accordingly, their employment contracts basically are indicators of reciprocity: workers sell their labor in order to obtain financial equivalents for their own good. More specifically, they are said to conceive of themselves now more as consumers than as producers. And their main aspirations are said to shift over to the satisfaction of private wants in the leisure sphere.

Some, however, will read different meanings into the current situation. The fact that workers long have remained inactive politically indicates to those on the industrial relations front, the workers' resignation and indifference to their lot. While there is no doubt that workers today financially are somewhat better off than before, they see little change in their basic dependence on employment, their lack of privileges in property relationships, and they despair of the amenability of the social system to radical change.

Taking into account more recent data on spontaneous strikes and outbursts of political radicalism, still others have claimed that workers have continued to live in a state of tension between frustration against their working and living conditions and their desire to upset the existing structure of income and prestige. One even finds official evidence that the concentration of productive capital in the hands of the privileged few has remained unchanged.[18] On this basis, the eruption of wildcat strikes in France in 1968, in Italy and West Germany in 1969, and their continuation throughout recent years and months is taken as proof of the fact that workers had become more conscious of the persisting dichotomy in social life with workers representing the lower half and others representing the top half of the social system. At the same time, the will to interfere with this destiny is expected to grow and finally lead to active opposition to the established system.

The recent history of the worker then appears as a double transformation rather than an integration into a pervasive middle class mentality of the industrial state. As two French authors have pointed out, the first transformation had been that worker preception of his class status has been blurred by a certain amount of affluence.[19] The second transformation would have to be seen in a renewal of a dichotomous class preception, a revival of intransigence and a resumption of open class conflict. Prosperity in this view ceases to be the palliative and the bribe which it was supposed to be in the effort to win workers allegiance to such conditions as they are.

Evidence in support of this view extends well into trade union sources. From the same trade unions which represent the vanguard in the formation of European trade unionism come statements to the effect that the antagonism between capital and labor continues to persist and that not even codetermination can or should do away with this antagonism Union spokesmen who may soon take the credit for getting together a trade unions alliance on an EEC-wide basis will insist on the class-conscious statement that trade unions are instruments of struggle and penetration rather than partners in a joint venture. These are statements from the very labor organization which has often taken the lead in bringing about economic advances for the worker and, in fact assuring him a larger share of the overall affluence of the West German economy and society.[20]

CONCLUSIONS

In a sense, current efforts at the standardization of industrial relations as a special project reflect the difficulties confronting overall tasks of integrating assorted national economies. Generally speaking, such attempts run afoul of established traditions, local preferences, and vested interests of individual pressure groups. In spite of rapid social change, these obstacles continue to persist. The ideologies of class conflict, for instance, often survive even where class lines have broken down to some extent. At the same time, it proves unexpectedly difficult to bring to a consensus different parties who—such as the trade unions—would seem to share common material interests and social goals.

It is against this background that we must evaluate the current trend toward introducing a form of comanagement to European firms which is modeled after the West German *Mitbestimmung*-scheme. Codetermination represents a pattern made to order for the dominant unions of the Federal Republic: socialist in principle, legalistic in form, without significant threat to the efficiency of management and, in fact, to the property interests of the owners. Precisely because of such characteristics, comanagement of the kind now practiced is turned down or considered inadequate by Communist and Catholic trade unions which by radical tradition and doctrine are impelled to drive beyond the current solution, and by some white-collar unions which subscribe to liberal or conservative ideologies and would rather see the powers of blue-collar labor depleted (to their advantage).

As indicated in the German case, there is a certain overlap between traditional and local or national preoccupations. French trade unions, to a large extent, are steeped in class consciousness, and object to comanagement because of their Marxist orthodoxies. Belgian unionists adhere to notions of worker control, and Italian workers have shown a penchant for spontaneous or anarchic actions. Following such foreign conventions and convictions, some have branded codetermination a peculiarly "Germanic" arrangement. Exaggerated though they may seem, these local aversions and preferences represent powerful obstacles in the path of in-group integration, let alone the agreement between parties on opposite sides of industrial relations. They certainly put into perspective specific if successful steps toward supertrade unions of European dimensions.

Nor would it be adequate to view these controversies entirely as a product of unquestioning partisanship for one solution or another. The point has been raised whether the German comanagement scheme could be invented and thrive only in the special situation offered by that particular country at a certain time. In this context, references are made to unique conditions and contributions such as the industrial dismantling program of the Allies and managerial submissiveness in the wake of World War II, the tradition of "collegial" management in

German coal mining and the intermittent political involvement of the steel companies. There is no room here to evaluate the relevance of such references; but it is becoming clear that some of the skepticism toward codetermination takes its cues from the intrinsic features of this industrial relations system, notably its history.

Apart from the genesis of this system, its efficacy is subject to doubt. The very fact that codetermination has been praised by all sides concerned for its efficiency and lack of frictions, seems to support the charge by others who see in it a major pillar of the status quo. In particular, *Mitbestimmung* leaves unaltered the decision-making status of the individual worker: his official powers over the job continue to be nil. In this sense, comanagement does not interfere with the employee's basic position in productive relationships, seen as a structure of super- and subordination. At best, it appears to help create one more "new class," this one consisting of union officers and other labor representatives.

The question, of course, is whether we can have a workable industrial relations scheme, and one standardized on an EEC-scale at that, which would lead to a status quo plus, or to a situation which would lessen the chances of class conflict as it arises from iniquities in material and less tangible privileges. New hopes have been raised by recent experimentation with autonomous work groups. But it seems premature at best to forsake well-established solutions, even if flawed, for apparent panaceas. A more realistic procedure would be to search for mechanisms which will mitigate such incidences of alienation, subordination, authoritarianism as is common even under *Mitbestimmung*. A simple system of redress and repeal via mediators inside the enterprise, for example, might go a long way toward dealing with such problems. But there is no limit to what the European Community may propose by way of centralized and decentralized institutions of its own making.

On the one hand, then, this is a time to bring to bear some institutional imagination. Following the leads of Sanders and, in particular, of Lyon-Caen, industrial relations in the EEC should not just be molded into one common denomination. Next to the need for standardization, we should recognize also an opportunity to improve upon the existing institutions. On the other hand, the drive for institutional perfection must be promoted in full awareness of a new spontaneity among the labor force. Groups of employees long marshalled by organizations have taken it upon themselves again to wield some independent influence. If these developments slow down progress, they may also give new meaning to the long wait of old.

NOTES

1. Wilke Thomssen, *Wirtschaftliche Mitbestimmung und Sozialer Konflikt* (Neuwied and Berlin: Luchterhand, 1970), p. 14.

2. George Strauss and Eliezer Rosenstein, "Workers Participation: A Critical View," *Industrial Relations*, IX (February, 1970), pp. 197-214.

3. Guy Desolre, *Le Mouvement Syndical Belge et le Problème du "Contrôle Ouvrier,"* mimeographed, Second World Congress, IIRA, 20-70, Sect. II/C/e, September 1-4, 1970.

4. Ernest Mandel, *Die EWG und die Konkurrenz Europa-Amerika* (Frankfurt: Europaische Verlagsanstalt, 1970).

5. For an excellent synopsis, cf. Karl Otto Hondrich, *Mitbestimmung in Europa* (Cologne: Europa Union Verlag, 1970).

6. Friedemann Schuster, *Mitbestimmung, Machtverhältnisse, Klassenkampf* (Frankfurt: Verlag Marxistische Blätter, 1971), p. 7.

7. Otto Brenner, "Die Gewerkschaften in der Europäischen Wirtschafts- und Währungsunion," *Metall Pressedienst* (March 3, 1971), pp. 1-2.

8. Cf. a recent report by a government commission on Codetermination, *Gutachten Mitbestimmung (Bundestagsdrucksache VI/334),* Bad Godesberg, Heger, 1970.

9. Quoted in *Sozialpartnerschaft oder Klassenkampf,* edited by Autorenkollektiv, Universität Hamburg (Hamburg: Spartakus GmbH. & Co. KG., 1971), p. 39.

10. Cf. Heinz Hartmann, "Codetermination in West Germany," *Industrial Relations*, IX (September, 1970), p. 142.

11. For a case history, see Wolfgang Richard, ed., *Fiat-Streiks* (Munich: Trikont, 1970).

12. Serge Mallet, "La nouvelle classe ouvrière en France," *Cahiers Internationaux de Sociologie*, XXXVIII (January-June, 1965), pp. 57-72.

13. L. Greyfié de Bellecombe, "Workers' Participation in Management in France," *International Institute for Labour Studies Bulletin*, (June, 1969), p. 75.

14. Ernest Mandel, *op.cit.*, pp. 112-113.

15. Frank Deppe and Hellmuth Lange, "Zur Soziologie des Arbeiter- und Klassenkampfbewubtseins," 2. Teil, *Das Argument*, XII (December, 1970), p. 810.

16. Richard F. Hamilton, "Affluence and the Worker: The West German Case," *American Journal of Sociology*, LXXI, 5 (1965), pp. 144-152.

17. John H. Goldthorpe *et al.*, *The Affluent Worker: Industrial Attitudes and Behaviour*, vol. I ("Cambridge Studies in Sociology", no. I); *The Affluent Worker: Political Attitudes and Behaviour*, Vol. II; *The Affluent Worker in the Class Structure*, Vol. III (Cambridge University Press, 1968), Vol. I, p. 38 *et passim*.

18. For the case of West Germany, cf. investigations by the Federal Ministry of Labor reported by Hans-Ulrich Spree, "Das Produktivvermögen teilen sich nur Wenige," *Süddeutsche Zeitung* (Munich: August 3, 1971), Nr. 184, p. 7.

19. Andrée Andrieux and Jean Lignon, "L'ouvrier d'aujourd'hui," (*Recherches de Sociologie du Travail*), Vol. VI (Paris: Rière 1960).

20. Cf. quotations from union officers in Friedemann Schuster, *op.cit.*, p. 30.

4

THE DE WOLFF REPORT
ON THE MEDIUM TERM
ECONOMIC POLICY

Excerpts translated by

Steven J. Warnecke

The following selections are from a report on the European Community Medium Term Economic Policy (MTEP) entitled *Perspectives for 1975: Macroeconomic Development and Economic Problems in the Community*. It was prepared by a committee of experts headed by Professor P. De Wolff of the University of Amsterdam for the Commission of the EC and presented to the president of the Commission, Franco Maria Malfatti on April 21, 1971. The 300-page report covers the following areas. In the first part, the economic and political problems of the EC and the macroeconomic prospects of the Community are analyzed up to 1975. On the basis of this analysis the developmental trends of the member state economies are evaluated from the Community perspective. The second part is devoted to medium term projections and the coordination of policies in the individual member states. In addition, the two parts discuss in great detail the conceptual and methodological problems involved in defining goals, expressing them through statistical indicators, interpreting the indicators, and finally translating them through the available instruments and institutions into effective policies.

The excerpts are of interest for several reasons. They attempt to place the discussion of national economic policies in a larger framework by approaching them through a model of a European-wide economic system. Through the application of this model upon which the MTEP is based the De Wolff Report analyzes in depth the extent to which the social, political, and economic causal relationships necessary for the model to work exist in the present EC. This analysis raises two serious questions. If the institutional structures and relationships necessary for the European oriented model to function successfully do not yet exist, why should national governments be willing to shift important elements of their economic sovereignty to Brussels? The implication of this position for the supranational aspirations of the Commission is clear. In addition, how is the dirigist element in the MTEP to be reconciled with the voluntarism upon which it rests?

Although the De Wolff Report indicates the range of difficulties facing the EC Medium Term Economic Policy, these difficulties should not detract attention from the purpose of the MTEP. If the European Community is to deal adequately with the interdependence of the member state economies it must approach these problems through such instruments as the MTEP. In this respect the officials responsible for the MTEP as well as the members of the De Wolff Committee have considerably expanded the discussion of the policies relevant to a multinational economic community.

PART I: PERSPECTIVES AND PROBLEMS AT THE COMMUNITY LEVEL. EXPERTS' GROUP ON MEDIUM TERM ECONOMIC PERSPECTIVES, COMMISSION OF THE EUROPEAN COMMUNITIES, MARCH, 1971.

Medium Term Economic Policy and Projections at the Community Level

In the Treaty of Rome every member country has obligated itself "to pursue the economic policy necessary to ensure equilibrium in its overall balance of payments and to maintain confidence in its currency while ensuring a high level of employment and the stability of prices" (Article 104). It has also obligated itself to achieve "a continuous and balanced expansion of its economy" (Article 2). In order to facilitate the attainment of these objectives, member countries shall coordinate and pursue the gradual approximation of their economic policies (Articles 2 and 105).

In addition, at the Hague Conference of heads of state and government in December, 1969, member countries agreed in the coming years to press forward with vigor the necessary development and strenghtening of the Community's structure in order to transform the European Community into an economic and monetary union. The process of integration must lead to a "Community of Stability and Growth."

At its meeting on February 9, 1971, the Council of Ministers adopted a fundemental decision of the establishment by stages of an economic and monetary union and laid down concrete measures for the first stage and for the coordination of short and medium term economic policy. In respect to the aims of the Treaty of Rome and to the stated objectives of the governments of the member states conditions must be created without delay to ensure that this Community can function as smoothly as possible and that its objectives can be realized. The contribution to be made by the medium term economic policy on the Community level and the function of medium term projections for the drafting of a consistent Community economic policy to be adopted for the period until 1975 shall be explained briefly in the following sections.

With the conclusion of the twelve-year transition period and the completion of the customs union, the European Community has made important steps toward achieving economic integration. However, the Community still faces difficulties and contradictions inherent in the present system which stand in the way of achieving a genuine economic and monetary union. The increasing intermeshing and interdependence of national economies call for growing convergence and compatibility in economic policy. In practical politics, however, the centers of decision-making responsible for economic policy continue to exist largely on the national level. Lack of close harmonization among the most important economic policy decisions have repercussions on the internal development of member countries. Consequently, the chances of member countries to realize their objectives and aims are seriously jeopardized. In the present phase of integration the effectiveness and autonomy of national economic policy (at the national level) in the European Community is restricted in different ways:

With the completion of the customs union member states have renounced the use of certain instruments, such as tariffs, discriminatory obstacles to trade, and quantative restrictions.*

With the growing interconnection of national economies and the increasing mobility of goods, services, and capital, vulnerability to

---

*The renunciation of the resort to such measures would be reinforced if the currency union should materialize. The reason for this is that within a currency union member countries can no longer change their exchange rates.

disturbances and disequilibria emanating from neighboring countries is constantly increasing.

Past experience has shown that whenever any basic disequilibria occur emergency protectionist arrangements, exchange controls, exchange rate manipulations, etc. are invoked. For any one country to resort to such national measures might be an irritating vicissitude in its own economic development. In the construction of an economic community, however, such measures cause fundamental tensions and breaks as a result of which the previously mentioned purposes of the Community might be canceled. Such measures should they reoccur might even prove destructive to the Community.

The negative effects of disequilibria in the economic development of member countries and the resulting defensive measures associated with such disequilibria would be reflected in the following results among others:

By preventing an optimal division of labor within the Community and the flow of capital and labor toward the most productive employment since businessmen would hesitiate to orientate their investment decisions toward the European-wide internal market.

By obstructing the emergence of a common European money market as long as the movement of capital continues to involve uncertainties as a result of the continued possibility of fluctuations in exchange rates.

By hindering the achievement of both national and partner country macroeconomic goals if painful adjustments on national home markets are required in order to overcome any disequilibria in the balance of payments.

By rendering all the more difficult the decrease in structural rigidities and disparities, or even the creation of new structural difficulties since any overall disequilibria threaten to reenforce sectoral and regional disparities and cause specific efforts to intervene to occur in the wrong direction.

By straining the emerging sense of solidarity among member states since deficient and erroneous developments on the basis of past policies and disturbances and disequilibria in one country are bound to encroach upon developments in the other member countries.

The contradictions, conflicts, and divergences in the Community in the past have prevented the full exploitation of the dynamic, long-range advantages of a great common market, i.e., the optimal use and allocation of productive resources. The task of an effective medium term economic policy is to create the conditions for the maintainence of fundamental equilibria in each one of the member countries. The object of short term economic policy, therefore, is to defend overall economic equilibria, to control any fluctuations affecting the economic equilibria and to maintain a steady rate of development in each member country. The question remains whether such a balanced development in member countries—following the loss of autonomy in national economic policies as indicated above—can be achieved by nothing more than "progressively approximating the economic policies of the member states." In addition, there is also the question of what areas should be coordinated, adjusted, or harmonized by economic policy.*

The solution to problems of coordination does not depend on purely economic factors, conditions, and management devices alone. Economic policy extends far into problems of welfare and social structure. Consequently, the objectives of economic planning and action usually reach beyond simply the material improvement of living standards. Economic equilibria could be upset by social upheavals such as strikes and political crises. Deficient and erroneous developments may come about as the result of neglecting the education system, protection of the environment, investment in regional infrastructure, housing and town planning, etc. In the not too distant future these sectors, too, will require more or less stronger coordination on the Community level.**

The expert's group recognizes the great importance of all these problems. For lack of sufficient opportunities, however, it is compelled to confine itself to purely economic factors and conditions in its analyses and forecasts. In this context it appears relevant to refer to the following problems which stand in the way of achieving and maintaining economic equilibria, particularly equilibria in foreign trade in the Community:

The inadequate harmonization of economic and social policies of the member states.

The lack of coordination among member countries of the instruments of macroeconomic policy and the inadequate means for using such national instruments on the Community level.

---

*This includes the questions of whether, where, and when the instruments of economic policy should be employed by organs of the Community in order to permit efficient and coherent management.

**Since political, institutional, and social objectives and reforms have immediate repercussions on medium term development, the achievement of economic integration requires the approximation of welfare and social policies.

The divergent points of departure among member countries with regard to the "structural," i.e., sectoral, regional, and social problems.

The inadequate analytical and forecasting techniques through which deficient and erroneous developments and conflicts can be detected in time and appropriate measures taken and modifications initiated.

Whenever economic policy decisions are made by more than one authority it will be necessary to design a comprehensive system of priorities. This applies both on the national and the Community levels. An important coordinating function would be to approximate the priorities in member countries' overall economic and political policies to such an extent that they would become compatible with one another. Convergence in economic policy objectives would surely facilitate the guidance of economic development along the path of equilibrium, reduce the element of uncertainty in long-range decisions, and strengthen the factors upon which automatic adjustment in the mechanism of the market rest. A consistent system of economic priorities and preferences in the Community would be the prerequisite for a rational economic policy. The definition of objectives presupposes, however, a number of conditions. On the one hand, a decision-making and control system must exist which is capable of a political evaluation of economic priorities and can then set these priorities.* On the other hand, such a decision-making and control center must be capable of implementing these objectives through the appropriate means and also be able to assume responsibility for doing so. If one is not to lose credibility in the building of Europe, the European sense of solidarity and the political resolve to achieve certain aims must correspond to the ambitious extent of these aims. The more pronounced this consciousness and political resolve, the more ambitious the aims can be.

The adjustment and determination of quantative objectives, while a necessary condition, are only first steps. The coordination of overall economic and financial policies with the aim of achieving a durable fundamental equilibria in a steadily growing economy becomes all the more imperative for all the member states of the Community the closer their economies are intertwined and interdependent through the commodity and money markets. The coordination of overall economic

---

*A system of political decision-making would require the participation of the public and of labor and management in the "harmonization" of "European" objectives.

management within the Community would be adequate under existing conditions (continued existence of autonomous centers of decision-making and of sovereign national currencies) if, in the long term the following could be ensured:

The maintenance of foreign trade equilibria.
The optimal realization of internal objectives.

In an economic union only the Community's foreign trade balance as a whole and in respect to third countries would be of significance.* At the present stage of integration the orientation of macroeconomic management toward the union's external foreign trade balance and the neglect of foreign trade equilibrium among the member countries is as yet impossible. As long as fixed exchange rates have not been established among member countries, a unified or closely coordinated economic policy is lacking, and spontaneous adjustments by means of the complete freedom of movement for capital and labor or through the mechanisms of supporting measures such as interregional financial adjustments are not functioning or function inadequately, foreign trade balance must be achieved separately for each member state.**

The foreign trade balance must be achieved simultaneously with the achievement of internal objectives without resorting to protectionist measures and controls. In addition, parity changes within the Community should be avoided. The success of an overall policy oriented toward fundamental equilibria depends on whether conflicts between the foreign trade balance and domestic objectives can be avoided or whether the aim of a balanced foreign trade can be subordinated in every member country to domestic objectives such as growth, full employment and price stability.***

The attainment of fundamental equilibria through overall management is made more difficult by the different possibilities available in

---

*The disequilibria caused by surplus or deficit balances between member countries would then be reflected in divergent regional developments, i.e., a currency union would transform balance-of-payment problems into regional problems.

**In the event of continuing disequilibria the central problem—the coordination of economic development—could not be solved by the automatic or conditional granting of reciprocal loans.

***The compatibility of the goal of full employment with the achievement of a foreign trade balance again depends on the flexibility of costs and especially on wage rates.

member countries for flexible adjustment to "structural" changes. Structural changes result from technological progress and from changes in domestic and foreign demand. The rigidities of regional, trade, wage, and employment structures hamper the process of spontaneous adjustment and could jeopardize the tendencies leading toward the maintenance of overall equilibria. Such rigidities can be the result of deficient or erroneous economic developments in the past on the basis of prior policies, of social crises, and protectionist behavior on the part of the state and of business enterprises.

One might argue whether a "structural policy" is an essential prerequisite for overall management and coordination of the economy or whether it is only through an orientation of overall economic policy toward fundamental equilibria that makes an efficient structural policy directed toward regional development and economic growth feasible. Within the framework of a medium term economic policy the coordination of measures of structural policy on the Community level might prove difficult for the time being because of the type, and above all, the intensity of structural adjustment problems which differ markedly from country to country. This might result in a search for effective forms of intra-European financial adjustment and equalization and to the stimulation of the processes of spontaneous adjustment. Structural measures focusing on regional and employment policy, for instance, would be facilitated by a viable European money market which in certain cases would favor the maintenance of foreign trade equilibria.

In the present report it has been pointed out several times that one of the chief dangers standing in the way of achieving compatible developments is that the working hypothesis concerning the development of prices outside the Community turns out to be inaccurate. It is probable that on a medium and long term view the Community's option for stability of prices—while worldwide inflationary tendencies continue—could be achieved in relation to the rest of the world only by a more extensive Community oriented policy of flexibility in exchange rates.

This, however, presupposes not only that the Community's "identity" in the monetary sphere is carried a good deal further but also that economic policies in each member country should be about equally successful in defending the common option for stability. Applying past experience to the period under consideration, excessively divergent development of prices must be expected within the Community because of different business cycles and different degrees of "vulnerability" to price increases in member countries. Such price movements are in practice irreversible and threaten in the long-run to cause foreign trade disequilibria and exchange rate changes in the Community.

PART II: THE FUNCTION OF MEDIUM TERM PROJECTIONS AT THE COMMUNITY LEVEL

Medium Term Projections

Within the scope of the coordinating functions under discussion medium term projections of economic development are an instrument for an efficient and rational economic policy. Their significance as aids in macroeconomic policy is today recognized in all member countries. There are differing views, however, concerning what should be oriented toward and through these indexes. The reasons for these differences are to be found in the unequal starting conditions, in the heterogeneous social and welfare goals, social structure, and political and economic policy in the various member countries. These differences are exemplified in the procedures, the degree of detail, the direction and the institutional aspects of establishing medium term projections at the national level. Looked at in a somewhat simplified fashion, the function and purpose of medium term projections in market oriented economies would appear to be the following:

The description and interpretation of long term prospects for economic development with the goal of reducing through macroeconomic analysis the risks and uncertainties facing private and public decision-makers.

The provision of both a framework and instrument for drafting an economic policy of maximum coherence which seeks to harmonize the conduct of public and semipublic decision-makers (and under certain circumstances also of labor and management) by means of quantative indexes and planning objectives.

Both functions overlap in economic practice. The adoption—and publication—of a medium term strategy by a national government diminishes the uncertainties for the private sector. The distinction above indicates, however, the difference in degree to which the private and public sectors can be coordinated or "influenced" by "projections," "plans" and "programs." The views on "the logic or state of planning" or on the relationship between government and the private economic sector underlying long term projections cannot be dealt with here.

The Role of Medium Term Projections

At the Community level the role of medium term projections lies at present less in the reduction of uncertainties and more in the common exploration of future marketing opportunities for enterprises within the Common Market. This function is an important by-product of projections only to the extent that it might help steady discussions on economic policy. At the present stage of integration the importance of medium term projections lies mainly in the advanced coordination (*ex ante*)* of member countries' economic policies.

Definition and Harmonization of Medium Term Orientation Indexes and Objectives

The coordination of objectives introduced by the Commission's memoranda and in the Community's third program for medium term economic policy concern the following overall economic indexes and planning data for each member country:

foreign trade equilibrium
the increase in the general level of prices
the rate of employment or unemployment
the actual rate of growth for the entire economy.

It is obvious that there exists no direct, easily definable means-ends relationship between the various policies and measures directed toward a growth oriented structural policy and these four indexes. The greatly simplified considerations presented here in respect to medium term policy and macroeconomic management presuppose—

That no incorrect estimations have occurred in the determination of the orientation indexes concerning structural developments and relations as well as the effects of a growth oriented structural policy.

---

*In contrast to *ex post* coordination through the market in which corrections are only initiated after disequilibria (balance-of-payment surpluses or deficits, deficient structural developments, etc.) have occurred.

That excessive, much less, unpredictable and violent changes in national preferences and priorities have not occurred in the period under consideration.

That in connection with the business cycle medium term orientation indexes relevant to concrete measures for macroeconomic management are correctly interpreted.

Such incorrect estimations are not to be excluded, however, both in view of existing uncertainties of economic diagnosis and of economically irrational factors bearing upon the development of national systems of priorities.

The coordination of economic policy in member countries are generally confronted with the following uncertainties when attempting to achieve the medium term objectives outlined in the orientation indexes—

At the level of diagnosing the economic situation and the possible economic measures derived from this diagnosis (problem of diagnosis).

At the level of simultaneously integrating these measures in both the national and rudimentary Community systems of priorities and of the political feasibility of the concrete measures which have been selected (problem of decision-making).

And at the level of judging the effects of these measures on actual economic development (problem of effect).

The experts' group agrees with the Commission and the Committee for Medium Term Economic Policy that these four orientation indexes and their quantification for the period 1971-75 are not adequate in themselves to guarantee a balanced and undisturbed medium term development within the Community. The simultaneous determination and realization of these four indexes (in economic debates known as the problem of the "magic square"), implies a simplification of the function of economic policy coordination at the Community level. In the present situation this simplification must be looked upon—technically—as a preliminary stage for the efforts at projections by the member countries through which the harmonization of their economic objectives is to be initiated. Advanced coordination of economic policy is much more complex and the conceivable conflicts of interest go far beyond the sphere of the four indexes used here. Behind this harmonization there are hidden not merely the problems of the creation, distribution, and use of income, the direction of fiscal revenue and expenditure, and the harmonization of the diverse specific governmental objectives, but also the regional, sectoral, and social aspects of medium term development which might obstruct a covergence of overall economic objectives.

The quantification of the four orientation indexes in an effort to make them compatible among the member countries is to be regarded as an attempt to define orientation data for major economic equilibria. In addition, this effort provides a frame of reference for all future developments and economic policies. In order to reduce the degree of vulnerability inherent in the integration progress which inevitably arises from divergent objectives among member countries, economic policy will have to be more strongly oriented toward the general interdependence and compatibility of orientation indexes at the national and Community levels.

Thus, medium term orientation indexes have a normative or target character by which the margin of possible developments is to be realistically limited. Ultimately, an important function of these indexes would be to initiate at the Community level an unbiased debate among the public, the governments of the member states, and labor and management in order to make the necessary and the desirable better conform to what is feasible. Such a debate would also exclude the possibility that some countries, certain social and economic groups, regions or branches of the economy would look upon the inevitable process of adjustment and coordination with the Community as "a sacrifice to integration."

ECONOMIC RELATIONS BETWEEN THE UNITED STATES AND THE EUROPEAN COMMUNITY IN THE 1970's

5

THE ECONOMIC ISSUES BETWEEN THE EUROPEAN COMMUNITY AND THE UNITED STATES IN THE 1970's: AN AMERICAN PERSPECTIVE

William Diebold, Jr.

"The United States has always supported the strengthening and enlargement of the European community."[1] No one could quarrel with the historical accuracy of that statement in President Nixon's second "State of the World" message. And the words that followed could have been said by any President since Truman: "We still do. We welcome cohesion in Europe because it makes Europe a sturdier pillar of the structure of peace." No serious question could be raised that words like these correctly describe the main lines of American policy toward Western Europe since 1947.

All this is familiar, indeed commonplace, and so it risks becoming boring. (It is worth recalling, though, that when, in the late 1960's Washington did not reiterate its endorsement of European integration often enough, some Europeans began to worry.) Still, candor in speech, consistency in action, and coherence between the two over a long period of time ought not to go unnoticed when they appear in U.S. policy. But there is more to U.S. policy toward European integration than continuity. There are also elements of change. Over time there have been changes in some of the reasons for American support; the ways in which it was given and the conditions attached (whether explicit or tacit); and the specific features of integration with which the United States was primarily concerned (whether in actual achievement or expectation). Another thing that has shifted is the place of support for European integration in the gamut of U.S. foreign policy measures and its relation to other parts of that policy. About these matters there has been far less certainty, many more questions, and often a good deal more debate than about the general proposition supporting European integration. Sometimes the adaptation of policy to circumstances and sometimes a reflection of changes in thinking, these shifts in emphasis are highly relevant to appraisal of American relations with the Community in the present and the foreseeable future—another time of change.

What is involved in both an understanding of the character of American-European relations and a perspective in which to consider the problems of today. As users of the green Michelin guides have learned, it is easier to appreciate what one is looking at if one begins with *un peu d'histoire* however broadly sketched.

PAST CHANGES

On V-E Day the designers of American policy had a reasonably clear idea about the part Europe would have to play if there was to be security and prosperity in the world. War-torn economies would have to be rebuilt. Germany would have to be kept under control—and opinions differed as to how that could be done. Europe would have to play an active part in the world economy, for its own sake and because that was essential to the system. In all of this, but especially the last part, Britain had a key role as the center *par excellence* of international trade and finance. Nothing in American policy called for—or was premised on—a united Europe. There was little evidence that such a goal could be more than a distant ideal, and some Americans doubted it was desirable.[2]

It was only between 1947 and 1949 that the promotion of European integration became an aim of American policy. It is common these days to explain everything that happened in those years in terms of Cold War but this is simplistic and consequently erroneous. Of course the belief that a unified Western Europe would be stronger than a divided one and so better able to defend itself (politically more than militarily) against external pressure from Moscow and internal pressure from Communist parties played a major part in getting support for this view. But the initiation of the process—at least so far as the United States was concerned—lay a little closer to the operational needs of policy than that. In the speech that started the process Secretary of State Marshall did not set distant goals of European unification but insisted on the need for Europeans to cooperate more closely to make the most of their own resources and the aid he was proposing that the United States should give them. No doubt he also had Congress in mind. Something like $10 billion of aid had already been provided to

Europe. The British loan of 1946 had been presented as a necessary step to get the international monetary system going again and was plainly not doing that. Clearly the chances of getting major new appropriations would be better for a single cooperative program than for a series of national requests that would soon look unending to the congressional eye.

In their response to Marshall, the European governments had a lot to say about cooperation but showed only a limited interest in the idea of a customs union which had been suggested to them by Under Secretary of State William L. Clayton in his role as a "friendly adviser." This was probably the earliest precise American proposal for major moves toward integration and too much may not have been expected from it. The word integration itself was first used in its present meaning and as an objective of American policy by Paul Hoffman in the fall of 1949.* By that time the process had begun and Americans were very active participants in it, in Washington, in the national capitals of Europe, and especially through the mission to the Organization for European Economic Cooperation (OEEC). In this activity the potential conflict between American advocacy of European integration and other aims of American policy became evident for the first time.

It must be recalled that much of American foreign policy in the years after World War II was concerned with the construction of a new world order. On the economic side the objectives were the reduction of barriers to trade and payments, nondiscrimination, and close, multilateral cooperation among nations. The aviators of the approach were the International Monetary Fund and the General Agreement on Tariffs and Trade (GATT). GATT was originally seen as a temporary arrangement pending the working out of the more comprehensive International Trade Organization which in fact never came into existence. Before the European countries could take a full part in this process, they would have to rebuild their economies and overcome the multiple handicaps conveniently labeled "the dollar shortage." All this was foreseen in the GATT and Fund rules which permitted countries in balance-of-payments difficulties not only to restrict trade and payments but to discriminate in so doing. But, as the need for the Marshall Plan showed,

---

*He spoke of "the formation of a single large market within which quantitative restrictions on the movement of goods, monetary barriers to the flow of payments and, eventually, all tariffs are permanently swept away." *New York Times*, November 1, 1947. "Integration" may have been chosen because it was weaker than "unification" which was favored in Congress but seemed excessive to some in the Executive branch.

the period of transition was going to be longer than was originally expected and the effort to cooperate to make the best use of Europe's resources was leading to a more extensive and more systematic pattern of discrimination against the United States (and other hard currency countries) than had been contemplated. One of the OEEC's principal achievements was a program under which quotas were removed on trade among the European countries while being kept on imports from others. The development of intra-European trade and other transactions was then greatly helped by the creation in 1950 of the European Payments Union (EPU) which provided credit backed with American aid, permitted the multilateral settlement of accounts, and gave an international board certain powers in dealing with countries whose accounts were persistently out of balance.

Americans had had a large hand in devising these constructive measures, but some people in Washington worried about three points: 1. That vested interests would build up to make European trade discrimination permanent; 2. that the EPU would work in ways that limited the powers of the Fund (which was not playing as important a part in the world economy as had been expected); and 3. that shielding Europe from foreign competition would perpetuate trade barriers and the dollar shortage. The doubters were overcome and the victorious view was proved justified by the end of the 1950's when the major European currencies became convertible for foreigners and most discriminatory controls were subsequently removed.[3] Nevertheless, the need to make a choice was the first tremor of a new tension that was to arise in American policy between the objective of a multilateral nondiscriminatory economic system and support for European regionalism which called for some degree of discrimination.

In the same year the EPU was created, Robert Schuman proposed a coal and steel pool. Thus the process of European integration began with characteristics quite different from those of the measures taken through the OEEC. There is no need to retrace the familiar path from the successful negotiations for a coal and steel community, through the failure of the effort to form a defense community, to the *reliance* at Messina that led to the ratification of the twin Treaties of Rome. For present purposes it is enough to underline some of the differences between this process and the kind of integration that had gone on before. Permanent change instead of recovery was the objective. Because six countries were willing to go farther than the others, the deepening of integration was accompanied by the creation of new divisions in Europe. The motive power for the new effort came principally from concern with internal European problems—not least the German problem—and far less from consideration of Europe's place in the world. The American part in the process was small compared to what it had been in the recovery-oriented integration and declined from a secondary though significant role in adoption of the Schuman Plan through diplomatic failure in the EDC to a bystander's applause in the creation of the Common Market. A partial exception to the last two sentences which foreshadows an issue that will arise again is the hard-to-trace but undoubtedly real stimulus to European integration that came from the Suez crisis of 1956 and the discovery that the United States could be on the other side from its main allies on such an issue.

The creation of the Common Market—in practice rather than on paper—marks another shift in emphasis. European integration had achieved a sort of critical mass. One could see that it would have a significant impact on the outside world. American interests—not only trade—were directly affected and the United States for the first time had to decide how to respond to European integration. That need was met by the Trade Expansion Act of 1962 (TEA) and the lengthy negotiations of the Kennedy Round. In contemplating the result of that effort—the lowest level of tariffs on trade in manufactured goods among industrialized countries in about a century—we may ask ourselves how long it might have taken to reach the same point if the Europeans had not first created the Common Market (and EFTA). In the same vein, it is relevant to recall that the TEA not only represented the greatest advance in American trade legislation since the original passage of the Trade Agreements Act in 1934 but that for some years before it was enacted American trade policy had been in the doldrums with nothing in sight that seemed likely to restore the momentum which had made the United States the leader in trade liberalization during the whole postwar period. Not only did the creation of the Common Market lead to the Kennedy Round but the Kennedy Round helped shape the Common Market. The clearest example of this is the close interaction between the tariff bargaining with the outside world and the agreement on major features of the Common Agricultural Policy (CAP). But there must also be cases in which the decision about how far to reduce certain rates in the common external tariff settled questions that might otherwise have been postponed about the structure of industry within the Community.*

---

*Whether the need to present a common front and the use of the Commission as a single bargaining agent strengthened Community processes and the Commission is not altogether clear. Some believe so but a well argued case to the contrary is to be found in Frans Alting von Geusau, *Beyond the European Community* (Leyden: Sijthoff, 1969), Ch. V.

There are also negative features about the interplay between
European integration and Europe's relations with the rest of the world
in the 1960's. For example, the unprecedented power given the
President of the United States to eliminate tariffs entirely on certain
major segments of American imports could not be used because it was
premised on Britain's becoming a member of the Community. This
failure of the European partner to materialize also contributed to the
evaporation of President Kennedy's concept of partnership. The fact
that there was no single European partner did not, however, stand in
the way of active cooperation in monetary affairs in the 1960's. The
key there was the gain in European strength and a recognition of a
common interest in keeping the international monetary system functioning reasonably well which led European countries to give substantial help to the United States as it tried to come to terms with a
troublesome but somewhat misunderstood balance-of-payments problem. In this difficult but major expansion of cooperation, Europe did
not act as Europe or the Community as a Community. Instead national
governments and national central bankers made the decisions. The
possibility that the Six might some day act together and thereby
acquire greater influence on monetary affairs than they had in the past
is recognized by the agreement on Special Drawing Rights which gives
the Six a veto over what is done—provided they all vote the same way.
Whether this possibility—or its less formal equivalents in other fields—
will prove to be a significant factor affecting the course of European
integration in the 1970's is, as we shall see, a major question.

There is, however, one more comment to be made on the 1960's.
The debates of those days about the American interest in European
integration gave rise to a widely accepted commonplace which is at best
only a partial truth and can be quite misleading. The proposition is that
the United States wants Europe to be integrated for essentially
"political" reasons and is prepared, if necessary, to pay an "economic"
price for that result. The statement takes many forms. A rather refined
version appears in President Nixon's first "State of the World" message:
"We consider that the possible economic price of a truly unified Europe
is outweighed by the gain in the political vitality of the West as a
whole."[4]

The general tenor of this statement is clear enough. One would not
quarrel with some obvious applications. For example: "The United
States wants Europe to be strong; to be strong it must act together; a
good way to start acting together is to form a customs union; a customs
union puts those outside it at a disadvantage; nevertheless, the United
States wants to see Europe strong, etc." The wide acceptance of the
statement means that it has seemed meaningful and useful to many

people, some of them quite sophisticated in the analysis of policy. But except when applied to a specific case—perhaps whether the United States should have complained more when the Common Agricultural Policy was adopted—it is rather a meager guide to policy. While distinctions between the "political" and the "economic" are conventional in our speech and sustainable as illustrations of textbook definitions, they are of dubious value when they occur in general statements about a world in which governments are held politically responsible for the economic welfare of their people and a high proportion of the substantive content of international relations affects the creation, transmission, and division of wealth and income. A country that excludes certain foreign investments and thereby foregoes employment, production, and perhaps other benefits because it does not wish to have certain parts of its economy controlled by foreigners can indisputably be said to be paying an economic price for a political purpose. But when the United States, for over twenty-five years, lends support to European integration because it wants Europe to be strong, it is not making a distinction between economic and political strength. While the possibility remains that some forms of economic strength in Europe are disadvantageous to the United States in certain ways, this is not so generally or consistently the case that it forms a good premise for policy. Moreover, as we have seen, from the very beginning one of the main reasons the United States wanted a "strong" Europe was so that the international economic system would function better than if Europe remained in the condition it was before the Marshall Plan (whether that is a political or economic goal). It is hardly worth arguing about.

THE CHANGED PRESENT[5]

The changes in circumstances that made American support for European integration something different in the mid-1960's from what it was in the mid-1950's or late 1940's have not all given way to still newer conditions in the 1970's. Indeed, a good bit of what is relevant today took shape some time ago. It was 1966 when Harold van Buren Cleveland pointed out that "the ends which European union was to serve according to the classical doctrine have been accomplished by other means. . . ."[6] The ends he had in mind were recovery, security, and a reasonably good arrangement for embedding Germany firmly in Western Europe which appeared to have been attained without much political integration. Economic integration Cleveland thought might go on as before, that is to say, rather pragmatically. This reasoning is clear and sound, but it is important to understand that a drop in urgency does not translate into an argument against integration and does not imply that there is no connection between attainment of the objectives and the degree of integration that has been achieved. While Europe's security depends more on American nuclear policy than on cooperation among European governments, integration has undoubtedly contributed to European prosperity, political stability, the absence of dangerous quarrels, and the intermeshing of the interests of Western Germany with those of its neighbors. The blockage of the De Gaulle years showed that integration could survive delays and setbacks but no one is entitled to assume that if it were to stop altogether Europe's gains in other fields would remain intact.

Still, there is no escaping Cleveland's conclusion about reduced urgency—from the American point of view—of further steps toward European integration. His view is all the more pointed since he played a significant part in shaping American support for integration during the Marshall Plan days. This is just as well since the ability of the United States to promote European integration is not great. Exhortation and diplomacy could (and should) have, at most, only a marginal influence on decisions of great importance to Europeans that cannot be soundly and decently made except by them. The material inducements to integrate that once fortified American policy no longer exist on any scale. This is not news, since the shift was well started by the mid-1950's. A major exception concerns nuclear matters in which the United States has something to offer and leverage on recipients of its help. But this question lies some place in the future. American support, neutrality, or resistance can certainly make it easier or harder for the Europeans to take certain steps—for example, particular trading arrangements or measures concerning American investment. But this potentially important influence operates within the process of European integration, so to speak, rather than as a major shaping force. A related question is how much negative influence the United States might have if it were to resist further steps toward European integration. "Quite a lot" is the probable answer with the important caveat that American opposition carried beyond a certain point might become a spur to integration by convincing Europeans that the only way to escape from unacceptable kinds of dependence on the United States is to draw more closely together.

But why should the United States oppose or resist European integration? Because, some would say, we have had a taste of the way a partially integrated Europe can damage American interests and can expect a stronger, more integrated Europe to be more damaging still. It is easy to sketch the scenario. Among the key words are De Gaulle, nuclear independence, gold, preferential tariffs, investments, Common Agricultural Policy, and "inward-looking." The picture is the obverse of another which also exists only in the imagination: that of a United States of Europe that would open its frontiers to American trade and investment, carry its share of all the unpleasant burdens (without seriously challenging American judgment of vital issues) and generally think and behave like its trans-Atlantic namesake. Only unsophisticated American advocates of European integration ever supposed that, if Europe became one, its power would never be used in ways the United States did not like, that some American interests would not be subordinated to European interests, and that all friction would be minor. It is possible to believe, however, that without being a docile partner, a united Europe could have a good influence on American politics, requiring a just *quid pro quo* in bargaining, making cooperation the sensible way of reducing conflicts of interest, creating economic competition from which Americans as well as Europeans would benefit and challenging the United States to emulate its best performance. No such result is inevitable. In European integration, as in everything else, a whole series of contradictory forces would be at work. But sensible management on both sides of the Atlantic could direct the increased potential to more constructive rather than less constructive results.

The United States does not have the choice between one or another kind of Europe for the reasons set out above. It can, however, have an influence on what happens, less in terms of relations among the European countries than in their relations with the rest of the world. By any standard, it will lack the primacy it had in the non-Communist world in the 1940's and 1950's. Still the richest and the strongest country, the United States, without whose assent little can be achieved, has to share with others the devising and executing of ways of managing many aspects of the world economy. In these matters, Western Europe as an economic entity could often be a far more useful cooperator than a number of European countries acting separately. In these circumstances, there is little reason to reverse the judgment which lay at the heart of the Marshall Plan that the United States was better off with a strong and relatively independent Europe than with a weak and largely dependent one. Such a Europe, it can be taken for granted, will require a good deal of integration—almost certainly more than exists now.

Integration is ambivalent. While bringing the participants together, it at the same time separates them in certain respects from other countries. The United States supported integration as a way to strengthen Europe and permit it to play a better part in the world economy than if it were weak. But the world economy was to be open and nondiscriminatory. Consequently the fostering of integration, which created differences as well as removed barriers, inevitably generates some conflicts within American policy. Keeping the two tendencies in the right balance is essential to the dual policy. What balance is "right" changes over time. At the beginning, integration had to have priority. Once it was well launched—and especially when it was largely out from under American influence—the correct emphasis in American policy was to shift to the external aspects of integration. That shift which started in the 1960's meshes well with the decline in the urgency of the United States' interest in promoting integration and its ability to do so.

It is debatable whether the United States made any economic sacrifices to help the Europeans integrate. If it did, there is little doubt it could afford them in the 1940's and 1950's. Nowadays matters are not so clear. A new populist-nationalist rhetoric was introduced into American foreign economic policy in the summer of 1971. The opinion was widely held though hardly proved that the United States suffers more from the unfairness of other people than they do from its own unfairness. A traditional American suspicion was relived in the form of the assertion that throughout the postwar period the American government had given away more than it got in negotiations with foreigners. One can disapprove of these developments and still find it impossible to deny that now and for the foreseeable future (as indeed for some time past) the United States will have to give greater weight than it did in the early 1950's to exports, the balance of payments, the conditions of competition for private business, and, therefore, some of the probable short-run consequences as well as the long-run expectations of what is done in Europe. This is not a matter of black and white nor an open-ended sanctioning of mercantilism. The formula is not easy to apply as any good discussion of President Nixon's measures of August, 1971, will show. Difficult choices will have to be made in the future as in the past. The point is only that once again—as has happened before in American policy toward Europe—the weights have shifted.

How do all these shifts come into balance—those of the past sketched in the last section and the more recent ones described here? A statement of principles or guidelines about American policy toward European integration in the 1970's might look something like the following.

The United States has an interest in further European integration but cannot play a major part in bringing it about. That is up to the Europeans. The American interest is explained by a complex of fairly familiar reasons, some of which have lost their urgency, but one of which remains very important: An integrated Europe should be able to help more effectively than a divided one in managing the international economic system. Consequently, American policy will be especially concerned with the relation of an integrating Europe to the rest of the world economy. This focus is further emphasized by the fact that some measures of future integration will almost inevitably entail some short-run (and perhaps long-run) economic disadvantages for the United States and other countries outside the group. It should be an objective of American policy to minimize these disadvantages. The United States should also insist that if outsiders are to accept certain burdens as the price of European integration, these should be inescapable consequences of steps that truly move toward integration and not the by-product of half-way compromises reflecting the inability of the Europeans to overcome their own resistance to integration.

Any attempt to live by these principles will, of course, leave room for honest disagreement within the United States and between Americans and Europeans. Beyond that, friction from other sources is inevitable. American economic diplomacy should, therefore, be looked on as a difficult art to be guided by several considerations. Much of what the United States wants will be to the benefit of other outsiders as well, especially Japan and Canada. The United States should make this evident and enlist their help. Many people inside Europe want both integration and the kind of world economy the United States is advocating. American policy should be designed to rally their support. When possible, it should avoid posing issues so that there appears to be a choice between steps toward integration and measures to improve relations with the rest of the world. When it takes a negative view of things the Europeans want to do, it should propose constructive alternatives that take account of European interests. In these matters it will help to bear in mind that in economic matters "national interests" are rarely truly national. The main conflicts of interest cut across national boundaries and divide groups within each country. A well-designed diplomacy must play on these divisions, balance advantages and disadvantages, and so create politically workable combinations in several countries that support cooperative arrangements. In working out its policy toward European integration, the United States should conduct itself so that if a stronger Europe emerges, the prospects for cooperation with it will be better than those of conflict. This is not a matter of being nice to people but of demonstrating where the common advantages lie.

Finally, we must not let this article's emphasis on integration obscure the fact that Europe is only integrated for some purposes and in different degrees. This is true today when there is a Community and also an EFTA, and it will be true if there is only one large Community with some outsiders. As of 1971, monetary policy, many nontariff barriers, the treatment of foreign investment, balance-of-payments controls, and a whole series of other matters central to American relations with Europe hardly at all reflect integration (or are even settled by European compromises). By 1975 all or some of this may have changed—and may not. It follows that the United States must have a flexible stance. It has to be able to deal with a common agency on one subject, separate national governments on another, and agreed national positions on still others. As time passes it will have to shift from the one mode to the other for some things and not for others. It will somehow have to coordinate these activities because all parts of economic policy are increasingly drawn together, blurring traditional divisions between trade and investment and requiring that negotiation about agricultural trade and nontariff barriers reach back to the domestic measures that give rise to import restrictions and export subsidies. Oddly enough, there is a significant connection between the problem of dealing with European countries when they do not act as a community and the broader emphasis on fitting Europe into the world. Because policy has to deal with nations in a variety of circumstances, it needs some guiding principles. In this case both intra- and extra-European relations are involved. In short, the conditions exist for which the multilateral principles of Bretton Woods and the GATT were designed. These are the long-time foundations of American foreign economic policy that have come under so much strain in the effort to accommodate regionalism—and for other reasons.

THE CHANGING FUTURE

"More than at any time in my experience, opinion among Americans with respect to Europe and among Europeans with respect to the United States is dominated by illusion." Robert Schaetzel said that to a congressional committee in July, 1971.[7] It is a disturbing thought coming from someone who has been a close participant-observer of American-European relations thoughout the postwar period and for some years now our Ambassador to the Community. One wonders whether what may come to be called "the events of August, 1971" will dispel illusions or turn out to have been based on them. These events may even let loose new chimeras, prompting one to think of De Gaulle's remark to Malraux: "Perhaps politics is the art of putting chimeras in their proper place?"[8]

Why do the illusions persist? Ambassador Schaetzel suggests that the main cause of the trouble is "the degree to which each side of the

Atlantic is preoccupied by domestic affairs." He means, I suppose, that people do not see straight if their only view across the Atlantic is a backward glance over their shoulder. Perhaps the stress should be on the common tendency of political leaders to expect others to adjust to their problems rather than vice-versa and to imagine that what serves personal interests serves national interests and what serves national interests serves the common interest as well. Whatever the source of the illusion, it cannot be any great mystery about the main problems in economic relations that arise between the Community and the United States. These are not arcane but very clear and easy to describe. The difficulty is to get the right things done about them or even, some might say, to get the right people to pay enough attention to them so that anything useful can be done.

Perhaps this last aim will be achieved as a result of the broadening and deepening of the Community that may take place in the next few years.* But even that is uncertain thanks to the ambivalence that characterizes so many of the issues taken up in this paper. On the one hand, Europeans are inclined to feel that they should get on with the business of enlarging and improving the Community before devoting too much attention to American-European relations. On the other hand, the implications of adding members and enlarging the economic content of what the Community does seem to Americans to affect the Community's place in the world so deeply that they think both sets of issues have to be tended to at once. Without speculating further as to whether anyone will look, this paper concludes with some notes on what they will see if they do.

In the short run, trade remains at the top of the list. The enlargement of the Community widens the area within which American goods are at a disadvantage compared with those of European origin. The application of the common external tariff to the new members will raise some duties and lower others. GATT has a reasonably clear-cut system for balancing such changes by compensations of one sort or another. While the disputes about who is entitled to what will be neither mild nor unimportant, I think one is entitled to feel that the greatest difficulties between the United States and the Community do

---

*By broadening I mean the admission of new members; deepening refers to the intensification of integration, i.e., steps toward monetary unity, common policies in more fields, close coordination of national policies, etc. Conference and publishing schedules being what they are, this paper had to be completed in mid-September, 1971. To avoid a series of hypothetical discussions, I have assumed that Britain will enter the Community on the terms that seemed agreed on before the summer.

not lie in the realm of adjusting tariffs. "If they can't settle that, they can't settle anything," is a justifiable attitude. Far more difficult trade questions arise about agriculture, nontariff barriers, and the Community's preferential agreements with outside countries. (These agreements raise major problems for the United States which Mr. Malmgren is handling in his paper so I shall pass over them in silence except to note that the heavy weight the Community understandably puts on its relations with the Mediterranean countries is a reminder that the perimeter of the "Third World" has become rather indistinct and will be blurred still further as time passes.)

Whether the Community grows to seven, eight, or ten members in the next few years, there will continue to be European countries that do not belong to it but are in fact closely linked with its economy. The circumstances of these countries vary too greatly to be discussed briefly so the subject must be left aside with just one comment. It concerns the recent surge of interest in the possibility of establishing a free trade area for industrial products that would include the enlarged Community and the other Western European countries. Such a step would have the virtue of simplifying matters. It would also have an implication which to Washington could appear to be an opportunity. The implication concerns the common external tariff. Always it has been treated as something more than a national tariff. Repeatedly it has been called a political bond because it was for many Europeans the clearest—some would say the only—advantage they received from integration. To those who found this a rather unattractive argument—perhaps correct enough but not resonant with inspiration—the answer was given that sooner or later things would change. Has that time come? Surely not much can remain of the argument that the common external tariff is essentially a political bond if it no longer distinguishes the Community from the rest of Europe. But to draw anything out of this implication the United States would, quite naturally, have to make an offer. The obvious proposal is to get rid of all tariffs on manufactured goods—at least in trade among the industrialized non-Community countries—over a reasonable period of time. This is not a very revolutionary proposal considering what the last quarter century has achieved in the way of undoing the work of tariff-makers from the Civil War to the Depression. But historical logic is not always easy to translate into political fact.

The Common Agricultural Policy, though extraordinarily complex, is no exception to the proposition advanced earlier that the basic issues between the Community and the United States are quite clear. The CAP enlarges the market for certain products if they are produced in Europe and, by import limitations and export subsidies, narrows the market for the same products when they are produced (much more cheaply) in the United States. The European answer that American farm exports to the Community have grown in spite of the CAP is only a partial answer because: 1. without the CAP they might have grown more; 2. for three years after 1966 they declined as the CAP was reaching full effect and their expansion in 1970 may be due to temporary factors; 3. in spite of the 1970 expansion, products subject to variable levies—the most characteristic CAP device—have declined faster than others, which means that the policy is working the way one would expect it to.[9] More to the point are the European demonstrations that the shift of labor out of agriculture is taking place at rates that are quite high by historical standards and that the CAP and its financing reflect one of the fundamental political equations on which the Community is built and so cannot easily be altered.

The biggest compensation the United States has had for the loss of other farm exports to the Community is an extraordinary expansion of sales of soybeans. The result is a high risk of instability. On the one hand, free entry of soybeans can be seen as a gap in the CAP which aggravates some of the problems connected with surpluses of butter and wheat.[10] On the other hand, soybeans are now so important (40 percent of American farm sales to the Community in 1970) that an effort to plug the gap—such as was considered a few years age—invited American retaliation. There are other elements of instability as well, mostly connected with the CAP's almost automatic subsidization of exports that generates American import restriction at home and matching subsidies abroad. Because of the asymmetry of interests—farm products make up less than one-tenth of European exports to the United States and double that share of the reverse flow—such disputes are likely to spill over into other sectors of trade.

The situation is dangerous. The first task of diplomacy is to keep the inevitable disputes under control. The second is to eliminate conflict at the fringes, for example, by limiting the use of export subsidies. The third task is change. Here I suspect that European consumers, taxpayers, and finance ministers will be more effective than American farmers and negotiators. There is a good deal of pressure in Europe for reform of the CAP and many ideas for improving it; some are endorsed by the Commission. A few modest steps have been taken. Although the major disputes are internal—within countries as well as between them—there is a possibility that some of the pressures for change can be strengthened, and perhaps some of the reforms made more effective, if they are linked with international negotiations and agreements. These could hardly be simple, old-fashioned efforts to do nothing but lower trade barriers; these have failed badly in agricultural trade throughout the postwar period. But another kind of negotiation, in which agreement centers on domestic agricultural policies—support prices, income payments, other forms of subsidy, production control, and the like—could open the way for real change that would also affect import barriers. Proposed unsuccessfully in the Kennedy Round, extensively discussed and approved of by experts and officials, this method has yet to be given a trial over the hurdles of politics. Whether it could clear them is far from certain; but the alternative to trying is waiting for internal forces of change to operate. From the American point of view, one of the real difficulties about waiting is that the enlargement of the Community, by expanding the protected market, reducing surpluses, and enlarging the basis for financing the CAP, will reduce the pressure for change while further contracting American markets. Of course, the enlargement may also strengthen the forces making for reform by increasing—through the addition of Britain—the urban and industrial "interest" (to use an old-fashioned term) and also—through Denmark and Ireland—the number of specialized efficient agricultural producers. But these are relatively long-run forces and the political risks are sharpest in the short run.

"Nontariff barriers" is a popular but often misleading label for an aspect of trade relations that will almost certainly prove central in international negotiations for some time to come. A more comprehensive term is Robert Baldwin's "nontariff distortions"[1] but only a dip into the lists of specific practices can convey a sense of the extraordinary range of things being touched on. The immediate—and largely correct—impression is that we should not go on talking in general terms. But at some level we must. In relation to the Community, an odd situation exists. Most nontariff barriers remain clearly in the province of the national governments, not the Community as such; they have been little touched by the integration achieved so far and create divisions among the six countries as well as between them and the rest of the world. An effort to attack these barriers (and practices) should clearly be on a multilateral basis. There are other practices, however, which, though they also still fall under national control, may through the deepening of integration come to look like new forms of discrimination against the United States. That would be the case, for example, if the Community countries worked out a code for government procurement that eliminated national preference but created a Community preference. When a group of European countries gets together to establish standard specifications for electrical equipment, American producers complain of discrimination. They are no doubt correct, but to give American views of what standards should be the full weight the size of the market would suggest may not be easy and a failure to agree cuts both ways. The American reaction to the increase in border adjustments as Community countries began to harmonize their value-added taxes stands as a double monument: to the difficulty of getting agreement among honest men on what is a nontariff barrier to trade and to the futility of staging an international confrontation without having in mind a constructive alternative that might command adequate assent.

That there will be more misunderstandings and difficulties goes without saying. Whether there will also be progress in the removal or regulation of nontariff barriers remains to be seen. No single approach is promising. Even a group of like-minded nations determined to liberalize trade among themselves will soon find that many nontariff barriers or trade distortions result not from simple protectionism but from the pursuit of quite different objectives. Government efforts to safeguard health, make machines safer, expand employment in depressed areas, increase investment, for example, may all create trade distortions. Efforts to check pollution and improve the environment are almost bound to produce a large number of new nontariff barriers even if governments and international organizations press ahead with the efforts already started to establish uniform standards and avoid needless conflicts (not all conflicts are avoidable in these matters). In many cases trade distortion can be avoided only if governments follow similar or coordinated policies in dealing with a number of domestic issues, a notoriously difficult task. At least some of the efforts they make in that direction will raise one of the fundamental questions about regionalism (which in this context means Community action versus agreement on a wider basis, say as a group working through the OECD). The question is: Is it better to have a limited agreement covering a large number of countries or a more thoroughgoing one among fewer countries even though that introduces some new distortions in world trade while eliminating others. Answers are not obvious. Such principles as we might set down to judge the trade-offs hardly mean much except as applied to cases. The real alternatives may not fall into this simple pattern for any number of reasons but the chances are that issues of this sort will add considerably to the agenda of U.S.-Community economic issues in the years to come.

Among the important sources of nontariff barriers are the efforts governments make to deal with problems affecting one industry or another. The most common form of action in the past has been to shore up weak industries, but the development of new lines of production has also had its part. More and more people are thinking in terms of the need for a more broadly conceived "industrial policy." It is not easy to reconcile many of the devices customarily used—or even the objectives frequently sought—with the requirements of efficiency and competitiveness created by the openness of national economies to one another that has become characteristic of relations among the industrial countries.[12] Within the Community, years of effort to devise a common energy policy have produced modest results but an excellent demonstration of the difficulties of devising common industrial policies. Something more may be achieved in quite a different area of industrial policy, that concerned with the encouragement of mergers on a more-than-national basis and the creation of Community-wide enterprises. There may also be progress in cooperative scientific research and the application of advanced technology. The connections between such efforts and relations between the Community and the United States are obvious with the Americans acting as continuing stimulant and sometime target. But even if the Community fails to take common action on many of these matters, international economic relations (and, therefore, U.S.-Community relations) will increasingly be concerned with the effects of what national governments—including the United States, of course—do under that loose rubric "industrial policy."

Closely linked to concepts of industrial policy are ideas about the treatment of foreign investment. In these matters, European policies have been fairly liberal and the existence of the Common Market has sometimes served as a check on restriction (because what was denied by one country could be given by another and the American firm thereby gained access to the first market as well). This may change if the Community could agree on common standards for the treatment of American investment. What kinds of problems may result depends, of course, on what that treatment turns out to be. Almost certainly there will be more problems in the future than in the past even if the Europeans continue to be receptive to American companies and try only "to see to it that they have as strong an interest in Europe as in the United States and that they pay as much attention to the point of view of European governments as to that of their own."[13]

Faced with changes along these lines—and possibly more trouble-some ones—Americans have to answer a number of questions. Is the old standard of free access for American firms and treatment equal to that given domestic firms to remain the objective of American policy? If so, is Washington prepared to give up efforts to control American business abroad? Many businessmen are willing to accept less than their full legal rights rather than have their status become the subject of new disputes between governments. How far are they prepared to go in this kind of adaptation? Other Americans may ask how great a public interest there really is in having the government use its power and influence to improve the position of private firms abroad. Does the increasing importance of returns on investment in the balance of payments make it a matter of national interest to expand these activities? In a sense an increasing share of the American economy functions outside the traditional frontiers. How can this segment be made responsive to national policy? The answers to such questions (and the others to which they lead) may be different if European investment in the United States continues to grow at the rate of recent years. Will Americans come to share the worries of people in the rest of the world about foreign domination of certain sectors of the economy? Will the attributes of Europeans change as they increasingly become investors and not just the invested upon? At least the bargaining positions will have changed.

In contrast to hypothetical issues concerning investment, do the real ones, of the 1960's and today, involve the international monetary system. There is no room in this essay to condense the history or to explore all the possibilities about gold, the dollar, the American balance of payments, and whether the rest of the world's dependence on the United States is necessary or not. To try to look very far ahead in a paper written within a few weeks of the floating of the dollar and the new *défi américain* would be foolish. It will have to suffice to note bluntly how central these matters are to the themes of this paper. The Community is pushed toward monetary integration—a term that can cover a number of different arrangements—by both of the main forces making for European integration in general. The internal or European forces are those connected with the long-understood fact that to move from a customs union to a full economic union would require a high degree of coordination of monetary policies. The external forces are those connected with the equally obvious fact that if Europeans want to change the international monetary system they have to act together. While acting together and monetary integration are not the same thing, there is a relation between them and in the long run they probably converge. That the combination of these forces should not have produced a high degree of European monetary integration before now testifies to the extraordinary difficulties of the task, the widespread awareness of the fact that a true commitment to monetary integration would have strong implications in other fields and limit the freedom of action of governments, and the inescapable fact that governments responsive to different constituencies and facing different sets of circumstances will have different reactions to common problems at least as often as uniform responses.

The first setbacks to what appeared to be the Community's greatest step toward monetary integration—agreeing to a modified Werner Plan in early 1971—came from "internal" differences concerning the Deutschemark and the French franc. The differences were prolonged in the initial responses to the floating of the dollar, instead of being quickly compromised as one might have expected when the opportunity arose to strike a blow in favor of a system less annoying and frustrating to Europeans than the dollar standard. Perhaps President Nixon's action of August, 1971 (and its style as well as its substance) may yet prove to be a sort of Suez of monetary affairs and goad the Europeans to fuller integration. But one cannot be sure. The lesser but nonetheless real opportunities of the 1960's were passed up. Although it is widely recognized that, as George Thomson has put it, Europe faces the world "with its affluence out of all proportion to its influence,"[14] it is ironical that even in monetary affairs, where affluence gives influence, Europe should not make the most of its opportunities. It is true that relations with the United States are not uniform among members of the Community,* but it is unlikely that the United States could in the long run conduct a policy that both divided Europe on these issues <u>and</u> led to the creation of a workable international monetary system more acceptable than that of the past. Nor should that be the objective of American policy. While it is certainly not the responsibility of the United States to try to overcome the obstacles to monetary integration in Europe, Washington should not resist that long-run development (which is not the same as saying it should not do what it can to resist anything that strengthens the forces for undesirable changes in the system, such as restoring the importance of gold). The analogy with the general argument about European integration summarized in earlier pages is close: A European currency would "challenge" the dollar in some ways; it could be used in troublesome ways; but a monetarily unified Europe could also play a very constructive part in managing international money in the future.

What European monetary integration cannot do is to take Europe out of the international monetary system. There is a wide range of possible relations between a European currency and a dollar area and some of them are bad, but what is not possible are no relations. The creation of a European currency area could solve some of Europe's problems, but for the most part it would simply alter relations with the rest of the world. For a long time to come, at least the assent and usually the active collaboration of Europe, Washington, and, on most matters, Tokyo remains essential. Many of the problems will

---

*On the connection between the American troops in Germany and that country's willingness to hold dollars instead of gold, see the interview with Karl Blessing, former president of the Bundesbank, published after his death. *Der Spiegel*, May, 1971.

undoubtedly be approached differently on the two sides of the Atlantic and perhaps we will have to continue to analyze "the argument between the European regionalists and the American cosmopolitans."[15] Whether the Europeans are becoming more or less "regional" and the Americans more or less global in outlook are questions of high importance, but a discussion of them would be the start of another chapter instead of the end to this one.

NOTES

1. *U.S. Foreign Policy for the 1970's: Building for Peace* (Washington, D.C.: U.S. Government Printing Office, 1971), p.29.

2. For views that it was not in the American interest to have Europe united, see the report of the work of the State Department's Sub-Committee on European Organization in Hans A. Schmitt, *The Path to European Union* (Baton Rouge: Louisiana State Press, 1962), pp. 13-15. Among other considerations, not everyone had forgotten that an earlier movement for a United States of Europe was directed against an "American menace." See Jacob Viner, *The Customs Union Issue* (New York: Carnegie Endowment for International Peace, 1950), pp. 57-58.

3. A fuller account of the issues can be found in my *Trade and Payments in Western Europe: A Study in Economic Cooperation, 1947-1951* (New York: Harper & Bros., for the Council on Foreign Relations, 1952), pp. 107-110, 405-415. An authoritative inside view is provided by the principal author and champion of the EPU, Robert Triffin, *Europe and the Money Muddle: From Bilateralism to Near-Convertibility, 1947-1956* (New Haven: Yale University Press, 1957), Ch. 5.

4. *U.S. Foreign Policy for the 1970's: A New Strategy for Peace* (Washington, D.C.: U.S. Government Printing Office, 1970), p. 32.

5. This section is for the most part condensed from part of Chapter 9 of my forthcoming book, *The United States and the Industrial World: American Foreign Economic Policy in the 1970's* (New York: Praeger, for the Council on Foreign Relations). A number of other issues dealt with only briefly in this chapter (especially in the next section) are discussed more fully in other parts of that same book.

6. Harold van Buren Cleveland, *The Atlantic Idea and Its European Rivals* (New York: McGraw-Hill, for the Council on Foreign Relations, 1966), p. 132.

7. Testimony before the Foreign Economic Subcommittee of the House Foreign Affairs Committee, July 22, 1971 (mimeographed), distributed by the Public Affairs Office of the United States Mission to the European Communities.

8. André Malraux, *Les chênes qu'on abat. . .* (Paris: Gallimard, 1971), p. 181.

9. Statements 2 and 3 and some in the next paragraph are based on calculations from *Foreign Agricultural Trade of the United States* (Washington, D.C.: Agricultural Department Economics Research Science, 1971), pp. 6-15.

10. See the argument in Adrien Zeller in collaboration with Jean-Louis Giraudy, *L'imbroglio agricole du Marche commun* (Paris: Calmann-Levy, 1970), pp. 64-70.

11. Robert Baldwin, *Nontariff Distortions of International Trade* (Washington, D.C.: Brookings Institution, 1970).

12. An excellent analysis of the problems combined with a condemnation of past practices and proposals for new lines of action (with France largely in mind) is to be found in Lionel Stoleru, *L'Imperatif Industriel* (Paris: Editions du Seuil, 1969).

13. Rene Foch, *Europe and Technology: A Political View* (Paris: The Atlantic Institute, 1970), p. 53.

14. George Thomson, "Britain and the Common Market: The Political Case," *The World Today*, XXVII (July, 1971), pp. 277-285.

15. Charles P. Kindleberger and Andrew Shonfield, eds. *North American and Western European Economic Policies* (New York: Macmillan, for the International Economic Association, 1971), p. xv. In their introduction the two gifted authors have very interesting things to say about these two approaches. A number of the papers in the volume and the comments made on them by participants in a conference in September, 1969, bear on issues discussed in this chapter.

6

POSSIBILITIES
AND LIMITS
OF A EUROPEAN COMMUNITY
FOREIGN POLICY

Ralf Dahrendorf

In Turkey, the signing, on November 23, 1970, of the additional protocol to the association agreement with the European Communities touched off a domestic discussion on the basic direction of the country's policy which may pose additional ticklish problems for Prime Minister Sûleyman Demirel when the protocol comes to be ratified. In the Buenos Aires declaration,[1] twenty-two otherwise basically different Latin American states drew together, prompted by their joint determination to affirm their independence in world politics through closer links with the European Communities. The offer by the European Communities of a scheme of generalized preferences has led in India and Pakistan to grateful acknowledgement of the work of the Communities. Meanwhile, the Associated African States and Madagascar have complained in the Association Council and the Parliamentary Conference about an alleged loss of their preferential position. Algeria is perceptibly transforming its special relationship with France into a similar one with the European Communities, seeking a compromise between special bilateral conditions and the establishment of relations still lacking with some other Community countries. Japan's hesitating progress on the way into an international community of mutual dependence finds strongly felt expression—both symbolic and prac-

---

This chapter is based on a talk that the author gave in Bonn on January 25, 1971 to the Deutsche Gesellschaft für Auswärtige Politik.

tical—in the trade agreement negotiations with the European Communities. Yugoslavia's endeavour gradually to eliminate a substantial trade
deficit by strengthening cooperation with the Communities is also a
political option in the understanding of those responsible for it.

Progress of the membership negotiations, and the clear impression
that this time round all parties concerned wish to see Great Britain
enter, enable a few bolder strokes to be added to this picture of the
effects which the European Communities have on the outside world. In
Norway, there has been no end to the talk about a government crisis
because of differing views in the coalition over entry into the European
Communities. Australia continues the process of diversifying its relations, which it started at the time of the first membership negotiations
between Great Britain and the EEC, and begins to build up comprehensive regional links of its own. Canada is concerned about its special
political position in the triangle Great Britain-United States-European
Communities, which as such threatens to disappear. In many countries
the wish can be increasingly heard that close relations be established
rapidly with the European Communities in an effort to catch the
already moving train. The eighty-five ambassadors accredited to the
European Communities, who for some weeks now have had a *papal
nuncio* as doyen, submit a large number of suggestions, *aide-memoires,*
and requests for information and cooperation.

The effects of the European Communities often give rise to strong
feelings. In some cases, these are hopes: for the Associated African
States, the European Communities, despite the generalized preferences,
represent a great hope of development possibilities with no political
strings attached. The Latin American states are not alone in trying to
escape the polarity of the world powers by turning to Europe. The
motley—perhaps unduly motley—range of agreements by the European
Communities around the Mediterranean stands for so many hopes of
development chances that are free from military threat. No single week
passes without at least one Minister of a foreign government coming to
Brussels to emphasize his country's wish to establish closer relations
with the largest trading entity and the second largest economic power
in the world, the European communities.

The hopes of some must be set against the misgivings of others.
Those who today watch the European Communities with concern
include the United States. This country expressly maintains its support
for the European Communities, including their enlargement and
deepening, but skepticism about the policy of the Communities is
nevertheless mounting in the press, in Congress, and also in the
Administration. Around the turn of the year, diplomatic representatives
of the United States waited upon the six governments and the

Commission to voice their concern about the agricultural policy and the preference policy, particularly in connection with the enlargement of the Communities. This is an unusual yet very eloquent move, particularly since the complaints are at present not backed by any discernible economic reality. We understand the general concern of the United States about an erosion of the principles of world trade for we share its concern, particularly where developments in the United States itself are involved. But undoubtedly there is still more at stake. Sometimes the picture is drawn of a European Community which, along with the countries linked to it under preferential arrangements, has already a majority in GATT and which, after the entry of Great Britain, Denmark, Ireland, and Norway, is heading for a majority in the United Nations: there would be ten members, six remaining EFTA countries with still unclear links with the Community; eighteen African states associated under the Yaoundé Agreement and three under the Arusha Agreement,* plus at least eight English-speaking countries in Africa after the entry of Great Britain; currently seven Mediterranean countries with preferential agreements and soon maybe thirteen—making a total of fifty-eight states already. Are we faced here with the emergence of an almost coherent regional block from the Arctic Circle to the northern frontier of South Africa?

The misgivings of the Soviet Union are of a different yet possible also similar nature. Just now the Soviet Union has again protested against the wish of the neutral EFTA states to establish closer relations with the European Communities. Writing about Sweden, the press talked of a loss of independence through association. Austria was warned that association would imply an infringement of the State Treaty because, with the Federal Republic a member of the European Communities, it constituted a form of the "Anschluss" that was expressly prohibited. In such situations, there is all of a sudden great reality about the existence of the same Communities against whose recognition the Soviet Union expressly protested again only recently at the negotiations on the renewal of the International Wheat Agreement, while failing, however, to draw the logical conclusion for its own participation and that of the Commission on behalf of the Communities.

---

*The agreement on the renewal of the association agreement between the European Economic Community and the African states and Madagascar associated with this Community, signed on July 29, 1969, in Yaoundé (Cameroon), like the agreement on the establishment of an association between the Community and Kenya, Tanzania, and Uganda, signed on September 24, 1969, entered into force on January 1, 1971.

These examples should suffice. They have not been listed as a substitute for an analysis or a program. They are rather intended to provide the background for a political thought that is the starting point and guiding theme of the following comments.

THE COMMUNITIES: A REALITY IN WORLD POLITICS

One may wish this Europe or wish it away. One may be astonished or pleased to see that the European Communities link Hamburg with Palermo but separate it from Stockholm, to say nothing of Leipzig and Rostock. One may argue over whether the Communities are an incomplete federal state or a developing confederation of fatherlands. One may praise the expertise of the European Commission or may try to treat this body as a purely "technical" institution. What is more, one may desire a common foreign policy for the European Communities or may not desire such a policy. None of these controversies alters the fact that today already these Communities are an operative force on the world political scene. This means, however, that these member states, no matter what their interpretation of Europe's possibilities and requirements may be, cannot escape the effects of what they have created in the shape of the European Communities. Today already the Six are committed by the world political reality of the acts of their not always beloved child.

These considerations can be supplemented by a look at the examples given. Undoubtedly the effects of the European Communities are in the first place directly economic in nature. Partly they derive from unilateral actions of the Communities, for instance from the offer of generalized preferences to the developing countries. Partly they are the result of mutual arrangements made within the limits set by the treaties since the end of the transitional period, in particular by Article 113 of the EEC Treaty; an example would be the agreements on preferential imports of citrus fruit from Israel, Spain, and Morocco. Such direct economic effects are supplemented by far-reaching indirect effects. British membership will force not only Australia but also New Zealand to diversify its markets and possibly its production in the next few years, which means that the impact of the Communities requires another distant country to reorient its domestic and foreign policies. Here, then, we are already at the point where the effects of the Communities are no longer described by the treaties and by the interpretation which some like to put on them with Cartesian logic.

For countries such as Egypt and Algeria, Argentina, and many others, to take up relations with the European Community is a political option. Whether one likes it or not, whether one tries to deny it or not: when Egypt talks with the Communities about oranges, it makes clear that cooperation with the Communities offers a way out of the depressing choice between the superpowers. Similarly, when Argentina tries to obtain tariff concessions for frozen sides of beef, this is not without economic importance, but what is even more significant is the beginning of a diversification in the country's foreign policy. For many countries in the world, including the most powerful and most important, the European Communities are not only an economic but also a political reality. They determine the political moves of these countries, even where this happens on a mistaken view of the facts and is disapproved of by many within the Communities. The Communities, and the six member states which currently form them, must therefore also shoulder individually and jointly the political responsibility for the political effects of what they have created.

The discussion about Europe has long been dominated by two ideological themes, both of which are beside the point and misleading— namely, the themes of political union and supranationality. The demand for political union, like the criticism leveled at this demand, has blinded some people to the fact that today the European Communities are already a political reality and have indeed been such a reality from the outset, and that the only question, if there is any at all, is how rapidly and in what direction the Communities' policy should be developed. Rather than being something new, something that differs from current reality, political union is a process that set in long ago and will undoubtedly never come to an end. The dogmatic dispute about supranationality has sometimes distracted attention from the concrete decisions that have to be made by the insitutions set up under the treaties, and consequently from the question of what can be done to render these institutions even more capable of making decisions and, consequently, allow Europe to speak with a single yet binding voice, i.e., a voice that is binding for the member states as a whole and authorized by them. But much remains to be done here. Europe, the political entity that is the European Communities, is an active force in the world, but it fails to speak or speaks only seldom, and then in an enigmatic language of little elegance and often obscure meaning. The existence of the Communities, the political decisions which they are making all the time (and be it only through postponement and adjournment), and even more so the great options of the Hague summit conference,[2] have consequences for many countries in the world. These are economic consequences in the narrowest sense, as well as political consequences in the broadest sense. But the way in which, in the Community, the political will is formed in external policy matters fails to keep up with the Communities' effects in the external policy field. The Communities work with very incomplete knowledge of what they want to achieve and why they want to achieve it. They are a major force in the world, but sometimes they look like a powerless force, be it in the Mediterranean or in Africa, vis-à-vis the United States or the Soviet Union. The slightest movement of the fettered giant can be destructive, yet he is incapable of even picking up the borken pieces. To put them together again or create something spontaneously himself is downright impossible for him as long as great power and ability are there but his hands remain tied.

This is not said with a light heart and most certainly not with any feeling of satisfaction. The six European states have created a political reality which need not be defined as being something different from these states, but which, in accordance with the will of its architects, cannot be controlled by any one of them alone. This reality has effects on the outside world, whether decisions are made or not. The Six are therefore jointly responsible for seeing that what they have created does not adversely affect them individually or jointly, and above all for ensuring that it does not do damage in the world which the member states would hardly be able to repair. However, it is by no means always clear whether the member states see this joint responsibility of theirs as clearly as they see their individual responsibility in the world. As the political instruments available to the Communities are incomplete, it is at the same time technically difficult to reduce the wide gap between the effects and the actions of the European Communities. The task is not to evolve new theories about Europe or call loudly for amendment of the treaties, but to recognize the responsibility of the Communities, in the light of the treaties and the reality based on them, and translate this responsibility into decisions.

PROBLEMS OF COMMON COMMERCIAL POLICY

Under the treaties, the European Communities' external relations that are based on common decisions consist first and foremost of trade relations. There are the formal relations that date back to the European Coal and Steel Community and the first EEC Commission. There are technical and political questions raised by external relations in connection with Euratom, as for instance the multilateral discussions on the conditions to be met for the nonproliferation treaty to enter into force.

There are the beginnings of a common development policy supported by a development fund in the framework of the Yaoundé and Arusha Agreements. The starting point for a common policy, however, was in particular to be found in Article 111 of the EEC Treaty, which, last year, with the transitional period over, was replaced by Article 113, which goes much further and stipulates: "After the transitional period has ended, the common commercial policy shall be based on uniform principles, particularly in regard to changes in tariff rates, the conclusion of tariff and trade agreements, the achievement of uniformity in matters of liberalization, export policy and measures to protect trade such as those to be taken in case of dumping or subsidies." The Article also defines the relevant powers of the Commission, the Council, and the advisory body today referred to as the "Article 113 Committee."

The Council of the Communities realized at an early stage what multitude of questions the common commercial policy raised. On December 16, 1969, in an unusual decision of principle, it therefore adopted rules on a number of important points. These rules relate, among other things, to the tacit or express renewal of existing agreements, the procedure for the opening of negotiations on new agreements, and the familiar waiver concerning negotiations with certain nonmember countries until December 31, 1972. In the wording of the decision, this latter arrangement, made with the Communist states of Eastern Europe and Asia in mind, relates to nonmember countries "where common negotiations in accordance with Article 113 of the Treaty are not yet possible." It includes a consultation procedure that has so far been strictly adhered to by all. With regard to the content of the commercial policy, the Council has unfortunately been less liberal in interpreting the Treaty. The repeated reference to the "commercial policy within the meaning of Article 113 of the Treaty" is restrictive, or in any case hardly extensive, in nature.

Given the light in which Article 113 and the arrangements deriving from it appear today, particularly the first Council mandate concerning trade agreements, the Communities very rapidly reach the limits of their possibilities. Here, the unresolved contradiction between the political expectations of the Community's partners and what they actually can be offered is, in a manner of speaking, only the external shape of the problem. Internally, the same problem recurs. Under Article 113 as applied so far, the Communities are responsible for trade agreements that settle questions referring to tariffs, quantitative restrictions, and similar matters. But who today is still interested in such agreements? Was it not one of the meanings and effects of the Kennedy Round to make them superfluous? And the Kennedy Round was already conducted against the background of GATT. Both are supplemented by international commodity agreements. Strictly speaking, there are only three cases where classical tariff and trade agreements still have a certain meaning: first, with regard to Japan, where unilateral liberalization measures will by the end of 1971 admittedly bring a far-reaching adjustment to the other trading partners in the world; second, with regard to the state-trading countries of the East, where the economic system in principle impedes the development of trade that goes beyond primitive barter and in respect of which responsibility has moreover not yet passed to the Communities; third, with regard to agricultural products, which, it will be remembered, were exempted from the Kennedy Round but in respect of which the common agricultural policy also sets narrow limits to trade agreements.

Intepreted in a restrictive sense, Article 113 is therefore hardly a basis for a common policy of substance. This has been stressed repeatedly by the Commission. In May, 1970, already, the European Parliament, in an important decision adopted on a proposal of the Committee for External Trade Relations, emphatically stressed that "the Community must make progress particularly in the field of harmonization of the national policies on the modern aspects of trading relations with nonmember countries." The Parliament expressly mentioned matters such as credit terms and "scientific, technical, financial, and industrial cooperation." Indeed, it would presumably be difficult to find any country that would be interested in treaties if the agreements with the Communities did not provide for an instrument that at first sight looks unimportant but in actual fact is a crucial element of modern international economic relations: the joint committee. In the trade agreement between the European Communities and Yugoslavia, for instance, one can read: "The Joint Committee shall ensure the smooth working of this agreement and shall examine all questions that may arise as it is being implemented. The Joint Committee shall, in addition, in the framework of regular cooperation, make suggestions of any type to develop trade on a basis that is beneficial to both contracting parties." The very role of the Joint Committee (in the case of Yugoslavia it held its first meeting in Belgrade at the beginning of January, 1971), therefore, goes beyond the other provisions of the Agreement. Reference is made to "suggestions of any type to develop trade." It is indeed inevitable that on the sidelines of such committee meetings there should be discussions on a large number of wider ranging questions of common interest. The joint committee in itself is an instrument of "regular cooperation," and cooperation is possibly the linchpin of agreements of the sort we may expect now and in the future. This includes technical and industrial cooperation, outline conditions for joint ventures set up by enterprises, cooperation in nonmember countries particularly in matters of development policy, a system of direct settlement of disputes under a code of good conduct and, of course, also cooperation through loans and investment in the partner country. All this comes out clearly at meetings of a joint committee. This committee cannot, however, give an answer to the new questions. Here it runs into the limits of the agreement under which it was set up.

When the Treaties of Rome were being discussed, there was no means of foreseeing the way from classical trade agreements to cooperation agreements. It can therefore be assumed that in the provisions on the common commercial policy the Six would have taken account of this development if they had been able to foresee it. Indeed, they left a small gap in that they stipulate uniform principles "particularly in regard to" some classical instruments of trade policy and, consequently, do not exclude the incorporation of other more modern elements. Today, however, it is indispensable, starting from this gap, to widen the interpretation of the scope of commercial policy. The member states must again ask themselves what the meaning of their common commercial policy should be, not only because of the discrepancy, difficult to accept, between what the others expect politically and what the Six are able to give, but also because of the contradictions inherent in a policy that tries to act on the basis of the irrelevant factors of yesterday. The fetters of the giant would at least be loosened if in the process a common interpretation of the treaties emerged, which would provide fresh scope for the strengthening of cooperation with nonmember countries. It must be emphasized once again in this connection that it is also the interest of the member states that is always at stake here, for individually these states will in the long run not be sufficiently interesting suppliers for the East, as elsewhere, nor will they be able to repair individually what the European Communities which rest on them destroy through a strength they are unable to control.

THE JOINT RESPONSIBILITY OF THE EUROPEAN COMMUNITIES AND THE UNITED STATES

Not in all cases are agreements the proper instrument to govern relations between the Communities and nonmember countries. Examples include the relationship with the United States. The importance of this relationship in the pattern of the European Communities' external relations hardly requires any special emphasis. In their economic power, the two are still wide apart, the gross national product of the United States being double the gross Community product. With the same size population, and a rapid advance in productivity and production on the Communities' side, it is nevertheless likely that the gap will be reduced further. In addition, investments in both directions create links that are difficult to undo. It should not be overlooked here that the book value of direct American investment in Europe, at more than $10 billion, is over three times as high as that of European investment in the United States. Taking trade alone, the European Communities are leading the United States, which shows the traditional dependence of the prosperity of the European countries on international trade.

These economic relationships, too, obviously have more general implications and a more general background. In their interests, the European Communities and the United States face each other in many parts of the world, and very often they are competitors. After the entry of Great Britain, the two partners between them will control not much less than half the volume of world trade, which is a measure of their special responsibility. The economic and monetary union may affect the position of the dollar and thus touch a pillar of the international monetary system and at the same time a sinew of the American position in the world. The prospect of British membership already gives rise to the concern, mentioned above, about the formation of regional blocs. In Europe, the strings of common action in the matters governed by the Treaties of Rome and Paris, of defense policy and general foreign policy are, at least in institutional terms, not yet convergent. In America they are in one and the same hand. There are nonmember countries which make their readiness to admit American military bases dependent on the readiness of the United States to promote their relations with the European Communities. This is why the European Communities and the United States must develop frank and free relations of partnership. At present this does not always appear to be very easy. In the United States those bearing political responsibility, led by the President, are fighting an increasingly difficult battle against the spreading atmosphere of indifference to international affairs. With regard to the European Communities this is still a well-meaning indifference. But it is precisely here that a certain disappointment has been spreading, particularly as regards the discrepancy between great political aims and the comparatively small progress of economic integration. Many are those who no longer want to take the possibilities of Europe on trust. Developments in Europe are frequently no longer viewed from the world political angle but in the light of narrow interests. On occasion, for instance, one may almost get the impression that relations between the United States and the European Communities are not shaped by the White House, the State Department, or leading foreign policy specialists of Congress, but increasingly also by the California and Arizona Citrus Association. Nathaniel Samuels, Deputy Under Secretary of State for Economic Affairs, quite recently made it clear that the time was past when the United States was ready to trade short-term economic costs for possible long-term political advantages.[3]

There is no reason why the European Communities should pass silently over arguments that are advanced in defense of American interests. Even the much-discussed common agricultural policy is only one version of an admittedly liberal policy in an economic area where none of the large producers is liberal. That the United States should have chosen other ways of supporting its agriculture does not make these ways any better and, above all, does not make the rate of support any lower. American reactions to European policy in Africa and the Mediterranean are puzzling in their vehemence. They rest on an extremely weak economic basis, and politically one would have expected the contrary, precisely of the United States. True, there is nobody who can claim that he had always and at all times fully complied with the principles which we all acknowledged when joining GATT. But it is precisely for this reason that the United States, in its glass house, should refrain from throwing stones.

Despite the soundness of these comments and the need to stress time and again that we in Europe will shape our future under our own steam and by our own will, the dialogue between Europe and America cannot in the long run be confined to the listing of mutual sins. The effects of such an exercise in world political immaturity must in the long run be baleful. Already we are sometimes conscious of a climate of ill-humor whose cause does not lie in the matter involved but in a certain disappointment at the vanity of the dialogue. One day we may arrive at certain concrete results. The European Communities do not refuse to go on discussing citrus fruit and tobacco, chicken and lard. But even if in these questions of detail it were possible to find appropriate and mutually satisfactory arrangements here and there, this would not resolve the growing frustration in our relationship. To this problem there is only one solution that largely exceeds the bilateral relations, freeing them from strains and making them firmer again. We must jointly try to tackle certain major tasks where we have a joint responsibility.

In my address of January 19, 1971, to the European Parliament, I called for a new drive toward liberalization. I immediately added that at present there was probably little point in giving it the form of a worldwide "round," for lack of substance. But we can open the talk about nontariff trade barriers. We can take a look at world trade in farm products without calling into question the bases of the agricultural policies. We can jointly discuss the questions involved in the formation of regional blocs and clearly mark where the geographical and the fundamental political limits of the intentions of the various parties lie. We can jointly harmonize our development strategies. We can find appropriate solutions to matters that are a cause of new protectionist tendencies, such as the textiles problem. In other words, we can, in a joint effort, try to solve great questions for which both the European Communities and the United States bear a heavy responsibility.

Can we really? Domestic developments in the United States are not precisely propitious to such efforts. Already the parliamentary formality that Wilbur D. Mills, Chairman of the Ways and Means Committee of the House of Representatives, reintroduced his protectionist Trade Act on the first working day of the new Congress, will again provide a general defensive attitude throughout the world. But the question as to whether we are able to tackle major questions jointly is here mainly directed at ourselves, at the possibilities and limits of an external policy of the European Communities. The member states hesitate over far-reaching common decisions. They hesitate even more if the task is to take common initiatives vis-à-vis the outside world. In the history of the Communities there is no single example of a foreign policy initiative of world political weight which would have been perfectly possible under the treaties. Sometimes, one cannot escape the impression that the member states like to use the Communities as a shield which protects them for a while individually, as a defensive pretext for failing or not wanting to act themselves. This, however, is an attitude which is no longer compatible with the responsibility which the Community, as the largest trading power, has precisely toward the United States, among other countries. Here too, it is a fact that the European Communities always have effects on the outside world. If the member states do not assume their joint responsibility, this amounts in the final analysis to demonstrating to the whole world their individual irresponsibility. If one feels that one of the most dangerous effects at this point in time lies in the absence of a European initiative, then foregoing a common initiative is no longer justifiable. Battles cannot be won with a shield alone, but we should spare Europe the fate of offering the sorry sight of those whose shield disintegrates, and who then are helplessly facing the opposite side. We can act if we wish to do so, but we must wish to act if we still want to be able to act tomorrow.

SIX PROBLEMS FROM THE COMMUNITIES' EXTERNAL RELATIONS

These comments have not been made flippantly, let alone with the intention of being provocative. They flow solely from the wish not to see the great possibilities of joint action by the European states go to waste. Here, I am guided less by enthusiasm for Europe than by a look at the visible needs of today. The problems which the European Communities have to solve are with us already. They do not disappear because one refuses to tackle them or tries to cope with them with all too easy pragmatism. Below I simply list, without discussing them in further detail, six problems of the external relations of the Communities, in respect of which decisions of major importance have to be made, with no more than very tentative beginnings having been made so far:

1. The dialogue with the United States of America can lead to a relationship of unclouded partnership only if there is the determination to find solutions to problems of detail and the readiness to act jointly in matters of major importance.

2. The largest world trading power, the European Communities, also bears chief responsibility for the development of free world trade. Today, this responsibility calls for a drive toward liberalization.

3. The relationship between the European Communities and the Soviet Union and the other Communist countries has not been clarified. The postponement of direct relations by three years must not prevent us from making early moves to create, on the basis of an acknowledgment of realities by the Soviet Union, the conditions for adequate cooperation with Communist countries.

4. The European Communities have assumed the responsibility of making, within the limits of their possibilities, a contribution to long-term stability in the Mediterranean area. It is precisely here, however, that the disproportion between weighty intentions and limited instruments becomes apparent.

5. The Communities' development policy has so far been largely confined to trade policy measures. It is, however, in our interest not only to maintain geographical preferences or, to put the same idea differently, to fix priorities, but also, in choosing our means of action, to establish a more rational relationship between our possibilities and the needs of the developing countries.

6. One of the many problems that still have not been solved completely in connection with British membership is the Communities'

European policy, i.e., the long-term view of European developments by which we are guided, particularly in relation to the neutral EFTA countries. The first Council decisions in this matter did not yet get down to the basic point.

Our tasks are not confined to these great questions. Here, as elsewhere in foreign policy, individual questions may lose in importance while new ones may arise. The answer to the Buenos Aires declaration, for instance, can be the beginning of a new pattern in the European Communities' external relations. The impact of the accession of new members is moreover worldwide. Canada, Australia, India, Pakistan are only a few special examples of the countries affected directly. The European Communities will hardly be able to dodge certain decisions of principle on the implications of British entry for nonmember countries. This is not said for the sake of completeness but merely to emphasize the thesis that the European Communities have effects on the outside world, whether they want it or not. The member states cannot escape these effects, and are therefore required to face up to them politically. At some points the rather defensive policy of merely reacting is no longer sufficient. The instruments available to the European Communities must be reviewed and supplemented. There will be a need to decide on some very important questions in the appropriate form.

THE FOREIGN POLICY CONSULTATIONS OF THE SIX AND THE EUROPEAN COMMUNITIES

This brings up a last question. Is it possible or, to put it more cautiously, likely that in the foreseeable future the Communities will make the necessary decisions toward a deliberate policy on foreign relations? Where major common initiatives are to be taken, the Commission as a rule suffers from the disadvantage that its right of proposal is not only limited by the treaties, and the not very broad interpretation often put on them, but also tends to be somewhat at the discretion of the member states. With all the integrity and expertise of its members, the Committee of Permanent Representatives consists of officials who are bound by the instructions they receive and can hardly be the source of political initiatives. And the Council of Ministers itself has been so successful in developing its own unwieldiness that, although it manages sometimes to disregard the Commission and the Permanent Representatives, after such a feat of strength it lacks the energy—or is it the readiness?—for political moves of its own. This is also true of foreign policy matters, of which one should indeed assume that they occupy a particularly central position in the Council of Foreign Ministers.

Here too, the conference of the Hague marked a new beginning. Today, one can no longer speak of the possibilities open to the European Communities in their foreign policy without mentioning the formula for the cooperation of the Six worked out by the Committee headed by Vicomte Etienne Davignon.[4] This formula met with much criticism. Many found it much too meagre, too intergovernmental, too remote from the existing institutions. Today, we know that the Davignon formula has provided the most effective stimulus for a long time to European political cooperation. The meeting of Ministers in Munich on November 19, 1970, the talks of the political directors of the Foreign Ministries, the first common instructions given to the ambassadors of the Six in the capitals of the nonmember countries have already helped to strengthen the awareness of the need for coordination of the foreign policies of the member states of the Community, and to take the first steps toward such coordination.

If, indeed, there is any criticism to be leveled at the Davignon formula today, it is that it does not provide any pointer on how the new impulses for cooperation in foreign policy are to be translated into decisions by the institutions set up under the treaties. The new stimuli are welcome, but this is all the more true the more they are translated into initiatives of the European Communities. Perhaps President Georges Pompidou had this situation in mind when recommending at his Press Conference on January 21, 1971, that the extremely busy Foreign Ministers and their technical assistants, the departmental Ministers, should be replaced by Ministers for European Affairs who would be competent and permanently available and would derive their authority from their respective national governments. It would be easy to make a start with such a development today, if, at foreign policy consultations, the Commission of the Communities were not only an occasional guest but a permanent participant able to translate the results of these consultations into proposals to the Council. In any case, it will very soon prove inevitable to translate the new stimuli which the Hague Conference gave to Europe and which, in institutional terms, have found their reflection in the Davignon formula and in what is probably not only President Pompidou's thinking, into action by the Communities. This will be all the easier, the more factual needs take precedence over vanities deriving from relative position.

After the end of the transitional phase, and the related completion of the first major stage of European union, the Communities are still faced with three, and not two, major topical tasks: first, the strengthening of common action through entry into the lengthy and difficult process of economic and monetary union; second, enlargment of the Communities through the entry of new members, particularly Great Britain; and, third, the opening up of the Communities to the world, on which they already have such a pronounced impact today, but in which they still act with hesitation and indecision. External relations will in the future be the third major pillar of the Communities' activities. To make them stable and attractive is a task that neither the Council nor the Commission, neither the member states nor the Community institutions can escape. The future of the European Communities will, in no small part, be determined by the way in which they succeed or fail in shaping the picture of Europe in the world.

NOTES

1. See the wording of the declaration of the extraordinary ministerial meeting of the Special Latin American Coordination Committee (CECLA) in Buenos Aires on July 29, 1970, in *Europa Archiv, XXVI*, 2 (1971), p. D 54 *et seq.* (published in German).

2. See documentation on the Conference of Heads of State or Government of the Member States of the European Communities in The Hague on December 1 and 2, 1969, in *Europa Archiv*, XXV, 2 (1970), p. D 27 *et seq.* Also see the articles by Ernst Kobbert "Den Haag—eine Frucht der Geduld" (The Hague, a fruit of patience), in *Europa Archiv*, XXV, 1 (1970), p. 11 *et seq.* and Katharina Focke "Europa-Politik nach Den Haag" (European policy after The Hague), in *Europa Archiv*, XXV, 8 (1970), p. 267 *et seq.*

3. See *Vision* (Geneva), No. 1 (November, 1970), p. 29.

4. See the wording of the report of July 20, 1970, by the Foreign Ministers of the Member States of the European Communities to the Heads of State or Government on possible progress toward political unification, in *Europa Archiv*, XXV, 22 (1970), p. D 520 *et seq.*

EUROPE,
THE UNITED STATES,
AND
THE WORLD ECONOMY

Harald B. Malmgren

The rapid emergence of Japan as an economic superpower, and the evolution of the European Community into the world's largest trading unit, have transformed international power relationships in complex ways. Added to these developments has been the extremely rapid growth of world trade and investment, growing more rapidly than national incomes. The degree of economic interdependence between countries has been growing so fast that national autonomy is increasingly challenged by international economic activities.

This restructuring of influences and powers will be accelerated by the enlargement of the European Community. The enlarged Community will be larger than the United States in population as well as trade, and approach it in GNP. The sheer economic size of the Community would give it the edge of world economic leadership, if the Community chose to lead. If it does not overtly seize leadership from the United States, the fact remains that its weight will give it the ability, and the right, to say yes or no to any proposals to reshape international economic relations among most of the nations of the world.

This, however, is only one aspect of the European Community's power. If a common position could be found among the Six on any issue, the tendency has been for applicants for membership to support that position, or at least not oppose it. Other countries in Europe which do not wish to become full members do expect to enjoy some special arrangements for preferred access to the Common Market for their products. Such countries are very reluctant politically to take positions which differ from those of the Community. The poorer countries of the Mediterranean and of Africa are even less inclined to quarrel with the Community on economic questions, both because their leverage is small and because they have become dependent on discriminatory bilateral economic ties with the Community. The overall political and economic dimensions of this new bloc of Europe, the Mediterranean, and Africa, far transcend the awareness in the present Community of the power implicit in the international relationships which have been established.

The members of the European Community do not recognize the power of the Community. More often than not, the Community is seen as a fractionated group of national interests quarreling among themselves, struggling to reach consensus, but rarely achieving it. There is recognition of specific political achievements, such as the creation and maintenance of a Common Agricultural Policy; but the general progress toward full economic integration and political unification is seen to be very slow.

It is also evident that the members of the Community have seen themselves as independent from one another with regard to traditional foreign policy issues, such as relations with Eastern Europe, and security relationships in and out of NATO. There has been no connection made in national capitals between the political handling of these kinds of questions and the economic handling of commercial and financial relationships with North America and Asia. Yet this connection is increasingly important in the domestic politics of the United States, and its reactions to European policies, especially to what Americans call "burden-sharing." The foreign policy of the Community can only be an economic policy, because the Community is so far only integrated economically—and even then only partially.

These two facts, of power without awareness of power, and of the division between economic and political foreign policies, are critical characteristics of the Community.

EVOLVING U.S. FOREIGN AND DOMESTIC POLICIES

The vision of an integrated Europe held by U.S. foreign policy officials in the 1950's and early 1960's was simple. Europe was to become prosperous, politically stable, and unified. The integration of Europe would enmesh Germany inextricably with the French and other Europeans, which would reduce the chances of a resurgence of independent German militarism. The unification of Europe would provide a strong counterbalance to the Russian threat.

A considerable debate took place as to whether this conception was right, and if so what form it should take. When all was said and done, however, American foreign policy pursued unswervingly and with passion the objective of European integration, through support of integrative steps among the Six, and through encouragement of enlargement of the Community to include the United Kingdom and other outsiders in Europe. It was simply taken for granted that integration would sooner or later work out for the best interests of all countries, and that a unified Europe would prove to be a partner to the United States in managing international order. That partner would no doubt share in the burdens of economic and military responsibility for world order; and it would very likely collaborate with the United States, in developing international policies.

Historically, perhaps the last open-ended endorsement of the unification of Europe under any circumstances was made in President Nixon's first "State of the World" report in February, 1970:

> Our support for the strengthening and broadening of the European Community has not diminished. We recognize that our interest will necessarily be affected by Europe's evolution, and we may have to make sacrifices in the common interest. We consider that the possible economic price of a truly unified Europe is outweighed by the gain in the political vitality of the West as a whole.

Since that statement, there have been no others like it. It is doubtful whether there will be any more. The official positions of Administration spokesmen have slowly been shifting, to express doubts about the equity of the international economic system as it has evolved, and about the willingness of its partners to share the burdens of the common defense, and of development assistance, and of managing the trade and monetary system. The new mood is one of frustration, and disappointment, with the policies of Western Europe and Japan. As far as Western Europe, and the Community in particular, are concerned, it does not now seem surprising that the ardent supporters of the Grand Design may have been wrong in their assumptions about the likely evolution of European policies. There is little need to analyze yet again the inherent flaws in the American conception of the Grand Design. Professor Stanley Hoffman, and others, have amply diagnosed the defects.[1] /That the United States should be disappointed with the Europe on which it had spent so much time is to be expected. The Community has been inward-looking in its policies, preoccupied with matters of internal harmonization, and to the extent that there is any external policy at all, it is a policy of ad hoc bilateral reaction to bilateral and regional pressures.

The U.S. frustration and disappointment has not caused a change in basic policy. The official position is to continue to support enlargement of the European Community, and to take no steps which might interfere with progress toward that end. However, the frustration and disappointment is being added cumulatively to a number of other critical problems which the United States now faces. The persistent balance of payments deficits and periodic monetary crises have brought new frustrations. While it is often recognized that a major cause of this deterioration is domestic inflation, primarily due to inadequate financing of the Vietnam War, the feeling is common that other countries in persistent balance of payments surplus situations should have taken actions to ease the international economic pressures on the United States. Exchange rates should have been altered more often. Greater defense expenditures should have been made by European countries. Greater foreign aid programs should have been offered by Europe.

Arguments can be made back and forth about the amount of adjustment which should be made domestically, and about the obligations of countries doing well to make room for countries doing badly. This was not the only problem, however. At home the United States found itself with a resurgence of protectionism. The delicate political balance between inward- and outward-looking interest groups was disturbed by the leap of the U.S. labor movement to its new position of favoring restrictions on the outflow of capital and the inflow of imports. Labor had been for many years an important piece of the political coalition which favored liberal international trade policies. Its loss left this coalition with two key groups, the multinational corporations and the key farm organizations, and a scattered array of well-meaning, but economically powerless organizations. The remaining coalition could be called upon to impede protectionist legislation, but it did not appear strong enough to bring about a new, constructive, internationally oriented program. It did not provide enough strength to achieve passage in Congress of bills which would enable the United States Executive branch to implement understandings reached with other countries on economic matters./

The matters left in abeyance by the end of 1971 included the American Selling Price (ASP) package, the implementation of general tariff preferences for the benefit of developing countries, and the funding of the international development institutions such as the International Development Association (IDA) affiliate of the World Bank and the proposed soft-loan facility of the Asian Development

Bank. The United States government had in the United Nations supported the proposal that nations provide 1 percent of their GNP in the form of official aid and private investment for development assistance. Just at the time, in the 1969-71 period, when the other developed nations began to take this idea seriously, and even to define specific targets for official aid levels independent of private investment flows, the United States found itself backing off. Instead of committing itself to providing development assistance funds at a level of 0.70 percent of GNP, as recommended by the Pearson Commission, the United States found its percentage ranking as a donor country slipping rapidly. Once the largest aid donor by any popular measure of effort, the United States moved down below the top twelve countries in terms of its share of assistance to GNP. Not only did a restive Congress reduce AID appropriations, but the President lowered his requests for AID funds. When the August 15, 1971, economic crisis decisions were announced, the package included a 10 percent reduction in foreign aid expenditures. This action, which had only nominal effects on the balance of payments, could only be explained in terms of the domestic politics of foreign aid. Something could be gained politically by a gesture to reduce foreign aid, and additional political support apparently was seen to be desirable.

The new American mood, and the new protectionist efforts, gave rise to many abortive, but prolonged and painful, labors in the Congress over foreign policy issues. The Vietnam War frustrations are often blamed for the foreign policy problems which have arisen in other forms, but the new, basic sentiments described have their own reality, cumulatively enhancing the isolationistic reactions to war and the use of military power in faraway places. The increasingly strong efforts by Congress to reduce American troop levels in Western Europe must be seen in this light.

All of this is by way of introduction to the new circumstances the United States and the European Community face in their relations with each other, and with the rest of the world in the 1970's and 1980's. The United States can be said to be withdrawing from a predominant position to a new role as one of several major powers in a multipolar world, without any clear conception of how to handle this new role. The European Community can be said to be playing a major new role in the world economy without awareness of that role, and without application of political energy or time to defining specific objectives in relation to the world as a whole. On both sides events appear to be unfolding without any conscious design, and even without high priority interest of the political leadership in both areas.

EFFECTS OF COMMUNITY POLICIES ON
OTHER COUNTRIES

The Community itself cannot be said to have a foreign policy, or even a foreign economic policy, on a global scale. It does influence other countries through its actions internally as well as externally, but the foreign effects usually seem to be afterthoughts, or even accidental. The emphasis on internal integration and policy harmonization in the daily politics of the Six is understandable. The almost complete failure to recognize the effects of internal decisions on the rest of the world, and especially on the world system of rules and institutions, is less easily explicable.

The internal achievement of the Common Agricultural Policy (CAP) should be seen in this light. This ingenious system for harmonizing policies and sharing the economic burdens has shown remarkable vitality in surviving one crisis after another. The mechanics of the system have not been neutral as regards outside interests, however. The barrier to imports is only one aspect of the major external effects of the CAP. This system is designed to support farm incomes through support of very high price levels (for example, about double the world price level for grains). This in turn provides a strong incentive for increased production. To prevent imports from cheaper foreign suppliers from spoiling this supported market, import levies are assessed in an amount sufficient to bring the price of imports up slightly above domestic price supports. Imports thus become residual, filling needs only when there is demand in excess of domestic supplies. The added impetus of technological change has added to the domestic pressures, resulting in a tendency to generate domestic surpluses. The Commission of the Community as a matter of doctrine is opposed to production controls. Since storage facilities are not available on a large scale, the Community simply subsidizes exports by an amount sufficient to meet export competition and unload the surpluses.

To the insider, the system passes a large portion of the costs of the farm program to consumers. To the outsider, the system passes another large portion of the costs on to suppliers in other countries, by reducing their exports to the Community and by disrupting their sales in other markets of the world.

This is mercantilism in a rather pure form. Since the politics of agriculture is important in every country, what the Community is doing is passing political problems on to others wherever possible. Efforts of the United States and other exporting countries to persuade the

Community nations of the dangers of following this course have proven fruitless. There is no significant recognition within the Community that its farm program need take foreign interests into account.

The Community's relations with other countries have taken the form of bilateral arrangements to accommodate specific historical relationships, or to respond to particular political and economic pressures. The Yaoundé Convention is a reflection of historical ties. Its existence, however, generated concerns in the Community about relations with other African countries. The Greek and Turkish trade arrangements with the Community originated in a different type of concern for the independence of these countries relatively to the Communist countries. Once the Greek, Turkish, and Yaoundé Convention countries were placed in a special position, however, the other nations of Africa and the Mediterranean appeared to be discriminated against. These discriminatory arrangements in practice encompassed development assistance, and special access conditions for Community exports ("reverse preferences"). Other countries were gradually brought within the network of special association relationships, including Morocco, Tunisia, Spain, and Israel. Over thirty countries are involved in such agreements. If the British become full members, provision may have to be made for certain other countries, such as Mauritius, India, Pakistan, and the Caribbean countries.

Statements by present and former senior officials of the Community suggest that these special arrangements are believed to be politically necessary, and that the whole of the Mediterranean and most of Africa must eventually be included. Having come this far, it is difficult not to include the others. This has resulted in the development of a rather large economic bloc which looks to the European countries for guidance in the formulation of national policies. The formation of a bloc may not have been the intent originally, but it is now the inescapable conclusion to the proliferation of special arrangements. The key question which remains is whether the process of proliferation can stop with Africa and the Mediterranean. The answer to that is likely to be no, because of the need to accommodate Commonwealth Preference countries as the British become full members. How to draw a line thereafter becomes a far more complex question. Regional boundaries would no longer provide a natural limitation.

These special arrangements result in discrimination against the exports of other developed and developing countries. Sometimes the effect is significant. In any event, the principle of nondiscrimination and the rules of the GATT relating to it become almost irrelevant as a consequence of the sheer magnitude of the exceptions which these special arrangements bring about. This problem has become seriously compounded by the question of how to deal with the other countries of EFTA which do not become full members of the Community. It is already taken for granted in Europe that they will be offered free access to the Common Market for their industrial products, without requiring accession to the Common Agricultural Policy or to the political institutions of the Community. This may be a practical solution for the neutrals who wish to benefit from the economic progress of the Community but cannot accept the political implications of full membership. For other countries outside Europe, this consolidates yet another major piece of the new economic power bloc which favors insiders over outsiders.

Looking to the East, the Community found itself with a variety of national policies in commercial and financial relations with the Communist countries. Slowly, the Commission has tried to harmonize policies of the Six, but with limited success. It did bring about the agreement on the so-called Common Commercial Policy, which provides for special safeguards against import disruption by the products of the nonmarket economies. Even here, then, the Community chose to work up new, special procedures rather than seek a new multilateral understanding with the other countries not members of the Community.

This tendency to deal bilaterally, rather than multilaterally, is a serious threat to the multilateral economic system of rules and procedures which was so painfully constructed during and after World War II. Its consequences are far-reaching, since the shift to bloc problem-solving directly affects the long-term interests of Latin America, Asia, and North America.

There is no sign that a positive, generally applicable design for economic relations with the rest of the world is even being considered.

The European Community points to its record of trade with developing nations as evidence of a positive policy. In 1970, for example, the exports of developing countries to the EEC amounted to about $16.5 billion, while their exports to the United States only amounted to about $11 billion. The EFTA countries, moreover, took nearly $7 billion worth of developing country exports. This record looks somewhat different when viewed from a regional point of view, however. Of all EEC imports from developing countries, nearly half came from Africa, and only 10 percent from South and East Asia. Even the EFTA countries, with a more even distribution of imports from the different regions of the world, took about a third of their imports from Africa.

The record is also not adequate in terms of the industrial development needs of the poorer countries. Of its imports from the poorer countries, the Community takes very little in the form of manufactures (as compared with the United States, which takes well over one-half of all the manufactures exported by all of the developing countries). The high level of Community imports is attributable to the demand for raw materials from these countries, continuing the trend of colonial resource exploitation of past decades.

The Community can say that it has consistently supported the concept of generalized tariff preferences to benefit all developing countries, and that it was the first to go ahead with implementation of general preferences, in the summer of 1971. This action was taken when there was no indication of when, if ever, the United States would implement similar preferences. This apparently courageous step by the Community is not all that it seems. Based upon analysis of the specific mechanics of the Community scheme, Professor Richard Cooper has concluded that the Community's scheme will offer almost no additional incentive to developing countries to export.[2] The Community system is based on a tariff-quota safeguard system, whereby imports up to some quota level are allowed to enter duty-free. Once the quota is met, additional imports must pass the normal tariff barriers. The tariff quotas have been set at very low levels, with a small allowance for growth. The normal growth in exports from these countries will rapidly overtake, and in many cases has already overtaken, the stipulated import levels of duty-free access. What lies behind this is simply ᵗhat the political decision to give preferences was countered by the inge-nuity of trade technicians in creating a complex system which is designed to deter rapid growth of imports from the low-wage, de-veloping nations. In defense of the new system, Community officials have stated that the quantitative threshold levels would in practice be used only as a guide to what was happening. Official action to invoke the safeguards would be rare, usually only in the case of so-called sensitive products. This however means that the ceilings could be invoked at any time. They provide no predictable, continuing assurance to the developing nations that the market access conditions for their products would not alter unexpectedly. Politically, if experience is any teacher, domestic industries in Europe could be expected to make complaints about the level of imports, and could be expected to succeed in having counteractions taken fairly often. Since the new members of the Community will adopt the same scheme, and the Japanese have imitated it as well, the end result has been the creation of a complex technically ingenious trade mechanism which gives rise to many false hopes and few benefits.

There is even another damaging aspect to this system. Because many "sensitive" manufactures are to be treated as exceptions, with no preference, a number of products which have been export successes will be excluded. The countries which have so far been most successful in exporting manufactures on a competitive basis are the Eastern Asian countries. Thus it is Eastern Asia which will be kept from improving its access to Europe. Moreover, since the ceilings on preferred products are set so low, exporters of manufactures which are doing reasonably well, but not yet highly troublesome to the developed countries, would run into the ceilings early. These again would include many of the products of Eastern Asia. On the other hand, the Africans do not sell, nor even produce, many manufactures. They would "benefit" from preferences which they could not exploit.

The end result is to tend to maintain the present pattern of excluding Eastern Asia and welcoming modest increases from Africa. The Community's general preference scheme thus does little to end the privileged position of Africa and the Mediterranean, and other associated countries, and provides little of benefit for exports of manufactures from any of the developing countries.

While the overall development assistance effort of the European countries has been improving markedly since the late 1960's, most of the bilateral aid was disbursed to countries historically related to the donor nation, or tied through other economic arrangements. The Community has itself established the European Development Fund, which provides assistance to many of the poorer countries which have association arrangements. The need for assistance programs elsewhere is not recognized. Participation in multilateral development assistance has always been done reluctantly (although cooperation with other donor countries has been positive in the special consortia for the rescheduling of debts of certain developing countries).

These are only some of the problems posed by the Community for the rest of the world. There are many other manifestations of the tendency to design policies which solve specific problems and exclude other outside nations from the benefits of the solution. European efforts to develop Community technical standards, or to develop Community environmental policies should be seen in this light. Some of the nontariff barriers about which Americans complain so loudly are simply a result of the exclusive, internally oriented problem-solving approach of the Commission.

This tendency is quite understandable, as far as the Commission itself is concerned. The way in which a bureaucracy of this type can become a political power in its own right is to design policies which would have to be administered by it on a Community-wide basis. Since the Community institutions primarily concern themselves with economic questions, the Commission simply sticks to economic problem-solving as the means to the end of increasing its control over member states.

Where the problems confronted by the Community as a whole are ones of an internal character, or are related to regional political problems, the tendency to ignore external interests is somewhat understandable. The undercutting of international principles is not limited to these kinds of issues however. For example, the Community has been conducting negotiations with Japan on mutual liberalization of trade restrictions. These talks break down each time they are begun, in part because the Commission insists that special rules apply to the possible reimposition of restrictions after liberalization. The Japanese position is that the multilateral principles agreed to by all nations are sufficient to take care of special problems which might arise between Japan and the Community; while the Commission argues that special safeguards must be agreed to which are more restrictive than the multilateral rules would allow. The Community also maintains a large number of trade restrictions against Japanese and other Asian country products which it does not apply to imports from other parts of the world. In other words, the Community countries positively discriminate against Asia.

When the United States or other countries raise all these issues, the Commission of the Community answers that the actual trade results have been good since the founding of the Common Market in 1958. Even in agriculture, the Commission will say, imports have grown significantly since 1958. The preferential agreements do not in most cases affect the trade of other countries in substantial ways. Perhaps there is discrimination against a few American exports like citrus as a result of the Mediterranean agreements, but after all, the American trade in such product areas is small. In other words, the Community takes the position that the results count in the end, while the breach of principles do not count at all. The Community is pragmatic in its policy, and it can be characterized as being disinterested in international principles, except where such principles may provide some short-term advantage to the Six.

Regarding the actual results, it can be observed that most of the impact of the Community's commercial policies is only beginning to be felt. The main provisions of the Common Agricultural Policy did not really affect trade until 1966-67. The proliferation of preferences on a selective basis picked up steam only in the late 1960's. Looking to the future, it is only now that the Community is beginning serious work on industrial standardization, or on industrial regulation, or on industrial and regional economic policies. The tone of official documents on these matters is one of exclusive preoccupation with Community problems, or of concern with the threat posed to internal policies by outside interests which operate within the Community. The major role of foreign-owned enterprise in Europe does complicate life for European planners, but the answer need not lie solely in the construction of defensive policies aimed against these interests, or in preferential treatment of European enterprise. The Community could instead suggest some kind of multilateral approach to the regulation of international business activity. Nothing of that sort is ever proposed, however.

IMPLICATIONS FOR UNITED STATES-EUROPEAN RELATIONS

The trend of European policy therefore creates apprehension in the United States even where no trouble has yet arisen. This trend of policy is more important as it relates to the future of international principles than as it relates to specific economic dislocations. The profound interest of the United States in the establishment and use of international rules and institutions on a global basis is threatened. This is not a matter of theoretical, ideological enthusiasm for certain types of principles and procedures. The United States does have global political and economic interests. The global economic interests are best protected by rules of nondiscrimination which apply as widely as possible. The global political interests are best served by rules which restrain divisive economic nationalism. But there is even another element to the United States foreign economic policy position which is often not understood in other countries. The United States political system, based upon bargaining and compromise among economic as well as political and social interests, tends to ignore external interests. The fact that trade is only 4 or 5 percent of gross national product allows the luxury of ignoring foreign economic interests without fear of disruptive consequences. Policy makers have therefore generally believed that international commitments in the form of principles and institutional procedures were a necessary constraint to keep the United States itself from engaging in blatant mercantilism. The principles of the GATT have time and time again been invoked by the Executive branch to restrain the political inclinations toward protectionism in the American Congress. Many sophisticated experts in and out of the United States government fear a rise of short-sighted economic nationalism in the United States even more than they fear such a development in Europe, if there is further erosion of the multilateral economic system.

Since the recent trends in the United States have already shifted in the direction of reversing the world trade liberalization accomplished up to 1967, the erosion of what is practically left of the international mechanisms risks total collapse of international economic cooperation. It is easy to list the derogations of the United States, ranging from the unilateral imposition of new trade restrictions to the unilateral character of the August, 1971, international actions aimed at shocking the rest of the world economy into new policies. The political frustrations with European and Japanese policies, the fear of the job displacement effects of trade, the unpleasant experience of stepping down from a predominant position to a role as a member of an executive committee, the diminution of the Soviet global threat, all of these elements work to make a shift to neo-isolationism not only possible but relatively painless.

Thus within the United States one finds a state of high tension between the forces which are pulling toward a new isolationism and the forces which call for a continued commitment to the defense of Western Europe and to the process of political unification of Western Europe. The tension is increasingly bearing upon the positions of policy makers, at least in their public positions. Strong speeches criticizing the policies of Western European countries have become a matter of habit, mainly because domestic American politics require it.

These developments have come at a critical time politically and economically. Politically, the confrontation between East and West Europe has settled down to a *modus vivendi* which both sides accept as preferable to high tension diplomacy. Negotiating within this new context for more formal arrangements, whether they be aimed at reduction of military forces in the vicinity of the NATO central front or at more broadly defined security objectives, is difficult. Western Europe needs a continuing American troop commitment to make credible the Western European negotiating position as well as to make credible the United States nuclear guarantee. It also needs some continuing deployment of American tactical nuclear weapons, even if there is a substantial restructuring of the force levels. Yet the American commitment seems to be in doubt. Economically, the new forms of stress between the United States and Europe are impeding the process of multilateral economic cooperation, adversely affecting the interests of both, and perhaps even more important, the interests of everybody else. Multilateral cooperation in economic matters is more critically needed now than at any time since the immediate period after World War II. The rearrangement of the balance of powers and the rapidly increasing degree of economic interdependence combine to make a coordinated effort at modernization of the international rules and institutional procedures imperative.

If there were some explicit policy design on either side of the Atlantic the problems might be less acute. The United States is acting now unpredictably, taking sudden actions which abruptly transform the conditions under which other governments must calculate their own self-interest. Policies can alter quickly and commitments can erode in this context where the tension between home and foreign interests is great, and where disappointment in foreign actions is keenly felt. On the European side, decisions are taken which are insensitive to the positions of third countries. The decision process itself is ponderous and inflexible. A particular national problem is viewed pragmatically, and after a very long period of political gestation a negotiated decision is reached which cannot afterward easily be reopened or altered.

A change in the Community methods of dealing with problems is not likely in the near term. Part of the reason is the split between economic and political questions referred to earlier. Fractionation of all decision-making procedures is another factor, with the Council of Ministers the only true point of coordination. At the Ministerial level, with only occasional meetings, it cannot be expected that the detailed decisions will always, or even usually, fit into a broad policy framework. Technicians in governments and their counterparts in the Commission work out solutions to their own technical and political difficulties, at a fairly low level sometimes, and the overall policy design is simply the cumulation of myriad technical decisions. The Common Agricultural Policy is one example of this process at work, with technical decisions in the so-called Management Committee shaping actions which affect in a major way both internal and external economic and political interests.

The experience of international trade negotiations with the Community suggests that the involvement of Ministers does not really introduce greater flexibility and a broader view. It does however make the negotiating process painful in relation to the meager results obtained. Proposals by the Commission to the Council of Ministers are considered, and perhaps altered; once approved the positions are locked in. Complaints from other countries about the outcome of a particular Council decision cannot be taken into account, because there is no easy way to reopen the question. This inflexibility has caused numerous difficulties in the Atlantic which might never have arisen in a more flexible mode of relations.

The very slowness of the decision process helps to make major problems out of relatively minor ones. The unresponsiveness of the Community in the evolution of the trade and monetary crises during the last three or four years is the most important example. Significant changes were required in national policies, and in the international mechanisms themselves. The Community not only failed to change its own position, but it also strongly discouraged informal efforts by the United States to begin a new process of continuous economic problem-solving. As the negotiations with the United Kingdom and other applicants became active, the Commission said that it could not deal with other problems at the same time. Once the negotiations were completed, the Commission said that the enlargement must actually take place before the interests of third countries could even be considered. New negotiations, even on specific problems, would have to wait upon the entry of the additional members, and upon the negotiation of special arrangements for the other European countries which remained outside the Community. This unwillingness to work on two fronts at once constitutes a threat to the international economic mechanisms and to political and economic cooperation with the United States.

One alternative was proposed by Chancellor Brandt. The West German government would favor the establishment of a permanent, bilateral consultative committee between the United States and the European Community. While this suggestion represented a significant break from the previously inflexible position of the Six, it was not a response to the basic problem of how to move back into a multilateral context in which the interests of all third countries can be weighed on a continuous basis. The German proposal was really yet another prag-matic, bilateral response in the same pattern which has so characterized Community thinking about external affairs generally.

Will the entry of Britain and the enlargement of the Community to include other members, and associate members, make the Commu-nity more outward-looking in a global sense? Certainly this has been an underlying assumption in American policy. It is part of the political rhetoric of those in the United Kingdom who favor entry into the Community. Great Britain has a weak economy, and the outlook is only fair for a significant boost to its economy as a result of entry. Industry will need a period of consolidation before openings are made for outsiders after the initial shock of entry. Its agricultural policy is already under transition, from a system of income supplements which served as a good example to other countries to a system similar to that on the Continent. Once British farmers become accustomed to the higher prices, and the British government to the shift of some of the budgetary costs to consumers, there will be far less incentive to curb the excesses of the Community's policies. Britain's foreign aid is in some trouble, with government unwillingness to meet the international targets for official aid. Britain's preferential arrangements will have to be taken account of in the new Community. It is true that Britain shucked off Australia's special ties completely, and New Zealand was put into a transitional position as a result of the entry negotiations. But the other countries, including especially the developing countries now benefiting from preferential access, will have to be accommodated. Finally, the British government will have to demonstrate that it is "European" in attitude in the early period of its membership. Under these circumstances, the chances are slim of Britain exercising a liberalizing influence on the Community's attitude toward outsiders. What can be expected is that the Community decision-making process will be even more complex, fractionated, and ponderous in the absence of a reform of the Community procedures.

In retrospect, Stanley Hoffman, Henry Kissinger, and others were correct in their criticism of American foreign policy assumptions.[3] In particular, two key assumptions were implicit in the American view of a unified Europe as a collaborative partner. One was that willingness to assume global responsibilities is directly related to availability of resources; the second is that there is a common interest, and that it is self-evidently a global interest. These two assumptions are far more questionable now than they were just a few years ago.

A respectable argument for a policy of European independence from the United States can be and is made. In part this argument stems from a belief that Europe's economic interests are primarily in and around Europe, while America's interests are global. The worldwide investments of the United States, along with its global military and economic programs, are seen by some people in Europe as defining a different orientation. The European countries do depend heavily on international trade, but this dependence is primarily on trade with each other. Trade among the Community countries and between the Community and EFTA accounts for two-thirds of Europe's total trade. Since the formation of the Community, internal trade has been growing far more rapidly than trade with the rest of the world, and this fact is generally recognized in Europe. Europe's interest is sometimes described in terms of the need to build up its own enterprises, and its own pattern of relationships, so that it can grow out of what is sometimes felt to be an infant industry status relative to the American economic colossus. Finally, some Europeans view as self-serving the passionate American attachment to principles of nondiscrimination and to the global institutions conceived at Bretton Woods. America has global interests, while Europe does not, and that, so the argument goes, explains the policy conflicts.

This line of thought must be given far more consideration than it has in the past. While the American interest in a global orientation is self-evident, the interests of Western Europe in what happens in and to countries not affiliated with Europe is far less evident. In the very long-term, the Community's economic interests may pull it toward a global orientation, but the incentives to make decisions with such an orientation now seem to be very small.

There are essentially two options for the United States and Europe. Either of these options profoundly affects the interests of most other countries. One option is to allow the emergence of a bloc orientation in all world economic relationships.[4] Western Europe will consolidate, in this option, special ties for the whole of Europe, the Mediterranean, and most of Africa. The United States would have its relations with Latin America. Japan would hopefully become responsible for the Pacific, or at least East and Southeast Asia. Russia and China would be imponderables, as they are now, with the potential to play some kind of complementary or counterbalancing role with one or more blocs. The Asian subcontinent of India and Pakistan would end up essentially as orphans.

This pattern is promoted by some American policies. While there are no formal preferential economic ties with Latin America, the United States continues to act as if there were a special relationship. The United States has posed a condition for granting general preferences (if and when the United States implements a general preference scheme), that it will not give preferences to any developing country which gives "reverse preferences" as part of a bilateral relationship with a European country. The chances are small that these countries could improve their trade with the United States sufficiently to offset the loss of benefits under existing special preferences of the United Kingdom or the European Community. Thus the American position may ironically promote the further consolidation of the bloc it wishes to loosen.

The bloc option could prove viable for some years, with the major multilateral economic institutions like the GATT and the IMF providing a referee or arbitrating function between the big blocs. It is a pattern which locks some countries together in a painful, if not deadly, embrace. Latin America, for example, is now increasingly seeking ties with other areas of the world, to diffuse the dominance of the United States. Many policy makers in the United States itself would encourage more Latin American ties with Europe and Asia, to ease the North-South tensions. The bad experience of American business with Latin America, and vice versa, should be another lesson to those who advocate bloc formation. Japanese domination of Eastern and Southeastern Asia would be likely to create similar tensions, in addition to constituting a formidable provocation to the People's Republic of China. On the whole, a world of discriminatory power blocs is likely to prove unstable, as much for reasons of internal tensions as for the external frictions which are likely to be generated.

The other option for the United States and Europe is to accept joint responsibility for shaping the world economic system in a deliberate manner, aiming in the long run at making the system more equitable and more open, and less discriminatory, for all countries.

This option would be based upon a conception that economic nationalism and regionalism are politically divisive, and that international rules and procedures are necessary to minimize conflicts between major powers. It would involve realistic recognition that the present rules and mechanisms had been outgrown, and that reform of them was necessary. It would entail a major effort by the Community and the United States within a multilateral context to initiate, and give impetus to a new series of negotiations on international economic problems and on the institutions required to deal with them.

The European Community does not perceive that it has a strong incentive to move in this direction, especially now when it is so involved in the enlargement of the Community. Yet the broad political-security considerations could be a source of motivation, if properly understood. The interaction of political and economic issues in the minds of Washington's policy makers is likely to grow. The economic questions will less and less be seen as instruments to be employed toward the objective of European political integration, and more and more as ends in themselves. The pressure for military disengagement will be intensified as the lack of Atlantic economic cooperation becomes increasingly evident. Europe can allow this to happen in an uncontrollable way only as its own peril, in terms of its relations with Eastern Europe and the Soviet Union, and especially in terms of its negotiating position with the East. As the nature of the military threat to Western Europe alters, and its conception of the role and functions of NATO changes, the Western Europeans could continue to hold American concern for European defense by offering greater cooperation in other spheres. In other words, it has not been, and is not now sufficient to refuse all of the American proposals for greater defense efforts in Europe and for different structural military relations, and to refuse to pay a higher proportion of the defense costs consequent to the deployment of United States forces in Europe. There must be a positive side to the European posture. For political and security reasons, even if for no others, Europe should place multilateral economic cooperation on a much higher priority. In the longer run, however, this kind of shift would serve the economic interests of Western Europe best, too. Europe's investments in other parts of the world are growing rapidly, as the European economy reaches an advanced stage of development. The wider its interests, the more need it will have for the protection provided by principles of nondiscrimination and by institutional procedures which channel national decisions in ways which minimize their adverse international effects.

These two options appear to be conflicting alternatives. Yet they both face a common set of problems. These same problems would also have to be faced up to by those who favor a return to economic nationalism, and the weakest forms of confederalism within blocs. Clearly, many of the policy decisions taken on a national or regional basis affect the interests of other countries. A decision to protect or promote European agriculture or some industrial sectors will have an effect on non-European farmers or industrialists. A mercantilistic decision will necessarily result in "bumping" other countries. Some of the costs of special nationalistic actions are incurred by foreign governments. Political costs are also passed on, in the form of treading on foreign interests in order to pacify home political pressures. This transference of economic and political costs to other nations has to be controlled, or at least moderated.

It is sometimes argued that industrial policy in France, or in the Community as a whole, cannot be effective if there is openness to the outside world. As governments become increasingly responsible to electorates for employment levels, inflation rates, and income distribution, the international aspects must be considered a threat to effective management of local interests.

THE CHALLENGE OF ECONOMIC INTERDEPENDENCE

Such an argument can no longer be realistically made in that simplistic form. Economic interdependence is already far too great, and turning this backward would itself cause economic disruption to the countries attempting it. The problem which has to be faced up to is how to balance the solution of a domestic problem against the reaction which might be engendered externally. While this has not been seen as a central problem in Community decision-making in the past, it must now become increasingly apparent, in view of the protectionist trend of the American Congress, the strength of the congressional and public support for troop withdrawal from Europe, and the Presidential actions of August, 1971.

In other words, freedom to develop along certain lines internally, whether nationally or regionally, requires certain limitations on that action, so that the system as a whole may provide the basis on which free action may take place. National decisions have to be channeled. The bumping of one nation by another's decisions must be subject to clearly perceived restraints. There have to be international rules of the road, and procedures for consultation to avoid periodic collisions of interests and intentions.

This requirement for a system of perceived, effective restraints would benefit the major powers, but it is crucial to the less strong nations. They have far less leverage to use in protecting their own interests. Their high dependence on external economic forces makes them especially vulnerable to the transfer of economic shocks generated by the great powers. The system on which they have relied in the past was the Bretton Woods system, defined primarily by the United States and Great Britain. In the future, they must look to whatever the United States and the Community develop between them, because that is where the power lies—the power to change, and the power to refuse to change. Japan of course is an increasingly important element in the Western economic power center, but thus far the other two have reacted defensively to Japan, and now they are both constructing new economic restraints against Japan and its economic satellites in Eastern Asia. Japan's influence will not be great until it becomes an initiator of global ideas and negotiations. Politically this is yet some time off.

For the United States and Europe, the resolution of mutual difficulties may seem in the short run the primary political problem. However, it is really the overall system of principles and procedures which is most important to each in the long run. This is not a matter of a shared concern for other countries, of a shared sense of responsibility and benevolence. That is where the simplified conception of the Grand Design left off. Instead, the shaping and the maintenance of an orderly system of international economic relations is a matter of self-interest for each. However, a certain degree of order requires the consent of other nations to participation in the system according to its rules. The incentive is small to go along with a coalition if a country is a relatively weak or economically small member. The leader, or leaders, of a coalition must sometimes reward smaller members to keep them within the group, and to keep them from deviating from the rules in order to seize momentary opportunities. There is a price for leadership; and leadership is beneficial to the leader if he is prepared to pay the price. If there is no leader, and no agreed rules, there can be no stability in relations. This in turn will mean frequent bumping of one by another, frequent disruption of local political balances by decisions taken elsewhere.

Looked at in this broad perspective, the United States concern for the principles of international conduct is a correct concern. The pragmatic answers of the Community relating to actual trade or payments effects miss the entire issue.

With enlargement, the Community and its affiliated bloc countries will cover over half of world trade. It may or may not share American concerns, or agree with American objectives. Its own interests are nonetheless at stake. Thus, my conclusion is that there are some points of common interest, whatever the conflicts, and that the two powers should recognize this. They will collide unless they manage their mutual relations better.

The practical management of these mutual relations will in practice determine the nature of the international system within which other countries operate. The two powers can nudge each other along constructively, to the benefit of all other countries; or they can proceed in neo-mercantilistic directions with the certain effect of damaging each other, and disrupting the system as a whole.

It is not clear that the management of their relations with each other, and with the rest of the world, can wait another few years, while Europe consolidates itself internally.

This paper in a sense is an old debate revisited. It agrees with the doubts of some earlier analysts that a natural conclusion to the Atlantic relationship is burden-sharing and common objectives. It tries to define the problems which have arisen between the United States and Europe in terms of their general economic and political effects, with special attention to the international principles involved. In the end, it concludes that there is a common interest in working within sensible, mutually agreed constraints. These constraints will in practice provide the operational principles for most other countries, unless there is to be chaos, with consequent economic and political cost to all nations.

The separation of economic and political questions in the Community allows it to operate without taking into account these broader considerations. When the outsider complains to a member state, he is referred to the Commission—for it is said to be a commercial policy question. When he complains to the Commission he is told this complaint is a matter of political policy, determined by the member states. Neither accepts, nor recognizes responsibility, and neither is susceptible to concentrated pressure from the outside. The normal checks and balances, of rewards and penalties, does not apply to the Community process of decision-making.

One solution is to put somebody in charge of everything, politically speaking. That is not in the cards for a while. The other solution is for individual Europeans, and for other countries, to force the Community into an international framework of rules and procedures which effectively limits the present freedom to act aimlessly.

The same types of alternatives, the same questions of how to manage the relationship, apply in the security field as well. In fact, the economic, political, and security relationships are inseparable. In the final analysis, it is a question of conflict management, of avoiding political collisions. The need for explicit understandings on rules and procedures in the economic area is greater, however. Tacit under-standings in the military context are backed by commitments and the visible deployment of forces. Tacit understandings in economic affairs are backed only by good sense. Threats of economic war do not so readily touch the sensibilities of individuals as wars of devastation.

That is where the Community, the United States, and the rest of the world economy have a common interest—in the preservation and use of agreed rules, institutions, and procedures on a global basis, or short of that, on as wide a basis as possible.

NOTES

1. Stanley Hoffman, *Gulliver's Troubles, or the Setting of American Foreign Policy* (New York: McGraw-Hill, 1968), especially Chapter 12.

2. "The European Community's System of Generalized Tariff Preferences," unpublished paper, 1971.

3. Stanley Hoffman, *op. cit.*; Henry Kissinger, *The Troubled Partnership* (New York: Council on Foreign Relations, 1965).

4. An excellent, somewhat different analysis of this possible outcome is Theodore Geiger's "A World of Trading Blocs?," *Looking Ahead*, National Planning Association, Vol. 19, No. 2 (April, 1971).

8

ADVANCED TECHNOLOGIES
AND THE EVOLUTION OF EUROPE
IN THE 1970's:
LESSONS FROM THE COLLAPSE
OF ROLLS ROYCE

Christopher Wright

ADVANCED TECHNOLOGIES AS AN INTEGRATING FORCE

The interplay of advanced technological opportunities, political interests, and economic constraints more often reveals their seeming opposition to each other than their inherit complementarity. A new technology is often seen as a future determinant compelling responses by political institutions and economic systems rather than as a possible basis for new options. Whether or not we know it in advance, some of these options will benefit society while others will not. Political decisions and the institutional infrastructures that support them are more often than not seen as impediments standing in the way of a rationalized economy and optimal use of advanced technologies, rather than as focal points for making hard decisions when no simple solutions are available. As such they may be in need of modification, if not a steady evolution. The scale and scope of their responsibilities and response to situations requiring policy decisions may be inadequate, but in one form or another, political forums are essential if societies are to take advantage of technological capabilities and opportunities beyond those that are accommodated through crude trail and error processes and the "hidden hand" influences of the economic market place.

So, too, the ultimate tests of economic viability through the balancing of measurable costs and benefits of particular production and trade patterns tends to obscure the fact that the form of these accounting measures may well change as more advanced technologies are adapted by a society. There is relatively little difficulty understanding and measuring the effects of incremental changes in the prices of well-established commodities and services. There are not as yet equally good measures for the characteristics of economic activities which may be most affected by the use of advanced technologies to meet human needs and aspirations. At the very least, efforts in Europe to exploit advanced technologies tend to dramatize the essential interdependence of political, economic, and technological considerations and point to opportunities for effectively differentiating and integrating its institutions so as to achieve a more highly evolved Europe.

In the quarter century since World War II, there have been many efforts to use advanced technologies in order to strengthen the sense of common purpose among Europeans and reduce the risks of destructive divisiveness. Advanced military technologies were used to provide a sense of security against external threats. Such technologies also provided an effective means by which one nation might advance its particular view of the form which European collaboration might take. Although not geographically a European state, the United States clearly had such effects through its defense policies and its position on collaboration has been variously amplified and attenuated by the advance defense systems and strategies developed by the various European nations.

Starting in the 1950's, there were a number of conscious efforts to view advanced technology as a source of opportunities by which to demonstrate the political will to cooperate and the advantages of doing so, assuming the particular project was justifiable in the first place. Many collaborative programs for military weapons development, the European Center for Nuclear Research (CERN), an organization to develop satellite launching rockets (ELDO), and ultimately, the treaty between Great Britain and France to share equally in the development of the Concorde supersonic aircraft led to closer cooperation in areas where the differential national, political, and economic considerations were carefully balanced or neutralized. But such politically motiviated technological initiatives have inherent limitations. They are less viable in areas of advanced technology, such as nuclear power, where the programs are likely to have continuing if not differential economic implications for cooperating nations.

In recent years, programs to exploit advanced technologies primarily for international or transnational political purposes have been subject to increasing scrutiny and occasional abandonment based on their lack of relevance to viable economic enterprises. Programs related to outer space and to pure science of even the military defense systems have come under such scrutiny. An increasingly selective approach to advanced technologies is reflected in decisions of the British government to encourage some industrial technological initiatives, such as the Rolls Royce bid to provide engines of advanced design for the Lockheed airbus (L-1011 Tristar) in 1966 and to discourage others, such as the later British Aircraft Corporation proposal to build a somewhat comparable airbus (BAC 3-11) and requests to participate in the European airbus scheme, which France and Germany continue to advance following earlier British withdrawal on economic grounds.

While advanced technology has moved from the center stage it occupied in the 1950's and 1960's as a specific vehicle for international influence or collaborative endeavor, selected technologies may now come into their own as critical testing areas for the capacity of European nations and industrial organizations to create and participate in more highly evolved systems of organized activity.

In this respect commercial aviation provides an extraordinary arena in which to view the interplay of technological, political, and economic forces. The collapse of Rolls Royce as a private company exposes to plain view the limitations of systems of air transport. It serves to identify issues and objectives that will influence the evolution of Europe in the next decade and the overall capacity of European organizations, public and private, to exercise enlightened social control of technology.

Commercial aviation can be viewed as a set of competing or complementary systems each involving two major elements: airlines endeavoring to meet the needs of and expand a consumer market; jet engine manufacturers ever interested in possibilities for developing new engines that, when attached to suitable airframes, will better meet the needs of the airlines. So long as there is competition among airlines and the suppliers of aircraft, the viability of a particular air transport service will depend on customer preferences. They will ordinarily patronize the service which offers them the fastest travel at the least cost. The generally recognized trend in commercial aviation has been to reduce travel costs between major population centers by increasing the carrying capacity of planes, hopefully also increasing speed and reducing noise levels and other environmental disturbances so as to minimize strains on terminal facilities or disruption of normal activities. Presumably this trend will continue.

Just what a particular air service can provide at some future date depends on decisions made many years in advance. Those made in the early design stages are highly dependent upon estimates of future markets, and hence the ideal size, range, speed, cost, and other specifications of the aircraft. The design problem of matching various specifications and technical opportunities so as to produce the right plane for the right market at the right time is further complicated by the different lead times required for designing and developing the various component parts and arranging appropriate funding. In this process the engine to be used becomes the most critical, expensive, and least assured component since it requires the earliest specification and detailed design and the largest investment in research and development. Indeed, the real possibility of a major breakthrough in engine power, efficiency, weight, and quietness sets the stage for each new generation of aircraft and reduction in air travel costs. As aviation systems become more advanced, increased elapsed time from original design to final production and deployment also increases the unreliability of estimates of total travel demand for that time in the future. Moreover, demand for particular aircraft is, of course, the most uncertain element to predict since it must take into account competition among aircraft manufacturers and ultimately the attraction of passengers by the airlines. The distribution of these risks through securing advance orders from airlines is now an essential feature of aviation systems.

This essential coupling of advanced technology in engine and airframe design with the civilian economy puts commercial aviation in a special position among those areas of advanced technology in Europe that have been looked to as the means of advancing European integration. The advanced planning and political decisions regarding policy that are so essential in these areas indicate and to some extent help to determine the characteristic evolution of Europe.

In Europe, and especially in the United States, a great deal of advanced technology, including aircraft developments, has been closely tied to military requirements. Many expenditures, especially for research and development, have not been subject to the usual economic constraints of the civilian market or the test of specific utility. While advanced weapon systems are increasingly being compared with each other on the basis of cost-effectiveness and cost-benefit, few if any are ever tested in terms of actual performance and usefulness in the war conditions for which they are intended. In this sense many advanced technological systems are replaced by still more advanced systems without really ever being used. While the design and development of these systems, as well as of such specialized systems as high energy accelerators for physics experiments, are sufficiently complex and expensive to invite collaboration among European nations and institutions, the collaboration required for such limited purposes is not clearly extendable to the kind of continuing interaction and interdependence required by a viable commercial aviation industry.

A closer analogy is to be found in nuclear power and in the computer industry, where hardware, software, and the markets for both must be orchestrated in a viable manner. The distinction between those advanced technologies which can become an integral part of a civilian economy and those which cannot, is increasingly important as the interest in using any available science and technology to further European integration gives way to an economic realism based on consumer willingness to pay.[1] The lessons to be learned from analysis of commercial aviation in the light of the Rolls Royce experience is thus of increasing significance in the Europe of the 1970's.

While the need for an economically viable base remains essential in commercial aviation, governmental involvement also increases. The increased cost of research and development for new transport systems places governments in multiple and sometimes conflicting roles, as interests in technological or economic development and in regulation or political control interact. Governments are called upon to underwrite the huge investments in the development of critical elements such as jet engines. Through the many nationally owned—but often quite independently managed national airlines—governments are also concerned with the acquisition of the best equipment to serve the needs of a particular market. And as the political entity identified with a particular nation, a government must take into account certain more or less overt "buy national" preferences in its decisions to promote or discourage a particular technological development or certain equipment for operational purposes. Thus, the extent to which a national government can acknowledge situations where the enlightened self-interest of the nation goes contrary to the promotion of home-made products is a question which comes clearly to the fore in any analysis of commercial aviation as an indicator of the prospective evolution of European institutions.

THE ROLLS ROYCE COMPANY: A CASE STUDY

Early in 1971, the Rolls Royce company was forced to declare its bankruptcy.[2] It no longer had or could acquire the resources necessary to continue development and delivery of the RB 211 advanced design jet engine to the Lockheed Corporation. It appears to have been obligated to do so at a fixed price and on a set schedule tied to penalty clauses. In the end it was clear that the cost of production would exceed the sale price, thus eliminating the basis for further borrowing of funds or for replenishing expended capital.

The immediate cause of the Rolls Royce collapse was the unexpectedly large development costs and the refusal of the British government to continue underwriting them as it has done for its share of the Concorde's development. Part of this expense was due to the failure of a promising new technology employing carbon fibers (Hyfil) for certain fan blades in the engine. It has also been suggested that management and bookkeeping practices contributed to the final outcome and that the original Rolls Royce bid was precariously low. In any case, there seems to be general agreement that even with the disappointment over Hyfil, in terms of power, efficiency, relative quiet, and simplicity of design, the RB 211 engine constitutes a major advance in jet engine design. As one of the three major jet engine manufacturers, along with General Electric and Pratt and Whitney in the United States, the engineering skill of Rolls Royce was unsurpassed. The roots of the failure are thus to be found in the broader management and policy decisions guiding the company and the British government and in how these in turn are influenced by changes in the character of commercial aviation.

The absolute cost of developing a jet engine such as the RB 211 is on the order of ten times what it costs to develop first and second generations of jet engines. This escalation seems characteristic of advanced technologies, although there is no theoretical basis for it. In any event, it leads to demands for public financing to supplement or replace private funding. It also changes the relationship between development and total production costs. As the engines increase in power and fewer units are sold for any one market, there are compelling reasons to increase the demand and reduce competition. In the extreme, as with the first Western supersonic aircraft, it appears that there will be only one design and that will have been produced by governments with relatively few assurances that there will be customers for it. If the underwriting arrangements for the Concorde program and for the RB 211 had been reversed, the former would have been terminated long ago and Rolls Royce would not have gone bankrupt. Thus, while the fate of a particular contract may be determined by cost overruns, failure to meet delivery dates, and bankruptcy, if one looks at the complete system of commercially viable air transport it can be assumed that all necessary development costs for a superior engine can and must be absorbed by the system.

In the absence of more fundamental evidence, it is unreasonable to assume that commercial aviation in Europe or worldwide would be better off without Rolls Royce as a supplier of advanced jet engines or that the company's disappearance from the field is necessary to the operation of a free economy.

The circumstances and decisions leading to the collapse do not adequately reflect such a judgment. Moreover, there is not now a reasonable mechanism for long-range planning and allocation of required resources for commercial aviation in the European context. The 1965 Report by Lord Plowden's committee on the aircraft industry urged such planning in European terms.[3] While decisions of the British government affecting aviation may well take some account of this general need and there exists a European Civil Aviation Conference in which the United Kingdom participates, there has as yet been little evidence of concerted effort to develop an authoritative overview on an multinational or transnational basis. Issues are faced on a piecemeal and ad hoc basis. It is still left to independent observers to consider critical questions having to do with the viability and goals of the overall system.[4]

The contractual arrangement between Rolls Royce and Lockheed must be understood in the context of the system of manufacture and uses centering on the L-1011 Tristar and of the proposed systems most competitive with it. Integral to Lockheed's use of Rolls Royce engines in the Tristar was the offsetting arrangement for British interests to purchase a substantial number of completed aircraft, thus completing a funding cycle within this particular system of commercial aviation. The significance of such financial arrangements is that they are relatively immune to extraneous influences related to international balance of payment problems. It is noteworthy that following the nationalization of Rolls Royce and new negotations between Lockheed and the British government, it appears that neither Lockheed Corporation nor the United States Congress, when it eventually agreed to underwrite further loans to Lockheed for the Tristar, gave as much consideration to the substitution of American-made jet engines as one might otherwise have expected and General Electric certainly desired. To do so would, presumably, have not only delayed production but reduced the order for the Tristar below the level that would justify any production.

While the integral funding of development, manufacture, and airline purchases of aircraft is becoming one of the clearest forms of integration across national boundaries, it by no means ensures the inherent viability of an operating air transport system Assuming general agreement on the usefulness of an aircraft meeting certain general design specifications, the number of orders for any particular craft depends upon alternative competing sources of supply. In this instance, six different aircraft had been designed, at one time or another, by at least four combinations of interests. The all-American entry and the first to be delivered to airlines was the Douglas DC-10 utilizing a General Electric engine. Two all-British entries, the British

Aircraft Corporation's BAC 2-11 and later the BAC 3-11 utilizing a version of the Rolls Royce RB 211 engine, were turned down for support by the British government despite the wishes of British European Airways. The decision against the BAC 3-11 came in late 1969 along with the government's second refusal to help underwrite an official contribution to the European airbus (A300B), which had started as a joint British, French, and German venture and still involves substantial British industrial participation. This dual decision reflected an informed judgment that British industry should concentrate more on aircraft engines than on the manufacture of airframes. It also signaled a determination that the European airbus was not likely to be a commercial success and the the L-1011 was an acceptable alternative to the BAC 3-11 for use by British European Airways.

Whether the French-German airbus utilizing a General Electric engine will in fact be successful, is still not clear. What is clear, is that fundamental new problems are created when national prestige considerations become subordinate, and logic dictates a reduction in the total number of different aircraft to be produced and a reconciliation of the various industrial, commercial, and financial interests in a viable total system. In this context, advanced technology is not so much an independent interest as it is a source of innovative pressure which must be taken into account by these primary interests. The demise of Rolls Royce as a private manufacturing entity with the independence to advance major new engine designs on its own initiative is especially interesting for these reasons. Its engineering capabilities and high standards of performance were unsurpassed. Moreover, as the leading jet engine manufacturer in a region where air transport is increasing rapidly, it is important to understand why these advantages did not save the Rolls Royce company but may still call for its distinctive involvement in a more integrated European aviation system. Whether or not such a system develops depends in part on specific interest in it, a parallel rationalization of air transport with other forms of transport (especially with the increased development of STOL and VTOL aircraft) and the extent to which the industrial engineering resources represented by Rolls Royce among other organizations are redirected.

Looked at in terms of strategies for a private company, this case suggests that Rolls Royce, having striven to maintain its lead in jet engine design by entering the American market and also maintaining its position in Europe, succeeded in losing both markets. By this view it was certainly a mistake to bid so hard for American business and to enter into a contract which appears not to have provided for important contingencies. The mistake of gambling so heavily on a technological breakthrough with Hyfil was compounded by later engineering design and development efforts, just as the original financial arrangements may have led to questionable accounting practices. Such isolated judgments about one company are, however, inadequate. They presume the company can and should operate as an autonomous business entity, with only the most formal and precise interactions with other parts of a larger system.

The decisions of the British government first to allow the collapse of Rolls Royce and then to negotiate a new contract between the nationalized Rolls Royce Ltd. (1971) and Lockheed can also be viewed as serving further notice that British industries, no matter how highly qualified and prestigious, must not be complacent and expect development air production subsidies, unless these can be rationalized within a broader system. In these terms the decision can also be seen as one taking advantage of a "once in a life-time" opportunity to escape some of the penalties of an unfortunate contract and to pave the way for new kinds of collaboration between a much less awesome private company and potential partners in Europe.

Interpretations of the immediate causes and rationale for the events affecting Rolls Royce thus must be viewed in the larger context of an unending need to sort out from among competitive human activities those which would seem to be most valuable in the larger European context.

The decisions which entered into the promotion and demotion of four rather competitive short and medium range airbus systems must be considered in terms of each other and in terms of related programmatic and nationalistic considerations. The British government's disinterest in the schemes involving BAC 3-11 and the French-German A300B was not only related to interest in the L-1011 but also to having extensive prior commitments to collaborate with France on the Concorde. The U.S. government's interests in saving Lockheed Corporation may have been for reasons that have little to do with salvaging the Tristar program and Rolls Royce participation in it and yet the latter fact is likely to have a very important affect upon the future of European commercial aviation.

Underlying these considerations in the area of commercial aviation there are fundamental ones which have as yet received even less careful analysis. Some of these have to do with the viability of any particular high technology company and the dominant perception of its proper business and goals. In defense of the risks taken by Rolls Royce to enter the American market, the chairman of the company has pointed out that while real risks were involved, the company could not survive otherwise.[5] When does "buy national" cease to become important and on what basis is it to be replaced by such propositions as "buy

European" or "buy American"?[6] Others have to do with a national government's perception of its national interests when traditional favoritism to domestic enterprises may run counter to the rationalization of commercial aviation in the context of Europe and the North Atlantic.

For analytical purposes at least, it is useful to recognize that the industrial engineering and financial resources of Europe, the demand for air travel, and the demographic and geographic characteristics of Europe can be viewed by attentive observers independently of the particular organizational arrangements into particular centers of private or public planning and decision-making. And since intra-European air travel is coupled with transatlantic air travel the whole of North American and Western Europe can and should also be recognized as elements of a commercial aviation system potentially rationalized on a still broader scale. The net effect of particular private and public plans and decisions and the perceptions underlying them is to superimpose a set of human constructs on situations which have some of their own imperatives. It is becoming increasingly evident that these superimpositions can be very fragile indeed. And yet, there is as yet no orderly way to affect the evolution of these forms or even to study the possibilities of doing so in a fully effective manner.

It is clear that the directors of Rolls Royce perceived the company as being in the business of manufacturing jet engines and that therefore they had no choice but to continue in this business and at all cost to attempt to penetrate the American market for engines. While it seemed inconceivable to the management that it should abandon this commitment to jet engines, with the benefit of hindsight and an excess of gloom, an editorial in *Nature* following the collapse stated: "It would have been much better for everyone, Lockheed included, if Rolls Royce had swallowed its pride and put its technical prowess into typewriters or sewing machines."[7]

Governments have just as much difficulty recasting their perceptions of what is possible alone or by specific agreement. One has only to remember the cancellation of the American Skybolt air to ground missile which Britain had so counted up to realize that the history of military defense systems in Britain and elsewhere clearly illustrates the prevalence of excess complacency. In the 1970's the consequences of such complacency may well be more serious in such areas as commercial aviation than in defense systems. Problems of modern defense and weapons systems can be so overwhelming as to leave a nation virtually helpless against many forms of attack. In such circumstances a symbolic defense or retaliatory capability may be little more than an expensive luxury. In commercial arenas, however, there are many more options for the reallocation of industrial engineering talents and for the maintenance or even growth of technical capabilities in a viable context, provided adaptations are not inhibited by preconceptions. The loss of autonomy in commercial aviation need not result in an absolute loss of resources or of profits from their optimum use within a larger framework. And yet, it is not clear just how appropriate redeployments of resources are to be identified and brought about. A degree of common understanding, argument, and coordination is required which cannot be achieved by one company, industry, ministry, or national government alone. Nor do equitable and mutually satisfactory allocations of human or natural resources necessarily assure viable exploitation of technological opportunities or even that the scope of the challenge has been properly identified. Perhaps in terms of commercial aviation the North Atlantic community must be seen as a single integrated entity, in which case the tendency of some European industrial firms to look to the United States for partners and protection against European competitors is understandable. But in the absence of contrary proof, there is every reason to believe, that Europe has the resources to meet its own future air transport requirements and to play its proportionate role in overseas transport. It does become a challenge to the political and economic units in Europe to fulfill this promise and to take full account of important new features of advanced technology.

Perhaps a more questionable premise for the 1970's is the feasibility of considering a European air transport industry apart from the broader context of all forms of European transport. With the resurrection of Rolls Royce there is discussion of its design for a new generation of quiet but powerful engines appropriate for short takeoff planes and intended for transport to more central urban locations.[8]

NEED FOR NEW PERSPECTIVES

The Rolls Royce case makes it clear that the most salient new features from the point of view of institutional development in Europe include a trend away from the independent management of separate components in favor of better orchestrated systems of air transport hardware and services. Moreover, these systems are not just subject to continual incremental technological improvements. Provided all innovative initiatives are not eliminated by reduced hardware competition, one must expect further major "quantum jumps" that may well assume their own imperatives and come about all too frequently for the equanimity of the human institutions involved. Every jump has its institutional as well as financial costs. In social evolution as in biological evolution there may be no place for the unsuccessful challenger for leadership in any particular area. The question is whether the forum for such challenges is unalterably determined or whether a potential challenger, in this case Rolls Royce, can redirect its talents and resources in order to avoid lethal competition except where this is absolutely necessary.

The unquestioned advantages of significant competition in human enterprises need not determine the arenas in which it takes place. The dramatic collapse of Rolls Royce suggests that advanced technological opportunities tend to alter both the geographical scope of competition and the goals of particular industries related to commercial aviation. If nations can no longer compete with each other in the production and operation of commercial aircraft, the competing units will tend to be composed of systems identified either with Europe or the United States or else with various combinations of organizations drawn from the North Atlantic community as a whole.

If the various organizational units can no longer each pursue its exclusive mission—be it full utilization of its capabilities for innovative design in one area for engine or airframe production or for expanded air transport services—then some overriding guidelines, if not actual vertical integration of managements, is clearly essential. It is still much less clear how authoritative guidelines can be developed that will encourage voluntary conformity by public and private organizations on the basis of enlightened self-interest.

While national political interests and responsibilities may well provide an essential motivating force for activities within the nation-state there is no doubt that they also provide one of the principal impediments to the kinds of adaptation evidently required in such areas as commercial aviation. In the events surrounding the various aspirations of the Rolls Royce Company it is clear that British fear of dependence on European manufacturers for part of an air system and French doubts about the rationale for seeming to aid Britain and a company as dominant in its field as Rolls Royce contributed to an atmosphere unconducive to the full utilization of European industrial engineering capabilities or satisfaction of air transport needs with European aircraft of advanced design.

The existence of European national airlines also reflects a certain built-in bias, but they also provide a means for maintaining an equitable distribution of profits from air transport services of roughly equal importance to Europeans without regard to nationality. Moreover, the discipline imposed by competition for passengers has led to considerable objectivity on the part of these airlines when it comes to the definition of their equipment requirements and the sources from which to acquire them.

The airlines accept, and the aircraft manufacturers welcome, the proposition that it is in everyone's best interest to move commercial air transport in the direction of cheaper mass transit. The technological opportunity to build larger shorthaul airbuses has created an irresistable opportunity to move more people at less cost with fewer flights, thus putting relatively less strain on terminal, traffic, and maintenance facilities. Major assessment of these guidelines and their implications has hardly begun.

The collapse of Rolls Royce and subsequent nationalization of its jet engine facilities clearly indicates that future accommodations to these technological and European imperatives is not likely to involve large private companies. Opportunities for independent initiatives and contractual arrangements made with the blessing and financial underwriting of national governments are now more limited. At the same time there are likely to be fewer ad hoc agreements among governments to advance specific technological programs and to contract with various industries to do the work. This is the pattern followed by the British and French governments for the development of Concorde. In terms of funding and management it has proved to be as unsatisfactory as did the private agreement between Lockheed and Rolls Royce. Neither arrangement provides sufficient opportunities for continuing analysis and responsive control and decision-making, given the unpreditables encountered in the realization of advanced techno-human systems. The inadequacy of these two types of arrangements highlights the need for vertically integrated policy planning and management. Whether or not national governments or private enterprise share in the financial and managerial aspects of such multinational corporate entities is of less importance than the existence of new independent centers of initiative with rather broad mandates.

The nationalization of Rolls Royce does not in itself foreclose future multinational technological cooperation on either an ad hoc or more permanently integrated basis. But the collapse of the Rolls Royce initiative signals the end of an era in which the benefit of the doubt is given to a new technological venture that has at least a minimum justification in economic or prestige terms. If the 1970's are not likely to provide opportunities for direct political initiatives leading to new levels of political unity in Europe, neither are they likely to be a time when advanced technologies will serve either as the catalyst or the symbol under which such political initiatives take place indirectly.

Because the new realism with respect to advanced technologies emphasizes control and use in terms of inherently viable opportunities, these may in fact lead to increased and more assured political awareness of common European interests. Viable technological enterprises may in fact tend to transcend narrowly perceived national interests. Thus, while it is no longer meaningful to create an M.I.T. of Europe, as was suggested in the early 1960's, in order to accelerate integrative activity, the time may be at hand when exactly such developments will arise out of a new sense of genuine need, regardless or even in spite of parochial national concerns.

The assessment of advanced technologies in terms of civilian economics may well blunt the impetus for technologically related changes once provided by new weapons technologies or the "big science" enterprises of the science community interested in nuclear physics, space exploration, oceanography, or molecular biology, for instance. But whereas those technologies closely related to national security or prestige interests tend rather to be used to extend national influence and those related to science at least serve to extend the political influence of the science community, the corollary of such developments is an insistence on incorporating a measure of national parity in any cooperative venture. This leads to redundance in the development of special competences, as in the case of the Concorde program, and to a disregard to the inherent advantages to be acquired by a well-understood and properly orchestrated integration of significantly different engineering, productive, and financial capabilities.

It must be recognized that the very attractiveness of such integration from a technological and economic point of view tends to make it unattractive from a political point of view, for it appears to foreclose opportunities for choice. Quite apart from political considerations of vested interests and their protection, the political arena can only work effectively where there are real choices available to be made through legitimate political decision-making processes.

In fact, advanced technologies closely coupled with ongoing human enterprises, such as commercial aviation, do provide many opportunities for major policy choices and development. The disruption if not loss of technological resources occasioned by the bankruptcy of Rolls Royce need not constrict opportunities for choice. It serves rather as further clear evidence of the need in aviation and no doubt elsewhere, to advance the art and science of overall policy planning, if not implementation on a transcendent scale. The interests of particular organizations, whole industries, and nations in response to major advances in technology and the new opportunities inherent in them must be placed in new perspectives.

While the mechanisms for such study appear to be at hand, it is not clear that any ideal model must be followed. One model may be the "impact statements" now being produced in the United States in order to provide advanced assessments of the environmental impact of certain proposed projects. The particular bearing of advanced technologies on the evaluation of Europe in the 1970's may well depend primarily on the degree to which open, informed, and timely assessment of technology-related programs is encouraged. Program assessment of this kind can now be seen to be a missing but essential component of any advanced technology related to ongoing human activities.

NOTES

1. For a comprehensive discussion of both forms of technology which does not, however, emphasize this distinction, see Christopher Layton, *European Advanced Technology: A Programme for Integration*, Political and Economic Planning (London: George Allen & Unwin Ltd., 1969).

2. For a general historical account see Robert Gray, *Rolls Royce on the Rocks: The Story of Rolls Royce* (London: Panther Books, 1971).

3. Report of the Committee on Inquiry into the Aircraft Industry (appointed by the Ministry of Aviation under Lord Plowden, 1964-65) Cmnd. 2853 (Her Majesty's Stationery Office, 1965).

4. Editorials and signed articles in *Nature* and in *The New Scientist* provide running commentary on various advanced technologies and their implications for Europe. For example: The Rt. Hon. Anthony Wedgewood Benn "Science, Europe, and a New World," *New Scientist and Science Journal* (February 18, 1971), p. 348 and "European Technology in Disarray," editorial, *Nature*, Vol. 230 (March 26, 1971), p. 198.

5. Gray, *op. cit.,* p. 82.

6. See for example Layton, (*op. cit.* p. 262) for a brief in favor of "buy European."

7. "Not Delivering the Goods," editorial, *Nature*, Vol. 229 (February 12, 1971), p. 441.

8. James Hay Stevens "Rolls Royce Design for Quieter Airlines," *New Scientist and Science Journal* (August 12, 1971), p. 376.

FOREIGN RELATIONS BETWEEN THE UNITED STATES AND A UNITING EUROPE: RIVALRY OR COOPERATION

9

EUROPE AND AMERICA
IN A
PENTAGONAL WORLD

Andrew J. Pierre

The title does not refer to Melvin Laird and his entourage. It refers to the new shape of world politics in the 1970's. We have now entered a transitional period in which five power centers—China and Japan, in addition to Western Europe, America and the Soviet Union—will be the principal actors on the stage of international politics. Japan's emergence to its new postwar status is the result of its gradual though impressive evolution in the 1970's to the rank of the third most powerful economic country in the world. Although Japan's strength today is primarily measurable in economic terms, history teaches us that such strength is sooner or later translated into political and military power. For the People's Republic of China the process of emergence has been quite different: the end of the cultural revolution has stimulated a new desire to enter the world of multilateral diplomacy. This has fortunately occurred at a moment when the Western states, and in particular the United States, have finally decided to deal with this nation of over 800 million people on the basis of reality, rather than of ideology or legalisms.

A five-sided table will make for a complex, messy, subtle, and sometimes inscrutable game. Each power center will react to the other and billiard-ball like clashes and causations may not become uncommon. Unlike a billiard game, however, the balls will not be of equal weight. The tendency will thus be for the growth of a complicated global balance of power, with fluctuations or shifts of differing relevance and import from time to time.

Such a world will have a marked impact on relations between Western Europe and the United States. The trans-Atlantic relationship of the past quarter century has been built upon the construct of a bipolar world. A perceived danger from the East led to the creation of NATO and underpinned much of the benign rationale for American assistance to the economic recovery of Europe. The Cold War in Europe in its harsh phase lasted into the 1960's and remnants of it exist to this day. Although an intentional and massive Soviet incursion into Western Europe is now considered almost totally implausible, the West European sense of security is still subject to real erosion. Western Europe will therefore remain dependent for its sense of security upon the United States until either Moscow's aims are perceived to have undergone a fundamental revision, or until an independent and adequate European defense capability comes into existence. Neither of those two contingencies are as yet within sight.

A qualitative change is nevertheless occuring in East-West relations in Europe. The sense of danger which spurred the Atlantic institutions in the past has now receded. A process of détente—a limited détente to be sure—has set in and continues despite Soviet intentions as revealed in the Czechoslovakia incident of 1968. The signs of détente are everywhere in the air: the Berlin Agreement, the Bonn-Moscow and Bonn-Warsaw Treaties, SALT, discussions about negotiations on mutual and balanced force reductions, and an eventual European security conference. This détente has already and will continue to have a transforming effect upon the European-American relationship. Together with important changes which are occurring or will occur in the domestic societies and foreign relations of the other power constellations, détente in Europe will result in a modification of responsibility and roles in the Atlantic security community.

In order to discuss the substance of this modification we must begin by briefly examining the probable evolution of the five centers of power. Such important factors as changes in the American military role in the Pacific, Sino-Soviet relations, the growth of Japan's defense capabilities, the political spillover of Britain's entrance into the European Economic Community, and the changing domestic consensus on American foreign policy will all have a significant impact upon the European-American relationship of the future.

THE FIVE CENTERS OF POWER

In the new era of international politics the <u>United States</u> will, at least initially, be preoccupied with healing its Vietnam wounds. During this recuperation period the attention of the nation will be turned to its own body politic. Problems concerning the cities, poverty, the pollution of the environment, race relations, crime, drugs, and so on through this dreary list, will receive priority. In foreign affairs the priority will be placed upon relations with the Soviet Union and probably China, for it is there that the principal threats to peace are likely to originate or receive decisive support. The limitation of strategic armaments and the avoidance of war in the Middle East will be aims of active diplomacy. But in other areas of foreign policy Washington will seek to maintain a low profile. Military intervention in disputes in the Third World will be avoided like the plague and will only be easily justified when, for example, there exists an immediate threat involving an unambiguous treaty commitment. Such standards of selectivity and reserve would probably rule out armed interventions similar to those of the United States in the Dominican Republic in 1965, Lebanon in 1958, or even Vietnam in 1965.

The broad domestic consensus which supported American foreign policy from Pearl Harbor until the 1960's has now virtually collapsed. Until a new consensus emerges, or coalesces, an American President is not likely to embark upon a large size armed intervention (save in the direct defense of the Northern Hemisphere and Western Europe) without the support, perhaps an overwhelming one would be needed, of the American people. At the same time public support for the defense budget has notably decreased. The Nixon Doctrine is a response to this changed American mood and can be seen as part of a fundamental reevaluation of the American role in the world. Despite all its ambiguities and uncertainties the doctrine does assume disengagement and a reduced American presence abroad. Thus far the line has successfully been held by the Nixon Administration on the issue of the level of U.S. troops in Europe. It is not difficult to envisage circumstances, however, under which support for Senator Mansfield's call for a 50 percent reduction of these troops would hold the majority in both houses of Congress. This could well come about, for example, should there be a further deterioration of trade and monetary relations between Europe and America.

In the Soviet Union the composite of foreign policy is likely to be more complex. The nature and direction of policy toward Europe may be of a different order than in the extra-European world. In the latter Moscow has embarked upon an imperialistic trust seeking now to establish itself and be recognized as a global Superpower in addition to its status of a nuclear Superpower. This is the explanation for the development of a worldwide reach with new conventional air and sea capabilities. The expansion of the Soviet navy in the Mediterranean and into the Indian Ocean is designed to underpin foreign policy through military power utilized for political purposes. A danger will arise that the outward momentum of Soviet political-military power, when in contrast with the inward retraction of American power, will create instabilities, or opportunities for dangerous miscalculations of each other's aims, intention and resolve.[1]

In Europe, on the other hand, Soviet policy will be essentially defensive. Two preoccupations of the Soviet leadership serve to dampen the past inclination to seek actively political gain in Western Europe. The first is a rising concern regarding China. President Nixon's visit to Peking cannot but rekindle fears of a Sino-American reapproachment to the detriment of Moscow. The Chinese courting of Rumania and Yugoslavia, and the long established ties with Albania, are further signs that the Soviet position of leadership in the Communist world is under increasing challenge and stress. Moreover, those Russian officials responsible for the defense of the homeland are acutely aware of the steady growth of the Chinese nuclear capability and the emphasis being placed upon the development of intermediate range ballistic missiles which would be capable of reaching targets in Central Russia and Asia, though not the United States. It is not for nothing that the Soviets have amassed approximately one million soldiers on their Chinese border.

A second preoccupation arises out of pressing domestic needs. The slow growth of the Soviet economy, hamstrung by a rigidly centralized industrial structure, impedes the production of long-awaited consumer goods for the population. Agricultural productivity has been lagging persistently. More important still is the continuing need for advanced technology, which is to say the importation of Western technology, trade and management methods to revive and stimulate the Soviet economy.

These concerns, among others, have forced an important revision in Soviet goals in Western Europe. The long-term aims may still hold good: the elimination of the United States military presence in Europe and the reduction of American influence so as to place the entire continent under Soviet influence, if not directly as in Eastern Europe then through a gradual process of political accommodation leading to an eventual "Finlandization." But these aims have now, it would appear, been put on the back burner. The European Economic Community is increasingly accepted as a functioning reality. In Central Europe the intention is to stabilize the status quo through a series of negotiations and agreements and perhaps an eventual European Security Conference. The Moscow-Bonn and Warsaw-Bonn Treaties of 1970 are designed to open the door to increased trade and technology in a "controlled" manner, that is, without permitting to pass through the same door the infectious spread of Western liberalism and ideas. The restlessness of the Soviet intelligentsia—the Sakharovs, Amalriks, and Solzhenitsyns—may be a source of concern, but they can only be a minor one because of their limited influence and visibility within the Soviet Union. More worrisome, no doubt, are the continuing signs of instability in Eastern Europe where the Soviet military and political role is threatened by powerful, economic, social, and intellectual forces not susceptible to total control.[2] Nevertheless the primary result of the important Soviet decision to enter into agreements with the West by being responsive to the Brandt Government's *Ostpolitik* and by signing a Four Power agreement on Berlin is to help stabilize East-West relations in Europe and to permit an era of negotiations presumably designed to reduce tensions and the confrontation at the center of the continent. The danger does exist and should be recognized, however, that the Western nations in the spirit of détente let their guard down too much or too suddenly. Such an erosion of the will to defend would only be destabilizing, since it would open new opportunities for Soviet incursions and mischief-making.

Western Europe in the early 1970's is no doubt at the stage where further evolution toward political unity is no longer an unreasonable expectation. After seven years of relative stagnation the passing of De Gaulle and the arrival of Brandt, among other factors, made possible the conditions which are likely to lead to the enlargement and deepening of the Common Market. The Community with its membership expanded to include Britain, Ireland, Denmark, and Norway will have 260 million people and a GNP of $600 billion, making it more populous than either America or the Soviet Union and richer than any country in the world except for the United States. Moreover, the economic power of the Community of Ten will be impressive since it will be the largest trading entity in the world.

For the next several years the European Community is likely to be preoccupied with problems relating to its economic and monetary integration as well as the effects of its expansion. By the mid-1970's, however, a second stage will be reached and it is then that the question of further progress in political consultations and defense will be most acutely posed. The fundamental impetus behind the quest for European integration has never been primarily economic. It has derived from the surprisingly rapid loss of power of the European states in the midtwentieth century and their recognition that only by banding together might they exert real influence in the international political environment of the future. With the United States increasingly turning its activity, if not its attention, to other parts of the globe and to its own domestic problems, and with Soviet-American relations increasingly becoming an essentially bilateral matter as in SALT, the Western European states will have sufficient incentive to deepen political relations and develop common foreign and defense policies.

More will be said about defense later in this chapter. A start on coordinating foreign policy took place following the Hague Summit meeting with the recommendations of the Davignon Report calling for periodic consultations on foreign policy by foreign ministers. The first meetings were held on the problems of a Middle East settlement and the Soviet proposal for a European Security Conference. As might have been expected these meetings led to little more than a restatement of government views which were already clear from their exposition in other forums. Foreign policy is still very much a sovereign matter jealously guarded over by individual national governments, often following differing interests and objectives. The growing interdependence which is evident among the advanced industrial states in matters of economics and technology does not extend as readily to gut political issues. Nevertheless, this modest start is a recognition that there are many interests which bind the West Europeans together and that these will be growing.

It is too early to speak of the exact content of a "European foreign policy" but not too early to visualize with what it will be concerned. Such a policy will be more "regional" than "global," with attention devoted to the European continent and its adjacent areas, as well as to the United States. A coordinated if not common approach to the Soviet Union and Eastern Europe would be likely. This might also be coordinated with the United States, especially on issues involving security and arms control. Similarly a common approach to the underbelly of Europe in the Mediterranean, Middle East, and North Africa could be envisaged. In Asia, Africa south of the Sahara, and Latin America, however, where European political (in contrast to economic) interests have greatly diminished, a common foreign policy is less likely. Past American efforts to achieve NATO-wide accord on policies toward the Third World, in the Congo and Cuba for example, have been singularly unsuccessful. The European states may eventually again play a global role, but this will require a far greater European supranationality than is likely to be achieved within the present institutional framework.

The opening of a totally new chapter in Sino-American relations in 1971 with the invitation extended to President Nixon to visit Peking, preceded by the easing of trade and travel restrictions, signals the intention of Communist China to move onto the world diplomatic stage as one of the leading actors. This was ratified by an early invitation to the People's Republic to occupy the Chinese seat on the Security

Council of the United Nations. The playing by Mainland China of the role in world politics which by most criteria it should have had some time ago will complicate the multipolarity of tomorrow's world.

China appears to be more ready now than in the past to participate in the international community, principally because the internal turmoil and disruption created by the Red Guards and the Cultural Revolution is over with. The aging Chinese leadership, moreover, is anxious to complete the Chinese revolution by receiving the recognition of the outside world before passing on its mantle to a younger and less ideologically inspired generation. But fundamental geopolitical factors are also at play. China appears to be strongly motivated in its still limited "normalization" of relations with the United States by two deep fears. One stems from the growing hostility with the Soviet Union, which now seems fundamentally unreconcilable except under conditions of grave threat to both nations emanating from a single source. Serious Chinese concern about a nuclear war with Russia, as evidenced by the vast nuclear defense tunnels in the major cities, or anxiety about a "surgical strike" against its nuclear facilities should not be underrated. Nor should one underestimate Chinese worries about a Russian launched "preventive" war along the extended border growing out of the frequent clashes there. A second fear arises out of Japanese prosperity and its economic penetration of countries on China's periphery, especially Taiwan and South Korea. With the expansion of Japanese economic influence, it is believed, will grow a renewed militarism. Fear of encirclement by an aggressive Japanese military state and a hostile Russia, with both nations someday possessing nuclear weapons, appears to be of greater concern to Peking than is the United States, which is now in the process of substantially reducing its military bases and forces in Asia.

With Communist China seeking—perhaps accepting is more apt—contact with the United States in order to balance Russia and Japan, we are entering a new phase of multipolarity. Moscow worries about collusion between Washington and Peking against its own interests—while the Chinese equally fear a Soviet-American alliance against them. At the side sits Japan, ready to develop closer ties with Peking but feared by China's leaders—a Japan which remains closely allied to the United States but which some feel will be tempted to strike out on its own. As for the United States, in the coming years it is less likely to focus its policies on the "containment" of China. Such a change of perceptions, involving a downgrading in official Washington of the "Chinese threat," preceded ping-pong diplomacy and the announcement of Nixon's trip. The Nixon Doctrine of disengagement and reduction in America's overseas military role in effect rules out the continued close-in military containment of China with bases and forces on its borders. Entrance by China into the United Nations equally rules out a policy of attempting to keep the People's Republic politically and economically isolated. The new pattern of great power relationships may be more complex and differentiated, but it is possible that in this global system there may also be found additional elements making for international stability.

As for the meaning of this for Western Europe, China's emergence will further divert the attention of the Soviet Union from its Western to its Eastern borders. The Chinese in turn are conscious of the potentials of Europe for their own purposes. The winds emanating from Peking toward Brussels have recently become warmer. The Common Market is now seen as having a double value, initially as a source of trade but perhaps even more important as part of the political mechanism with which Peking hopes to balance the Soviet Union. Creating such a balance has long been the aim of Chinese policy in Albania and the new attention given by Peking to Rumania and Yugoslavia must be seen as an attempt to strengthen further the political mechanism by increasing the strings limiting Soviet freedom of action.

The fifth side of the Pentagonal relationship, Japan, has been and is continuing an economic growth more rapid than any major nation. During the coming decade it could surpass the Soviet Union to become the second strongest economic power in the world. Japan's important economic position is already placing it at the center of international negotiations on trade, aid, and investment. Its technology and economy have become interdependent with those of the other advanced industrial nations, a fact which is symbolized by its membership in OECD. In addition Japan's industry and investment is extending outward to many of her Asian neighbors, which in turn gives her political influence in these countries.

The extent to which this growth in economic power will be matched by growth in military capacity and international political influence is difficult to assess. It is unlikely, however, that there will not be considerable "spill-over" into the military and political fields. Japan's potential military power is very great, indeed, and already estimates of that potential enter the calculations of policy-planners in foreign affairs ministries.

There is little question that Japan could become an operational nuclear power in a short time, perhaps in only twelve to twenty-four months, once such a political decision had been made. Both the existing civil nuclear program and the Japanese missile capability are highly developed. In recent years Japan's "self-defense" military forces have been considerably enlarged and equipped with sophisticated weapons.

The proportion of the GNP spent on defense remains a low 1 percent, but given the present 11 percent annual growth of the GNP even that provides for significant increases in defense capacities. There are, moreover, several reasons why the enlargement of the armed forces can be expected. The partial disengagement of the United States from Asia as it withdraws from Vietnam and in keeping with the Nixon Doctrine could be seen as creating a void; limiting such a vacuum would be all the more desirable because of the increasing Japanese economic stake in the area. The return of China to an active political role in the region, as well as the constant growth of the Chinese nuclear capability could be seen as requiring some redress. Finally, the famous "nuclear allergy" and the public opposition to defense forces appear to be receding with the rise of a more nationalist younger generation less effected by Hiroshima and the experience of World War II.

We can therefore expect that Japan's political and diplomatic stature will increase; it has been lagging behind her economic status but it is likely to catch up. Although the Japanese-American security alliance will continue, the military dependence upon the United States will diminish. This would be in keeping with the rising nationalist aspirations of those who want Japan to take a stance more independent of the United States and more reflective of the political leverage to which she is entitled by her economic power. On the other hand, the end of the Japanese-American security alliance would be unfortunate, if not disasterous, for the stability of Asia. Should the American nuclear umbrella be closed, it is likely that Japan would "go nuclear," a step which might then be followed by India, Australia, and perhaps others.

There are many in Japan who do not want to see the country undertake a greater world political and military role. Some are moved by moral considerations, while others are struck by the advantages of the present situation of economic prosperity without equivalent international responsibilities. It is unlikely, however, that Japan can avoid stepping further out on the diplomatic stage. This may be necessary to protect her economic stakes in Asia and it may be the precondition for the organization of a regional system to assure stability and peace in the Western Pacific area.

The international system of the 1970's (and beyond) will be dominated by five centers of power: United States, Soviet Union, Western Europe, China, and Japan. This is a different system from the one which set the parameters of world politics for the first quarter century following World War II and which provided the base for the construction of the postwar Atlantic institutions. What we are witnessing is the erosion through various stages of the relatively simple bipolar system and its transformation into a pentagonal multipolar system (which still contains some important elements of the old Soviet-American bipolar confrontation). The new system will be more complex and difficult to manage. It will require more subtle and sophisticated diplomacy, reminiscent perhaps of the nineteenth century balance of power.

EUROPEAN-AMERICAN POLITICAL RELATIONS

We must now ask what effect will the emerging Pentagonal system have upon European-American relations? The remainder of the chapter will be devoted to answering this question. We shall concentrate on issues primarily stemming from political power and security, since the important matters of economics are discussed elsewhere in this volume.

American diplomacy will have an increasingly global rather than Atlantic outlook. Attention will be devoted to worldwide accommodation and arms control with the Soviet Union and to developing a relationship with China and Japan that will help assure peace and stability in the Pacific. Within the Atlantic concept, Washington will seek to shift the United States from a position of predominance to equal partner in the sharing of common responsibilities.

This is not to suggest a general withdrawal or a loss of interest in Europe. There can be no such thing. Western Europe will always remain "number one." There is no other part of the globe which can match the historical, cultural, political, economic, and psychological ties with the United States. Two world wars have now been fought by America on the premise that a free Western Europe is essential to our own security and this premise is not likely to be altered. It is well to recall, also, that whatever friction may exist between Europe and America, and whatever be the risks of a trade war and monetary crisis, trade across the Atlantic remains the world's greatest; mutual investments are substantial, especially American investments in Europe; exchange of technology is high, as is the flow of tourism. No other international (and transnational) relationship shares as great a number of mutual interests.

World conditions and the overriding need to maintain peace will nevertheless lead the United States to devote much of its attention to global accommodation with the Soviet Union and regional stability in the Pacific. In addition, coping with and ameliorating the manifold problems of American society will drain energies which in the past, before these domestic needs were understood and recognized, were spent on foreign policy. Moreover, it is now recognized that foreign and domestic policies are constructs of the same body; that an unhealthy society at home does not provide the necessary base for an enlightened external policy. Finally, an additional item on the foreign policy agenda of the future which will consume increasing amounts of attention and resources will be the global problems resulting from science, technology, and the environment. The growing interdependence of states in dealing with these issues, and the pressing need for modified or new international institutions will be another item of priority in American foreign policy.

We can therefore expect, with some confidence, that the United States will press for a substantial devolution of its security responsibilities in Europe in the 1970's. We must then ask: what should be the response of a "united Europe?"

The conclusion I have reached is that Western Europe needs to develop additional or revived institutions if it is to handle successfully the challenges which will be placed before it. Not to develop new or changed institutions would, I believe, lead to a farther erosion of the influence of the West European states in world politics, including influence on the important process of negotiations with the Soviet Union and Eastern Europe on the outstanding issues of European security. It would also create new and more serious difficulties in the trans-Atlantic relationship with the United States.

The challenges facing Europe will be, first, to create a European sense of common identity in matters relating to its own security. This involves cooperative efforts in defense affairs and eventually a certain amount of integration of national military efforts. Beyond this is the more fundamental psychological need to be able to speak with one voice to the United States. Europe needs this in order to retain its confidence and self-respect. The United States desires it because of its need for an *interlocuteur valable*. One could go even farther and suggest that Europe is more likely to keep the United States constructively involved in securing its welfare the more it is able to express its will with one voice to Washington. A quarreling or passive Europe is less likely to engage the attention of Americans. Contrary to the views of some revisionist historians or polemicists of the radical left, the United States does not wish to keep Western Europe weak and divided in order to maintain its hegemonic and entrepeneurial position. Recent and future economic difficulties between Europe and America notwithstanding, the long-term aim of a United Europe which has animated U.S. policy since the close of World War II will remain valid.

A second challenge will be to make further progress toward a European settlement. The present situation of a European continent sharply divided politically, economically, and militarily, with a massive confrontation of armed forces and atomic weapons can be lived with if necessary, but remains a second best alternative. It would be a disappointing way to close the twentieth Century. This was explicitly recognized in the past decade by De Gaulle's vision of "détente, entente, et cooperation" and the *Ostpolitik* of succeeding West German governments; it was implicitly understood through the great public longing for détente. Developments within the Soviet Union may make it possible to undertake a wide range of negotiations aimed to reduce the confrontation, possibly through a series of European security conferences. The task for Western Europe will be to orchestrate its détente policy among its member states and with the United States. The divisive nature within the Western Alliance of separate and uncoordinated roads to Moscow became clear in the 1960's prior to the intervention in Czechoslovakia.

Third, and most uncertain and problematical, will be the need to find a way for Europe to play a role beyond Europe. Europe may sink into the provincialism of a large Switzerland, but such a role would be unworthy of its past heritage and present talents. One should not expect, on the other hand, a "third force" Europe capable of playing an independent Superpower role. This requires far greater political cohesion within Europe than we can presently see on the horizon—and that is precisely the point. Europe must make further progress in political integration if it is to be an active participant in the pentagonal world. This will require both new institutional mechanisms and political courage. Such mechanisms should include a far greater capability than presently exists to intermesh the economic, political, security, and social aspects of policy. The way by which economic disputes between, for example, the EEC and a non-EEC country can undermine political relations is now coming to be understood, but "economic policy" too often still remains separated from "foreign policy."

A "European" Europe, one which has evolved a regional identity and political capacity, need not be a bane for the United States. It should rather be in a position to accept new tasks and compensate for the devolution of responsibility from the United States. In a world of greater multipolarity it will be all the more crucial that the Old and New world collaborate together on common goals. For Europe not to face up to the challenges of the future would mean a gradual demoralization and eventual accommodation with the Soviet Union. In sum, we would than have a quadrilateral world! On the other hand, a "European foreign policy" will not always be completely aligned with that of the United States—and an active and imaginative American foreign policy should not seek to maintain such a close alignment at all times.

EUROPEAN DEFENSE

The defense institutions which are needed would be modest ones designed to create a European defense grouping of limited functions and power. The authority of such a group might be extended if Western Europe makes further progress in political integration. An excellent opportunity for progress in defense coordination will come about in the years after Britain's entry into the European Community. There are some persons who argue that if the aim of European political unity is to be pushed further, a start will first have to be made on a closely integrated defense. Although this claim has great merit it must also be recognized that security touches quickly upon sovereignty and that a high degree of integration in defense presupposes agreement among nations on fundamental questions of national security, on the nature of any threats, and the best methods of dealing with them.

A European defense grouping must therefore be "modest" because Europe itself is still at a rudimentary stage of political development. The other side of the coin is that for at least the next decade or two, Western Europe will remain ultimately dependent upon the United States commitment to its security. As long as there is a perceived threat to Europe from the Soviet Union and so long as the western end of the Eurasian land mass is not politically united, the United States must continue to act as the balancer. The only alternative to the American nuclear umbrella is a full-scale European nuclear deterrent, and this is not feasible for as far ahead as we can see. The military requirements of such a deterrent are roughly equal to the panoply of nuclear forces of the superpowers; the political requisites are even more daunting. The control arrangements for such a force would require a political authority capable of deciding on its use in behalf of Europe. Perhaps only a President of Europe with full authority in a nuclear crisis could endow a European deterrent with full credibility.

For this reason a new European defense grouping must be within the Atlantic Alliance framework and should not be a competitor of NATO. This would argue against placing it within the formal EEC machinery. Conceivably it could be an expansion in authority of the present Euro-group within NATO. Another possibility would be basing it upon the existing Western European Union which consists of Britain and the present EEC members. It would be important, probably crucial to its success, that France be a participant and this would be a critical factor in coming to agreement upon the proper institutional setting.

Such a grouping—let us call it from here on the European Defense Commission—would be involved with the whole range of defense capabilities, especially conventional forces, nuclear forces, and the procurement of armaments. With respect to conventional forces the Commission's prime task would be improvements of a qualitative rather than quantitative nature since a substantial increase in European forces is unlikely at least as long as the present climate of détente persists. A good deal could be done, nonetheless, to make the West European armed forces more effective through rationalization and integrative methods. This would include combining logistic systems, coordinating mobilization plans, joint training exercises, and common reserve policies. In addition a common Western European "offset" arrangement with the United States to alleviate the costs, especially in the balance of payments, of the stationing of American forces in Europe might help lessen pressures to reduce them.

The reduction of American combat troops in Western Europe during the 1970's, is, in my opinion, inevitable. The Nixon Administration thus far has successfully resisted attempts in the Senate to reduce forces unilaterally. Past pressures have stemmed from balance of payments concerns, the feeling that Western Europe is now prosperous and should be carrying a greater share of the burden of its own defense, the whole question of "national priorities," the squeeze on the Pentagon budget, the tendency to shed responsibility resulting from the traumatic experience of Vietnam, and a certain amount of Midwestern "Mansfieldism." What I believe will now be added to this will be a growing consensus within the Executive branch of the U.S. government that these forces should be reduced in order to avoid less desirable cuts in other parts of the defense budget. In addition there will be a reexamination of NATO strategy which will place less value on the Kennedy-McNamara concept of controlled and flexible response.

There is virtually no chance the U.S. troops will be totally withdrawn as has been sometimes unthinkingly suggested and unknowledgeably feared. American forces are living hostages to guarantee to the West Europeans that the United States would be involved in a conflict in Europe. But neither is there some magic number below which the number of troops cannot descend. The "hostage" function would no doubt be as well performed by one-third of the present level of 300,000. The "permissable" amounts of reduction which can be safely made will be dependent upon the political psychology and confidence of the Europeans, taking into account their reading of Soviet intentions. Another criteria will be the manner of the reductions and whether they are made in concert with a parallel reduction in Warsaw Pact forces. An important function of the European Defense

Commission would be to assure that any American reductions are made as a result of a collaborative approach with the West European nations. A secondary, but critical, task would be to take the lead in the drawing up of a new NATO strategic doctrine if the present flexible response strategy becomes no longer adequate or feasible because of the reduction of forces.

Discussion of the nuclear component of a European Defense Commission raises controversial and complex issues, but I do not believe that they can be avoided indefinitely. The devisive intra-Alliance debate on the multilateral nuclear force (MLF) proposal by the United States in the early 1960's has resulted in nuclear questions being swept under the carpet. Clearly the MLF illustrated the folly of the United States attempting to impose a totally new and elaborate weapons system upon its Allies on the assumption that this is what they wanted or needed. Nevertheless, the defense of Western Europe will continue to rest in the final analysis upon a strategy of nuclear deterrence. One must consider that: 1. In the pentagonal world the credibility of the U.S. nuclear guarantee, especially if there is a SALT agreement, will be subject to further erosion; 2. the British and French nuclear forces will not be allowed to wither away and their future will greatly effect the future of West European security; and 3. in the long run a "uniting Europe" cannot acquire a sense of confidence based on greater autonomy without coming to grips with the intricacies of its nuclear defense.

If the present SALT negotiations between Russia and America lead to an agreement prescribing quantitative limitations this will result in the codification of rough strategic parity. It is then likely that Europeans will have still less faith in the credibility of the American nuclear deterrent. A convincing argument can be made that the first use of nuclear weapons by the United States in behalf of Europe became implausable when America became subject to Soviet missile retaliation in the late 1950's. What counts, however, is people's perceptions and beliefs and most (excluding De Gaulle, but for different reasons) were prepared to accept Mr. McNamara's contention that it was the U.S. nuclear "superiority" which did much to make the guarantee credible.

A United States-Soviet Union agreement in SALT would be welcome to the West Europeans because it would be seen as curbing the arms race and adding to world stability, but it may also further erode the nuclear guarantee. On the other hand, the failure to reach a SALT agreement could be even more unfortunate from the European point of view. If the two Superpowers were unable to agree on limitations they might then proceed to build and deploy ABM systems. This would leave Western Europe—which, because of the expense, problems of command

and control, and geographical proximity to the Soviet Union, would be unlikely to build its own missile defense—with a sense of nuclear nakedness. Either way, therefore, the Europeans will be forced to reexamine the extent of their nuclear dependence upon the United States.

Part of this reevaluation for Britain and France will involve their independent strategic forces. These nuclear forces exist and will not be renounced. The lesson of the extensive European nuclear debate of the past two decades is that London and Paris will not accept a non-nuclear role, leaving Western deterrence solely to the United States. Even if the abstract logic of some strategic analysts suggest that "rationally" these forces should be abandoned—that they cannot be employed against the U.S.S.R. without inviting holocaustal retribution—the political, military, bureaucratic, psychological, and security incentives and pressures which led to their creation and maintenance points elsewhere. These nuclear forces will, however, need to be modernized and new generations will have to be constructed, particularly if there is further ballistic missile defense deployment in the Soviet Union. This would present the opportunity for an imaginative cooperative undertaking, involving the non-nuclear states of Western Europe as well as the United States.

The task, as challenging as important, would be to harness the existing nuclear forces in the service of all of Western Europe. This would have to be done with the active and participating support of the non-nuclear states of Europe and in close collaboration with the United States. Earlier I have stated that an independent European nuclear deterrent, capable by itself of balancing the Soviet Union, is not feasible mainly because of the problem of its control. But a greater European nuclear role within the framework of the Atlantic Alliance is possible and should be given serious consideration.

My proposal, outlined in greater detail elsewhere,[3] would involve the creation of a "European Nuclear Committee" and a new set of nuclear relationships between Britain, France, and the United States. The French and British nuclear forces would be jointly placed at the service of the European Nuclear Committee (ENC) on which they and the non-nuclear European countries would also sit. The main purpose of the ENC (which could be part of the European Defense Commission) would be to formulate political guidelines on when these nuclear forces should be used and to plan for the numerous contingencies which might be entailed. Since almost all such contingencies would also involve the activation of the American strategic forces, such guidelines would be worked out with the United States but they would have the advantage of presenting a unified European position to Washington.

The central element of command and control could not be delegated to the ENC without there existing a highly integrated, politically unified "Europe." But British and French targeting plans would be coordinated with each other, and in turn coordinated with the United States in the same manner as British plans have been in the past. Nuclear strategy would thus become a common undertaking and a matter of close consultations. In practical reality Britain and France would have three sets of target plans: "Atlantic Alliance," "European" and "National," the latter in the unlikely event that independent action should ever be desirable.

The European Nuclear Committee, in addition to being an appropriate forum for discussions of plans and strategy, could have an important role in the development of the next generation of European nuclear weapons. These weapons could then be built in "Europe's behalf." The non-nuclear states might be asked to assist in their manufacture or to make a financial contribution. Although ultimate control would remain with London and Paris, the participation of the other European states would grant them a vote on matters ranging from the choice of nuclear systems to general guidelines for their use.

Agreement on purpose and use of the forces would then make possible collaboration on their construction and manufacture. An "entente nucleaire" between Britain and France already has a great deal of logic. The technology of their nuclear forces is remarkably complementary and suitable for exchange. Britain has a great deal of experience and knowledge about warheads, but little about propulsion systems since it has bought American missiles for the past decade. France, in turn, has developed independently land and sea-based missile systems but is behind in sophisticated multiple warhead technology. Possible collaboration between the two has always run into difficulty because the United States, having given Britain a great deal of atomic information and assistance over the past two decades, does not permit this knowledge to be passed on to a third country. Although the British nuclear program developed a good deal of knowledge on its own (the first British atomic bomb, detonated in 1952, was manufactured without U.S. assistance), it is so intertwined with that of the United States that it would be impossible to identify the major aspects of the nuclear program which are solely of British origin. The ability to cut the Gordian knot therefore lies in the hands of the United States. Washington could free the British of existing restraints to collaborate with the French; or it could offer direct assistance to France and continue as in the past with Britain. In the mid-1970's relevant sections of the Anglo-American nuclear exchange agreement of 1958 will come up for termination or renewal. At that time it might be best to "Europeanize" the present nuclear relationship with Britain.

The proposal for a European Nuclear Committee based on the continuing British and French forces, as outlined here, would strengthen the European pillar of the Atlantic Alliance. It would be of special importance to the Federal Republic of Germany as the only major West European power without an independent nuclear capability. It would certainly require, and might make possible, the return of France to the integrated defense system since it would give France a prominent place in the major European defense undertaking. It would be in accord with the Nonproliferation Treaty since it would not include a transfer of nuclear weapons, or their control, to non-nuclear powers. For the coming period, it would have an important symbolic value—in time it could be the centerpiece of the security of a United Europe.

The joint procurement of armaments would be the third major task of a European Defense Commission. The need for a much greater amount of European cooperation in arms production than exists at present stems from the spiraling cost of weapons at a time of increasing sophistication in the technology of warfare. This coincides with pressure to maintain defense budgets at the present level, or preferably to reduce them. Such pressures are likely to continue if not accelerate if the present climate of détente continues and leads to a series of East-West agreements on European security.

The difficulties of the defense industries of the European countries are in many respects not unlike the broader problem of European nonmilitary technology as faced with American competition. Whether the "gap" be managerial or technological, or both, it is clear that without greater intra-European cooperation in high cost technology, such as computers, it is extremely difficult to compete with American industry. One of the particular problems of defense technology is the relative inelasticity of the demand. The national market is limited and often not sufficiently large. In the case of expensive weapon systems, such as aircraft, it is often essential that foreign orders be assured before a decision on production is made.

The history of joint weapons projects in Europe in the past fifteen years is a distressing one. Of all the projects planned more were left unfinished than were completed. Often the unfinished projects led to bitter charges and disputes between officials of the governments concerned. Equally often it has proven impossible to come to prior agreements on the weapons which were under consideration for development.[4] Two reasons can be cited for this: first the insistence by governments that they receive a "just return" on their investment in the form of orders for their industry of equal value to what they put into the jointly produced weapons; second, the difficulty that military services of two more countries have in coming to agreement upon the desired specifications for weapons.

The root of the problem is that agreement on weapons and their requirements presupposes agreement on strategy and defense policy. If Germany and the Netherlands, for example, are unable to agree on the tactical strategy for resistence to a frontal attack it is unlikely that they will agree on the specifications for an anti-tank weapon.

A European Defense Commission would help solve many of these dilemmas by requiring a far greater degree of European cooperation at all levels of defense planning. Once the basic European defense strategy was worked out (in concert with NATO), the Commission would facilitate agreement on common research and development, weapon specification, joint funding, production, etc. These functions might also become the responsibility of the Commission. European collaboration would thereby create a European-wide market, capable of producing armaments more efficiently and cheaply, and thereby better able to compete in the world market. This would be another big step in strengthening the European pillar of Western defense.[5]

EUROPEAN POLITICAL SETTLEMENT

The second major challenge facing Western Europe, we have noted, will be the negotiation of a European political settlement. This will involve a broad spectrum of political, economic, military, and technological issues; it will also draw into the process of negotiation the Soviet Union, the East European states, Western Europe, and the United States. Such a process has indeed already been well started with the Bonn-Moscow and Bonn-Warsaw Treaties, the Berlin negotiations, the informal exploratory negotiations concerning a European Security Conference, and SALT.

The starting point in the quest for reconciliation in Europe is the perception that the Soviet military threat to Western Europe has markedly declined. This view is widely held by the public, although the governments and bureaucracies are less confident of a risk-free world. Still the danger as now preceived is less of a military threat than a gradual political and psychological undermining. The very process of negotiation with the East is mistrusted by many persons because of the risk that it will lead to a false euphoria and "détente mindedness." This could induce an accommodation with the Soviet Union which would be disadvantageous to the West if its interests were not strongly upheld. At the same time it is instructive to note that by 1975 half of the voters in Western Europe will have been born since World War II. For this generation the Czechoslovakia coup of 1948 and the Korean War are dim and distant history. They see the military security of Europe as having been successfully achieved through NATO and possible future arms control negotiations. Political security is to be sought through some reconciliation with the East.

The road to a political settlement as seen by many West Europeans is the "normalization" of relations between the two halves of the continent. This became the policy of the West German government in the latter 1960's, especially after the SPD/FDP coalition came into power. After Brandt came to office he abandoned the last vestiges of the Hallstein doctrine of nonrecognition of states which had diplomatic relations with East Germany. Also abandoned was the previous "reunification first" policy as negotiations were entered into with the East. The Bonn-Moscow and Bonn-Warsaw Treaties, coupled with the Berlin Agreement, are in themselves significant first steps. But they bring only modest improvements in the long-term task of tearing down the partition of Europe. The diplomatic freeze of the postwar years has begun to thaw. West Germany can no longer be accused by the Soviet Union of being an aggressive, "revanchist" power. Access to West Berlin will be unimpeded and travel in East Germany has been facilitated. But Soviet troops remain stationed in East Germany, Czechoslovakia, and Poland; the Brezhnev Doctrine has not been renounced; Soviet hegemony in Eastern Europe is intact and the ugly Berlin Wall still stands. Peace in Europe remains, therefore, a distant goal.

One way to work toward the achievement of this goal is the negotiations of arms control agreements for Central Europe. The overall purpose of such arrangements would be not to radically change the present military balance, but to secure it with fewer armed forces and at less cost. Thus East-West negotiations on mutual and balanced force reductions (MBFR) must be carefully planned and executed so as to maintain, if not improve, the present level of stability. Another aim of arms control is to reduce uncertainty and the risk of the start of conflict by accident or miscalculation. A number of steps to assure this—the establishment of observation posts by NATO and the Warsaw Pact in each other's territory, the setting up of an emergency "hot line"—could be undertaken in Europe. Negotiations on arms control in Europe would be a European corollary to SALT. Although the Superpowers would of necessity have to participate, the dominant interest would be that of the Europeans, West and East.

A European Security Conference would in one way or another be concerned with arms control but it would also deal with a far broader range of issues. These would include trade, technological assistance, cultural exchange, and a number of East-West political understandings designed to clear up the underbrush of misconception and distrust. Such a pan-European conference would be limited in what it could achieve, if only because of the manifold issues to be discussed and the more than thirty nations that would participate. It is perhaps better to think of a European security conference as an ongoing process, as a series of meetings possibly with specialized subgroups working piecemeal toward a general political settlement. A permanent machinery, such as a European Security Commission, might be set up, perhaps in Berlin, so as to institutionalize the process.[6] For the East Europeans such a series of meetings would offer the advantage of increasing their flexibility and independence within the Warsaw Pact and COMECON. As to Western Europe, there is no reason why the process of East-West détente should divert attention from the movement toward European unity. A postwar settlement with the East cannot be given second priority to the evolution of the Brussels institutions, but should proceed side by side with the strengthening of a Western Europe less dependent upon the United States. Such a revitalized Western Europe may provide the best hope for the foundation of a stable peace.

Europe should be able to play a fuller global role in the Pentagonal world of the future. Following the events of the early 1970's the opportunity now exists for the growth of political and defense institutions and the coordination of foreign policy so as to achieve a common purpose. Whether Europe accepts the challenge now before it remains to be seen. A quarter of a century ago Europe lacked the necessary material resources to maintain its world role but still had the political interest. Today Europe has acquired the needed resources. Whether it also has the required political will and resolve depends upon its own discipline and political creativity.

NOTES

1. See Andrew J. Pierre, "American Down, Russia Up: The Changing Political Role of Military Power," *Foreign Policy*, No. 4. (Fall, 1971).

2. See Robert F. Byrnes, "Russia in Europe: Hegemony Without Security," *Foreign Affairs*, L, 1 (July, 1971).

3. "Nuclear Diplomacy: Britain, France and America," *Foreign Affairs*, XLIX, 2 (January, 1971), pp. 283-305.

4. The failure of the Anglo-French variable geometry aircraft is an example. See J. M. Ramsden, "Europe Learns Some Hard Lessons: Disillusion in Aerospace Cooperation," *Roundtable*, No. 236 (October, 1969), pp. 363-368.

5. For further discussion of armament procurement problems, see *Defense, Technology and the Western Alliance*, papers issued by the Institute for Strategic Studies, London, 1967, especially the paper by Alastair Buchan, "The Implication of a European System for Defense Technology." Also, Christopher Layton, *European Advanced Technology* (London: George Allen and Unwin Ltd., 1969); Walter Schutze, *European Defense Cooperation and NATO*, Paper No. 3 (Paris: The Atlantic Institute, 1969).

6. See Timothy W. Stanley, *A Conference on European Security? Problems, Prospects, and Pitfalls*, The Atlantic Council of the United States, Washington, D.C., 1970. See also Andrew J. Pierre, "Reconciliation in Europe: A Western Approach to the European Security Conference," *Interplay*, Vol. 3, No. 10 (July, 1970).

THE FUTURE
OF FOREIGN RELATIONS
BETWEEN THE UNITED STATES
AND A UNITING EUROPE:
A EUROPEAN PERSPECTIVE

Louis G. M. Jaquet

Europe will not be built within one day. It will not suddenly emerge as one great building. It will develop from concrete circumstances which will produce a factual solidarity.*

Efforts after 1945 to establish economic and political cooperation among some West European states were a response to the challenge caused by completely new postwar circumstances in the political as well as in the economic fields. Europe, impoverished and exhausted by the war, was faced with the tasks of trying to restore its prosperity and finding a new and suitable place for itself in the postwar world. It had to approach these tasks during a period in which the old type of nation-state seemed to have become obsolete because economic and social issues and problems surpassed the boundaries of these states. In addition, the approach to these problems were made all the more difficult because during this period West European states lost their colonial empires, world political leadership passed from the West European powers to the United States, and the Cold War started.

These developments created a bipolar world order. The two leading powers which emerged, the United States and the Soviet Union, enjoyed remarkable and exceptional positions for three reasons. First,

---

*Jean Monnet and Robert Schuman as quoted by Paul van de Meerssche in *De Europese Integratie: 1945-1970* (Antwerp, 1971).

they had overwhelming military superiority over their allies. Second, as a result of their victories in a partly power political, partly ideological war, they became the accepted ideological leaders of their blocs. Third, they had huge economic and financial resources which made their allies economically dependent on them. The Soviet Union used its position, especially in Stalin's time, to secure its hegemony over the East European countries. The United States exerted its leadership of the Western world not by suppressing its allies but by trying to build them up to junior partners.

A precondition for the success of such a policy was the economic recovery of the impoverished European countries. Such an economic recovery could not be attained without outside financial and psychological "injections." The United States quickly drew the consequences out of the requirements of the situation by launching the Marshall Plan in June, 1947. This was an act of determination and generosity as well as of well understood self-interest. Simultaneously, it was proof of American political wisdom to understand that permanent results from efforts at economic and political recovery would never be obtained by outside help alone. The United States was prepared to stimulate the process and to provide the tools. However, the Europeans themselves had to do the job.

In June, 1947, Secretary of State George C. Marshall declared:

> There must be some agreement among the countries of Europe as to the requirements of the situation and the part these countries themselves will take in order to give proper effect to whatever action that might be taken by this government. The initiative must come from Europe. The role of this country should consist of friendly aid in the drafting of a European programme and of later support for such a programme.[1]

The Europeans indeed went to work and set a process in motion which lead to the establishment of the Organization for European Economic Cooperation (OEEC) in 1948 and the European Payments Union (EPU) in 1950. Thus a combination of European readiness to respond to a challenge and American generosity and political wisdom produced the first coordinated economic cooperation between European countries. Such large scale economic cooperation was preceded by the agreement reached by the Benelux countries during 1944 to form a customs union and was followed in 1950 by the establishment of the European Coal and Steel Community (ECSC). The ECSC was the brilliant conception of the French statesmen Robert Schuman and Jean Monnet. On May 9,

1950, Schuman announced the French proposal to place the combined coal and steel production of Germany and France under one common authority. The organization would be open for membership to other European countries. Italy and the Benelux countries joined, whereas the United Kingdom did not. Thus, the so-called Europe of the Six came into being.

The establishment of the ECSC was of utmost importance because it raised the hope of the possibility for more intensive European political and economic cooperation. The approach was partly functional and partly supranational. It was functional in the sense that cooperation was restricted to a specific field—coal and steel—for which a common market was created by the abolition of import and export duties, subsidies and other restrictive practices on the movement of coal and steel between the participant countries.

It was supranational by creating a "High Authority" to administer the ECSC. This is a body with restricted but real powers consisting of members who, although appointed by their governments, were independent. The first important political implication of the establishment of the ECSC was the institutionalization of Franco-German cooperation. This makes future Franco-German military conflicts highly improbable. A further political aim was to pave the way for future European cooperation on a federal basis. The Schuman declaration on this point made this political aim perfectly clear.

> The pooling of coal and steel production should immediately provide for the setting up of common foundations for economic development as a first step to the federation of Europe. By pooling basic production and by instituting a new higher authority, whose decisions will bind France, Germany and other member countries, these proposals will build the first concrete foundations of the European federation which is indispensable to the preservation of peace.[2]

The Schuman initiative fitted in completely with the American post-1945 foreign policy goal of creating partners on the European continent. It aroused American enthusiasm and met with American support. The political imagination of Schuman and Monnet also caught the strong interest of the European continent.

The intensification of the Cold War after the outbreak of the Korean War further stimulated the already growing American and European cooperation. As a result of these developments the position of Germany and the possibility of German rearmament (proposed by the Americans, but received very skeptically by the French and the

British), came into the center of discussion. The result was the Plèven Plan to establish a European Defense Community. The plan was in keeping with Schuman's functional approach of integration by sector. Its provisions, however, for the establishment of an Executive Commissariat provided the EDC with a supranational incentive. In addition, by merging the new German army into a supranational organization, the French fear of the reestablishment of an independent German army and a German General Staff could be removed, while the American desire to use the German defense potential for a European and Western defense system could be satisfied. However, the plan went still further than only a European Defense Community. Article 38 of the draft EDC treaty provided for the possibility of creating a European Political Community with a federal and confederal structure. Europe seemed on its way to cooperation and unification. But reactions were bound to arise against these plans. Exactly as in the case of the ECSC, the United Kingdom decided not to participate. Then French politicians and parliamentarians had second thoughts. They became aware that by restricting German sovereignty in the military field through the incorporation of the new German army into a European Defense Community, France by implication would also have to transfer at least part of her absolute sovereignty in military and political matters to the new communities.

In spite of heavy American pressure culminating in the "agonizing reappraisal" statement of Secretary of State John Foster Dulles at a press conference during a NATO conference in Paris in December, 1953 (a statement in which the United States threatened to detach itself from its European commitments in case the EDC was not accepted), in August, 1954, the French Assembly rejected the treaty. This resulted in a serious political malaise. Supranationality had received a major set back. Under these circumstances the British government took the initiative by proposing the establishment of the West European Union (WEU) as an organization to be based on intergovernmental cooperation between the "Six" and the United Kingdom. The WEU made German rearmament and German entry into NATO possible, but the principle of supranationality was not reintroduced.

It was the so called "Relance Européenne" started at the Conference of Messina in 1955 which led ultimately to the Treaty of Rome establishing the European Economic Community (EEC) in January, 1958. The Dutch Minister of Foreign Affairs at that time, Dr. Beyen, together with his Belgium colleague Paul-Henri Spaak played a prominent role with regard to the preparation of the conference. The experiences with the disillusionment caused by the abortive EDC negotiations in 1954 apparently put their mark on the negotiations leading to the Treaty of Rome. The issue was now economic cooperation instead of the previous efforts directed toward political and defense cooperation. The approach was pragmatic. Political and theoretical considerations formerly in vogue were now shunned. As Spaak put it: "We talk on the basis of the list of practical necessities formulated in Messina and on no other basis."[3] Spaak was right. Introduction of politics would almost certainly have jeopardized the negotiations of the Rome Treaties.

However, the result was a treaty that greatly stimulated economic cooperation thus promoting prosperity within the Communities. But the treaty lacked long-range structural views. Its philosophy was that economic cooperation and economic union would by themselves lead to political cohesion and unification. But this "spill over" theory did not work out in practice. Practice shows that at certain important stages "political injections" are needed simply to keep the machinery— including the economic machinery—going. But in order to give political injections, a common political will is required. And a common political will presupposes agreement on basic policies. However, such agreement did not exist.

The handicap of an absence of long-range structural views and political agreement began to become clear at the end of the 1960's. The integration process had then reached a point at which at the least a strongly coordinated economic and social policy seemed to be required "to keep the machinery going." Besides, economic integration had reached the stage at which a major crisis could most probably no longer be met by "soft-pedal reactions." Moreover, growing cooperation between the members and applicant members of the EEC became increasingly desirable and urgent because of Western Europe's position as such as well as its position in relation to the United States (which was clearly endeavoring to restrict its commitments) and the Soviet Union (which was steadily expanding its military power and presence).

Nevertheless neither European economic cooperation nor even European political unification can be ends in themselves. The question has to be asked: "L'Europe pour quoi faire?" What is the grand design of European cooperation? What does it mean for internal developments in the economic, social, and political fields and what will be Europe's place in the world? The trouble is that too few Europeans have clear conceptions about Europe's future internal and external positions. And those who have often fundamentally disagree. However, efforts to build the structure of a unified Europe will ultimately fail unless the Europeans have clear conceptions of Europe's internal political, social, and economic framework and its external relations with the United States, and Soviet Union, and the non-Western world. The danger of such—in the long run useless—efforts could be that because of a technocratic approach Europe will, without being aware of it and without or perhaps against its political will, drift into a situation which will not be under its political control. Such a development could ultimately lead to a major political crisis.

Thoughts about a possible future structure for Europe have to take into account her relations with the rest of the world. In the first place this involves the United States, the Soviet Union, and the non-Western world. Europe's external relations will be influenced by the way Europe will be structured, but the structure of Europe can, on the other hand, not be seen as a function of its external relations only. While thinking about a possible European structure the question has to be asked: What can be done if a purely supranational cooperation will for the time being be an impossibility and a purely technocratic approach will obviously end in an impasse? To what extent will the present functional European integration be affected by a failure to develop closer political and military cooperation? Will further functional integration be possible without political integration? In other words is there a chance for the closer European cooperation which circumstances require in a form in between the ideal supranational and the possible intergovernmental cooperation?

In my opinion a solution could be found by introducing a system based partly on functional cooperation modeled on the present community method and parallel with it partly on intergovernmental cooperation. This means that under present conditions those supranational elements necessary to keep the process of economic and financial integration going must be injected. As for the remaining areas, cooperation, especially in matters of foreign and defense policy, should for the time being be implemented principally on an institutionalized intergovernmental basis. The communique issued after the summit conference at The Hague of heads of states or government and ministers of foreign affairs in December, 1969, and the subsequent Davignon Report seem to be examples of moves in this direction. The communique instructed the Ministers of Foreign Affairs to study the best way to achieve progress toward political unification within the context of enlargement. The Davignon Report presented to the member governments in the summer of 1970 outlined steps to implement these instructions. In the report the Ministers of Foreign Affairs stated their belief in the necessity that similar developments should take place in the political field as had already been the case in other sectors of Community cooperation "in order to expedite the moment when Europe will be able to speak with one voice." The Ministers recommended that in the third phase of increasing political cooperation efforts must be made to harmonize the foreign policy of the member states. The report recommended that the Ministers of Foreign Affairs hold conferences twice a year and that a Political Committee composed of the Directors-General of Foreign Affairs of the member countries be established to meet at least four times a year. In the event the activities of the Foreign Ministers might influence the work of the Communities, the European Commission would be invited to express its opinion. According to the Davignon Report the cooperation of the member states in foreign policy matters aims at:

1. Furthering a better mutual understanding with regard to the great international political problems by means of regular exchange of information and consultations;

2. Strengthening solidarity by barmonizing positions, coordinating lines of conduct, and, where possible and desirable, common action.

The Hague Communique and the Davignon Report are, in my opinion, encouraging moves in the direction I recommended in the preceding paragraphs: intensification of the existing functional cooperation in an enlarged Community and parallel with it an intergovernmental cooperation of the member states of the enlarged Communities in other—especially political—fields. However, the Davignon Report is no more, and could be no more, than a first step to compromise among the member states.

Aiming at possibilities rather than desirabilities it could be possible to go further in the field of foreign political cooperation than indicated in the Davignon Report. Moreover, I would also recommend the exploration of the possibilities for cooperation on a country to country basis in the defense field, although this is admittedly a more difficult undertaking.

COORDINATION OF FOREIGN POLICY:
INSTITUTIONAL MEASURES

My recommendations would be:

1. More extensive institutionalization of cooperation and coordination in foreign policy matters than recommended in the Davignon Report. To this end a permanent nonpolitical secretariat should be established in order to further the implementation of agreements reached by Ministers of Foreign Affairs.

2. An institutionalized cooperation of foreign policy and defense matters implies activities parallel with but not integrated in the organs of the European Communities. However, in my opinion, the European Commission should be consulted and informed more regularly than is provided for in the Davignon proposals as accepted by the Ministers of Foreign Affairs. Consultation with and information of the European Commission could be promoted by appointing a representative of the Commission as an observer to the meetings of Foreign Ministers and the Political Committee.

3. As long as the applicant members of the Communities have not obtained membership, the procedure of informing the applicant members, as proposed in the Davignon Report, should be changed to a procedure of consultation with them.

SUBSTANCE OF A HARMONIZED FOREIGN POLICY

Coordination and harmonization of foreign policy should include.

1. Relations with the United States;
2. Relations with the Soviet Union and Eastern Europe; and
3. Relations with the non-Western world, in particular, Africa and the Middle East.

There is more than one reason to expect that in the near future the foreign political "cooperation" among the member states of the EC will not surpass the consultation or at best the coordination level. The formulation and implementation of a common foreign policy will—with the exception of a foreign economic policy—be excluded in the foreseeable future. This seems also to be the gist of the Pomipdou-Heath understanding which laid the basis for French consent to British entry into the Common Market. The main reasons why the intergovernmental phase cannot be passed in the foreign political policy field are:

1. The nation-state may have become obsolete in the economic, technological, and social fields, but it is very obstinate and vigorous in the foreign political and defense fields. Few nations are willing to entrust their most vital interests to the arbitrary power of a supranational body.

2. Moreover, there is as yet no common outlook and no common political will among the members of the EC concerning basic problems of foreign policy.

It is possible and it is to be hoped that a common political outlook and will, will grow in proportion to the growth of common interests as a result of the success of functional economic cooperation. But as has already been mentioned in the foregoing, practice has shown that economic cooperation will not automatically produce political cohesion. This is as true in the field of internal politics as in external relations.

But the opposite is true as well. Without a clear political will to give up major parts of absolute sovereignty, the establishment of a monetary union (implying harmonizing economic, fiscal, budgetary, and social policies) will not be possible. But here the Dutch proverb: "Stagnancy implies decline" may be applicable. In the present phase of integration a failure to establish a monetary union may destroy the chances for an economic union and a failure to establish an economic union may adversely affect the maintenance of a customs union. Thus the challenge posed by developments may become so great that as a matter of necessity in order to avoid major crises a political act will be urgently needed and accordingly performed. But by the nature of the process the required political injections will be performed earlier in the areas of economic, monetary, and social cooperation than in the foreign political field. Unless major international crises would compel us to do so, a common political will with regard to our external relations will be a by-product of growing common economic, financial, and social interests as Linthorst Homan correctly remarks.[4]

3. Each new group in a society is confronted with two main tasks:
a. To organize its internal structure in order to guarantee its cohesion; and
b. To arrange its external relations.

The two can and should be complementary. But new groups can be so involved with the organization of the internal structure through which to keep the group together that they neglect to pay proper attention to their external relations. They are not willing to put the possible results of building their internal structure with too much at stake by attempting simultaneously to overcome their divergencies of opinion concerning their external relations. This can further the tendency of "leave us alone." But the modern world does not permit countries or regions of the importance of Western Europe to be left alone to escape into a kind of neo-isolationism. Therefore, the different countries cooperating in the European Communities will at least have to consult each other and to try to coordinate their policies concerning major aspects of international relations.

RELATIONS OF WESTERN EUROPE
AND THE UNITED STATES

The time has passed when Western Europe accepted the United States almost unconditionally as the natural military, economic, and ideological leader of an Atlantic Community. The time is also over in which the United States gave an absolute priority to foreign policy considerations in regard to its relations with the European Communities based on the assumption that European unity is contributing to Atlantic cohesion and thus serving overall American interests. The possibility that a United Europe one day might become an economic competitor was outweighed in postwar and Cold War days by political and military considerations. There has been growing skepticism in Europe about the credibility of United States commitments since the change of official U.S. nuclear strategy from massive retaliation to a flexible response. This skepticism has been encouraged by the American desire for troop reductions as well as the growing American tendency to look inward even though the United States is still deeply involved in the tragic Vietnam affair. In addition, the serious social and racial problems with which the United States is confronted might one day tempt American leaders to make a deal with the Soviet Union at the expense of Europe.

On the other hand, Americans are becoming increasingly annoyed and disillusioned with a Europe that up until now has failed to unite and that continues, ultimately, to depend on the United States for its defense without being prepared to make a sufficient contribution of its own in terms of manpower or finance. There is irritation about a Europe where, notwithstanding generous American help in the recent past and continuing military protection at present, a not unimportant part of public opinion is very vocal in criticizing and condemning American domestic and foreign policies. There is a growing apprehension in the United States that the enlarged European Communities which will be the world's largest commercial bloc controlling more than 40 percent of world trade, might become a serious competitor. But I wonder whether this apprehension is realistic. In the field of trade the Community philosophy that European economic cooperation would stimulate prosperity to such an extent that the market would—not withstanding tariff barriers—become more and more important also for outsiders has proved to be valid. As a matter of fact during the last ten years American exports to the Communities have more than doubled. This trade will grow even more rapidly after the entry of the United

Kingdom in the Common Market. Moreover, American business has profited considerably by its huge investments in Europe.

There is also skepticism about French foreign policy as well as German *Ostpolitik*. In the latter case it would be a task for American leadership to ensure that German *Ostpolitik* will be integrated in the general framework of East-West relations.

I think that as long as common sense prevails, one will have to acknowledge that common interests predominate over controversial issues. Because of the asymmetrical relation with the Soviet Union, Western Europe needs the American umbrella. When dealing with military relations I shall try to explain why Western Europe does not have the option to become a Third Force between the Soviet Union and the United States. Cutting off the Atlantic ties would imply becoming a greater Sweden or a bigger Finland. The Finnish type of neutrality would imply sitting for as long as possible on the fence between Moscow and Washington but being at the mercy of any Moscow-Washington understanding reached at Europe's expense. The Swedish model of armed neutrality could enable Europe to deter possible superpower pressure and threats in matters not so vital for them as to justify facing the possibility of small scale retalitation. Under such a policy the French and British nuclear weapons could play a role. This type of armed neutrality would most probably not enable Europe to withstand the combined superpowers' pressure. Such pressure would be a result of a previous agreement between the United States and the Soviet Union. A policy of armed neutrality of the "greater Sweden" type might—at least for the West European powers—be easier in a triangular or multipolar than in a bipolar world. The reason for this is that an agreement between three or more superpowers to impose their will on the smaller powers is less probable than an agreement between two superpowers. Therefore, a triangular or multipolar world might to a certain extent enlarge the freedom of action for the middle powers. Finally, being a member of an alliance with a superpower means being an active part of a political power structure and being able to influence the policy and decision-making process of a major ally. As long as a political will remains on the American side as well as on the European side, an American-European partnership is still the best policy for Europe as well as for the United States.

Two well-known Americans, Professor Zbigniew Brzezinski and former American Ambassador to NATO Robert Ellsworth have commented on common European-American interests in the coming years. In an article published in the April, 1971, issue of *Survival*, Ambassador Ellsworth wrote:

From the American point of view in 1971, while many places are important, there is no area of the globe—outside the United States itself—where American interests are more important or more extensive than in Western Europe. Our mutual ethnic, historical, sentimental and political ties are stronger and more widespread; our mutual trade is incomparably greater; our mutual investments are far more substantial, varied, and technologically advanced; our mutual monetary interdependency is more fundamental; the mass tourist travel of our citizens is far heavier between Europe and the United States than between any other comparable areas of the earth. Quite apart from defense, security and foreign policy, then, Western Europe and the United States constitute the largest and most intimate system of mutual interests in the world today.

And in the October, 1970, issue of *Foreign Affairs,* Professor Brzezinski wrote:

The American presence in Europe, moreover, is a fact. Recent years have seen an explosive growth in American economic investments in Europe and in the proliferation of large multinational corporations. In spite of American-West European difficulties in regard to tariffs—even in spite of a threatening tariff war—a kind of an Atlantic supermarket is developing, precluding American disengagement from Europe. Reinforcing this growth is the ever increasing scope of scientific collaboration, of educational-cultural ties, of an intensifying flow of communications and the cross-Atlantic movement of tourists.

The American military presence in Europe thus should be viewed not as primarily a perpetuation of Potsdam or of the cold war, but rather as a reflection of a common involvement.

President Nixon expressed similar views in his report to Congress on United States foreign policy for the 1970's "A New Strategy for Peace" when he said that:

As we move from dominance to partnership, there is the possibility that some will see this as a step towards disengagement. But in the third decade of our commitment to Europe, the depth of our relationship is a fact of life. We can no more disengage from Europe than from Alaska.

It seems clear that America and Europe need each other and that Atlantic partnership serves a common interest. However, this does not include a common global policy. The Atlantic Treaty is a regional treaty. Articles 5 and 6 of the Atlantic Charter restrict the treaty obligations to the NATO territory. And I think this is right. Outside the NATO territory, the partners do not have common objectives, common interests, and common views. Therefore, efforts to reach a common NATO global policy would undermine the cohesion of the alliance to a considerable extent.

RELATIONS WITH THE SOVIET
UNION AND EASTERN EUROPE

The existing political and military situation still requires a "balance of power" policy as an essential element in East-West relations. This implies that although bilateral contacts between East and West European countries can serve a useful purpose, the essential relationship between East and West Europe should be channeled through or at least coordinated by the existing alliances: NATO and the Warsaw Pact.

The essential element in a balance of power policy is the balance, not the level, of power. Accordingly mutual and balanced force reductions seem to be the only rational approach toward the problem of military security. Détente will not be furthered by unilateral measures or concessions but by a détente policy. The starting point should be the status quo, i.e., the tacit acknowledgment or acquiescence in the existing Eastern and Western spheres of influence. However, a situation should be avoided in which the "status" would be for Moscow and the "quo" for the rest of Europe. Or, to put it in the words of Pierre Hassner,[5] the West should not accept an Eastern "status quo plus" policy, i.e., a policy aimed at keeping the Eastern sphere of influence integrally intact and at the same time trying to hollow out the Western sphere.

However, seen from Moscow, negotiations for a détente are not of much importance if Western concessions are made anyway (for instance, for financial or internal political reasons). If the West reduces its forces anyway for financial or internal political reasons why should Moscow be interested in force reductions being mutual and balanced?

Making Berlin a testing point for Russian seriousness to start real negotiations on European security seems for various reasons a sound policy. However, it seems to me to be a European interest that a European Security Conference or a series of conferences should start as soon as the situation permits. The present German *Ostpolitik* should be backed by and integrated into a general Western East-West policy. In the long run since a "status quo" cannot continue to exist, a permanent maintenance of a security system based solely on a balance of power seems impossible as well as undesirable. Consequently, new elements have to be built into European relations which will provide better guarantees for peace than the existing system. Creating more common interests between East and West by furthering cooperation and joint ventures in the economic field, in matters such as environmental hygiene, and perhaps in the technological field, as well as solving or at least cooling off important political controversies, may contribute to this end.

RELATIONS WITH THE THIRD WORLD

Efforts to coordinate European policy are desirable with regard to important adjacent regions: the Middle East and Africa. Although the result of the first exercise of the Political Committee to formulate a common analysis of the Middle East situation does not give much ground for optimism, activities in this direction should be continued. More coordination in the field of technical, economic, and financial assistance to developing countries seems possible and desirable. The conclusion of trade agreements with outside countries will be a common responsibility after 1973 of the EC member states. As for the remaining areas, European countries should continue their bilateral relations with the rest of the world against the background of an overall consultation and coordination of foreign policy matters.

COORDINATION OF DEFENSE POLICY

Institutional Measures

An institutionalized cooperation and coordination of defense policy of EC member states should be set up by:

1. Organizing regular meetings of Ministers of Defense and Chiefs of Staff in the same way as provided for Ministers of Foreign Affairs or the Political Committee;

2. Setting up an agency for arms purchase, development, and production;

3. Forming an institutionalized caucus of EC member countries within NATO; and

4. Making use of the same permanent secretariat as the Ministers of Foreign Affairs.

Substantive Issues

My suggestions for possible defense cooperation start from the premise that a European defense and détente policy can only work when the Community operates in the defense field as an integrated part of the Atlantic Alliance. Under this proviso harmonization and coordination of European defense policy could include:

1. Coordination of European conventional defense and cooperation in the field of logistics;

2. Efforts to develop a common European policy with regard to arms development, arms production, and purchase of arms;

3. Formulation of a common European strategic doctrine inside NATO;

4. Insurance of a more important European voice inside NATO in matters of nuclear strategy as far as the defense of Europe is concerned; and

5. Nuclear defense as such should remain a NATO responsibility. The nuclear arms of the United Kingdom and France should preferably be assigned to NATO or otherwise be kept under sole national responsibility. They should not be used as a nucleus of a future independent European nuclear force.

An independent West European nuclear force should not be established because Europe does not have the option to become a Third Force between the United States and the Soviet Union. It must choose between being an ally of the United States and accepting the American nuclear umbrella or becoming a greater Sweden or a bigger Finland. In addition, as has already been mentioned, Western Europe does not have the option to become a Third Force because of her asymmetric relationship with the Soviet Union. The geographical situation, the lack of depth, the concentration of industry, and the density of population do not make a European nuclear deterrent credible. Nuclear war would be sheer suicide for Western Europe, since the short distance to the Soviet Union would hardly provide any early warning in case of nuclear attack. There is no reason why Western Europe could not spend the same amount of money for her defense as the Soviet Union and thereby build up a comparable defense apparatus. However, this would imply a shift of budget priorities to the benefit of defense and at the expense of social welfare, etc. It seems out of the question that governments of West European states would propose such a shift of priorities and that parliaments would accept them. Moreover, the establishment of an independent European nuclear force would poison relations with the Eastern bloc. Most of all because it would give the Germans, if not a finger on the trigger, at least a finger in the pie. It would also most probably cause frictions with the United States and would diminish or put at stake the American commitment. Finally, a European nuclear force could only be an instrument in the hands of a federal government of a United Europe to which the member states would entrust their most vital interests. Since the establishment of such a federal government is not in the offing, the possibility of the establishment of such a force is for the foreseeable future a totally theoretical one.

In certain circumstances a less theoretical possibility could be the coordination and division of tasks of the rather complementary French and British nuclear forces serving as a nucleus for a future European nuclear force. In case such a combined or coordinated French-British force would operate outside NATO similar objections could be raised as against a European nuclear force. The other non-nuclear countries would most probably be asked to pay their share of the nuclear burden without having a real say in the use of the force. (Taxation without representation.) This possibility involves a very important question. Why would the non-nuclear West European nations be willing to change the stronger and less biased American protection for the weaker and, in European affairs, more biased French-British one?

I share the judgment of the former British Defense Minister Healy who said: "An Anglo-French nuclear force would be destablizing and dangerous to peace." It would weaken the Atlantic Alliance, diminish the U.S. commitment and frighten other European countries. Moreover, one would have to choose between a not easily acceptable discrimination against the Germans or a dangerous German involvement.

As has been stated previously my conception of European defense starts from the notion that European defense should be integrated within NATO. But for a satisfactory implementation of this principle the active participation of two partners is required: the Europeans and the Americans. Although the present American Administration is on record as stating that "the United States would maintain and improve its forces in Europe and not reduce them without reciprocal actions of our adversaries,"[6] time and again uncertainty is created by publications, public statements, and most of all acts such as the Mansfield Resolution. I agree with Professor Brzezinski who also wrote in the October, 1970, article in *Foreign Affairs* that:

> There is, of course, no special magic to the present U.S. force levels in Europe. The point is to avoid the uncertainty and ambiguity bred by such perennials as the Mansfield Resolution. It sometimes appears as if the American Senate was bent on maximizing uncertainty concerning commitments of the United States to its allies. The real problem is financial. Though estimates of the actual costs of U.S. forces in Europe vary, a realistic figure appears to be somewhere around $3 billion per year.

This is of course no small amount, but no more than 4 percent of the total American defense budget. Moreover, this amount could only be saved if all the troops stationed in Europe were demobolized. Keeping the troops in reserve in the United States would in fact augment and not diminish the cost. Finally, if there is a political will to solve the important problems at stake, it must be possible to overcome the financial difficulties.

I think that those American pressure groups are wrong in thinking that in case the Americans step out, Europeans would step in to fill the gap. Exactly because Europe does not have the option to serve as a Third Force or a semi-Third Force (maintaining loose connections with the United States), President Nixon was right when he remarked in his speech of February 25, 1971, mentioned above, that in case of doubt about the American commitment: "They [the Europeans] would more likely loose confidence in the very possibility of Western defense and reduce their reliance on Western solidarity."

To conclude I would like to endorse Prime Minister Heath's statement in a speech on July 19, 1971, before the American Bar Association Conference in London that: "A permanent satisfactory relationship with the United States is essential both to our individual interests and to our joint endeavors."[7] Without such a relationship neither Europe nor American can fulfill its obligations to one another as well as to other nations.

NOTES

1. Quoted in E. H. van der Beugel, "The United States and European Unity," *Internationale Spectator*, XIX (April 8, 1965), p. 448.

2. Quoted in Ernst H. van der Beugel, *From Marshall Aid to Atlantic Partnership* (Amsterdam, Am Elsevier, 1966), p. 230.

3. Quoted by J. Linthorst Homan in "Which Europe?," *Journal of Common Market Studies*, VIII (September, 1970), p. 68.

4. *Ibid.* p. 80.

5. Pierre Hassner, "Change and Security in Europe," *Adelphi Papers*, Nos. 45 and 49.

6. *U.S. Foreign Policy for the 1970's: A New Strategy for Peace* (Washington, D.C.: U.S. Government Printing Office, 1971).

7. Quoted in the *London Times*, July 20, 1971.

COMMUNITY FOREIGN POLICY
AND POLITICAL INTEGRATION:
LESSONS OF THE
AFRICAN ASSOCIATION

Gordon M. Adams

The likelihood of a future common foreign policy among the member states of the European Community depends directly on the Community's experience of political integration during the past twelve years. It therefore seems almost fanciful to be discussing common policies, given the observation, by now commonplace, that the process of political unification among the Six ground to a halt some time ago. Nevertheless, the existence of this volume shows how observers on both sides of the Atlantic see or anticipate a major change in the international system as a result of the gradual integration supposedly taking place in the European Community. It is thought that some kind of transnational actor is emerging, although its form and powers are still unclear. This Chapter, however, puts forward the thesis that the expectation of an emerging European actor is highly unrealistic, as past experience within the Community shows.

The halt in political integration in Europe was noted before 1965, but it has been most clear since the 1966 Luxembourg agreements, which enshrined the principle of the veto in the Community's Council of Ministers. Even the prospects for British entry, it can be argued, have depended on the French realization that the British had no intention of working in the Community for the kind of political unity which might threaten the sovereignty of the member states.

This present reality in the European Community contrasts with some of the more optimistic expectations found in the early writings of students of political integration. There is no need here for an involved discussion of integration theory, but its divergence from Community experience is of some importance. In a general way, it seems to stem from the bias of early discussions toward seeing the political process in the Community as fairly automatic. Early writings overestimated the extent to which the member states of the Community would find themselves obliged to confer increasing authority on central Community institutions as the wider policy ramifications of their initial decision to form a Community became clear. Common decisions on customs duties, for example, were expected to necessitate common decisions on internal economic policy, as well as common decisions on external trading policy. The member states would simply feel themselves obligated to make more decisions in common as a result of the decisions they had already made. One of the many results expected from this process was the gradual emergence of a common world view, or foreign policy, among the member states. This last manifestation would be the most significant, for it would represent the emergence of an entirely new regional actor in the international system.

A major problem with this vision—here oversimplified but, I would argue, undistorted—was that it was based on very little detailed study of the day-to-day operations of the European Community. The research reported in this essay represents the conclusions drawn from a detailed study of those operations in one area of Community policy toward the outside world, the policy of Association with a certain number of African states. This research indicates that the obstacles to a common foreign policy among the Six are far greater than students of political integration have imagined.

The study shows that the obstacles to further political integration in the Community, especially in the area of external relations, are threefold. National interests, separately defined and defended by each member state, play a critical role in frustrating political unification in the Community. External demands and pressures on the Community, moreover, can exploit these divergent national interests to hamper even further the evolution of a common policy. Finally, both these factors have had an important part in changing the operation of the institutions of the Community, particularly the balance between Council and Commission in favor of the Council, and in leading to a substantial weakening of the impact of elite and interest group pressures on the Community.

Although the Six have made an explicit commitment to a common policy toward the African associates, one would expect to find pressures building for common stands, if the integration process produces the kinds of inevitable expansions of power the theorists expect. A good number of efforts have been made within the framework of Association policy to develop just such pressures, largely without success.

THE DIVERGENCE OF NATIONAL INTERESTS

The African Association was first established in 1958 as an integral part of the Treaty of Rome. It tied the overseas colonies and territories of the Six to the Common Market by creating a free trade zone between the two areas—gradually abolishing customs barriers confronting the exports of the African countries, and slowly opening these countries to the exports of each of the Six (with some safeguards for the Africans). The Rome Treaty also created a common development fund, administered by the Commission, which since 1958 has handled over a billion dollars in aid. Finally, the arrangement provided for the gradual extension of the right of establishment in the overseas areas to nationals and firms of the European member states.

Since the overseas countries were independent by 1962, the agreement was renewed for another five years from 1965 through multilateral negotiations including the Africans. New joint institutions were created and the entire arrangement was renewed again in 1969 to continue until January, 1974. On the surface, the Association policy seems to contain all the elements of what could be called an incipient common foreign policy for the Six: common institutions joining the Six and the Associated African and Malagasy States (AAMS); apparently common trade and establishment policies for the Six toward these countries; and Commission management of the European Development Fund (EDF). It is vitally important to note, however, that this entire structure of policy stands side-by-side along with the undiminished bilateral development aid policies of each of the Six, both toward these eighteen countries in Africa and toward the rest of the developing world. This was the first sign of the uncertain nature of the commitment by the Six to a common policy in this area. The ambiguity stemmed from the fact that the national interests of the member states in the Association diverged very basically from the start. The French were strongly committed to a Community policy toward their colonies in Africa, largely in the hope that they might find ways to share their aid burden. Moreover, it was difficult for the French government to define an alternative arrangement that would allow it to maintain close economic ties with both Europe and Africa. The French could hardly abandon their colonies for the EEC, though some of their European partners encouraged them to do so. Some way was needed to protect the African and overseas French interests while encouraging France's partners to "Europeanize" the more costly parts of French colonial policy, such as trading preferences in the European market, price supports for tropical agricultural exports, and development aid.

None of France's partners shared these interests. Almost uniformly they objected to the introduction of the question of association into the already complex negotiations in 1956 over the market. Only the Belgians supported the French proposal, more out of courtesy than shared interest. Belgian colonial policy in central Africa did not conflict with the common market, since free trade had existed in the Congo since 1885. At the most the Belgians hoped for some additional development aid for the Congo from the proposed development fund.

The German, Dutch, and Italian governments were firm opponents of the proposed association. The Germans had for some time been constructing a reputation in the developing countries as a non-colonial power, and had no desire to be tarred with the brush of French colonial policy, especially as manifested in Algeria. Moreover, few German trade and financial interests in the developing countries could be found in the proposed associates. The Dutch shared this reluctance for resisting the association. They feared reductions in the Community's commitment to the development of the Italian south if financial resources were demanded for the development fund for the Africans.

The Six were so divided on this issue that it could be resolved only at the highest level, at a meeting in Paris in February, 1957, between French Premier Guy Mollet and German Chancellor Konrad Adenauer. The French made acceptance of the association a *quid pro quo* for their signature on the Treaty of Rome in March, 1957, forcing their partners to yield for what was seen by both sides as a largely symbolic price: no Europeanization of bilateral French price supports, slightly lower EEC preferences for the AAMS than they received from the French (pegged to the lower common external tariff, rather than the French tariff), and special duty-free import quotas for German, Dutch, Belgian, and Italian imports of competing bananas and coffee from nonassociated developing countries.

These conflicts of national interest were bound to persist after 1958. On the one side stood the French, anxious to develop a European commitment to the narrow, protective French colonial policy. They gained allies subsequently among the independent African states and, to a large extent, in the Commission of the European Community. The French commitment to a truly European policy was, and still is, ambiguous. While they have tried to Europeanize the more costly parts of their policy, bilateral French aid, cultural programs and private investments continue to serve important national interests. On the other side, the Germans and Dutch strained to avoid any but the most vague and permissive Community policy toward the developing countries, whereby each member state could pursue its own interests as it saw fit.

These conflict have influenced every subsequent Community policy decision toward the AAMS. They are at the heart, for example, of the problems of the European Development Fund, of the inability of the Commission to harmonize bilateral development aid programs, and of the continual struggles over trade preferences among the Six.

Divergent interests were fundamental to the initial declaration by the Six (in Article I of the convention implementing the Association) that EDF aid was to be considered complementary to the bilateral efforts of the member states. The conflict has continued in the constant debates among the Six about the financing decisions of the EDF. France's partners are rightly afraid, for example, that French interests will benefit disproportionately from the EDF.

This conflict has been an important obstacle to the extension of Community competence over more general development aid policy. More will be said on this below, but it is useful to note that the Commission's effort to develop a common policy for technical assistance through the Technical Assistance Group (under the Council of Ministers) has led only to a minimal sharing of information about specific contracts. The Group has defined few joint projects, let alone a common policy covering all projects.

The original conflict of interests among the Six is continued in a very obvious way in the area of trade policy. France's partners have insisted that the details of the Association (if not the basic commitment) be renewed every five years. The Dutch and Germans, who already had special protocols for vital products, have used these renewals to whittle down the exclusive preferential access the AAMS receive from the Community. Each time the level of the common external tariff on several major tropical products has been reduced, which has meant declining preference for AAMS exports of coffee, cocoa, tea, vanilla, pineapples, and palm oil: The net result is to increase the export possibilities of developing countries where France's partners have important interests. Some officials in Brussels fear that this process will eventually empty the Association of its substance as far as the AAMS are concerned.

For each of the Six, bilateral interests in trade and aid with the developing countries are an integral part of their separately defined world roles. The benefits drawn from these interests in economic and prestige terms, far outweigh the cost savings or increased negotiating strength that might come from a common policy. Moreover, all efforts to define such a common policy flounder on the problem of determining which policies toward which countries. It seems absurd to have to point out that the separate national interests of the Six, in any area of policy, are a possible obstacle to integration and therefore deserve more serious analysis. Yet all too few studies of integration tackle these interests. The experience of the Association shows how important national interests are likely to be in frustrating a common foreign policy.

THE IMPACT OF EXTERNAL PRESSURES

Outside demands and pressures on the Community are also of great importance in deterring or encouraging future integration. These forces are likely to be particularly important in determining the evolution of a common foreign policy. Theorists have tended to assume, on the basis of the (presumed) influence of Soviet power on the original efforts to unify Western Europe, that external pressure will unite the members of a common organization in order to gain the strength to resist.

It is by no means certain that external pressures will unite the Six in a common foreign policy. The history of the Association shows how outside pressures can, in given circumstances, actually divide the members of a community and prevent political integration. The possibility of British entry into the Community in 1963, for example, widened the division that separated France, the Commission, and the AAMS from the Dutch and German opponents of Association. In the name of British entry (to facilitate it) and later in the absence of British entry (to prevent the French veto from closing the door to future ties with the developing parts of the Commonwealth) the Dutch insisted on reductions in the common external tariff for products of interest to the former British colonies, notably coffee, cocoa, tea, and tropical hardwoods. These reductions tended to reverse the commitment to a common preferential policy toward the AAMS.

In the same way, the Dutch, Germans, and Italians accepted the renewal of the Association in 1963 on the condition that France approve a common declaration welcoming applications for association from Commonwealth countries of a similar economic status. This has led to lengthy talks and eventual agreements with Nigeria, Kenya, Tanzania, and Uganda. Although these might appear to expand Community policy, officials lament the weakening of the commitment to the AAMS. Moreover, the creation of these separate association agreements tends further to dilute the chances of creating a coherent Community policy toward the developing countries.

A more recent example of the divisive effect of outside pressure on the Six can be found in the debate over generalized preferences in UNCTAD, the OECD, and among the Six. This is not the place for detailed discussion of generalized preferences, but in the context of this debate the Americans put considerable pressure on the Six to reduce their commitment to the AAMS in return for American agreement to the general system. The initial American price was an end to all preferential trading access in both directions. Later, this stand was reduced to demanding an end to the preferential entry the AAMS granted the Six in Africa.

This demand was bound to exploit the division between the French position on Association policy and that of the Dutch and Germans. The two latter governments began to put pressure on the AAMS to end the preferences they granted the Six in return for the generalized system. The French and the AAMS opposed this demand, arguing that the two issues were quite separate. The Africans were particularly committed to these preferences. They feared that ending them would make the Six increasingly less inclined to grant the important preferences the Africans needed in the Community. The issue became bitter and divisive during the 1969 Association renewal negotiations and led ultimately to a feeling among the Africans and in the Commission that the Six had weakened their commitment to a common policy by pressing the point.

External pressures can as easily exploit the divisions among the members of a regional community as they can unit them in a common stand. There is no guarantee that pressures from outside on agricultural or monetary policy, or even European fears about American investments in Europe will automatically unite the Six in the defense of a common foreign policy. The members may well feel they have more to gain by responding in separate, national ways.

THE CHANGING INSTITUTIONAL BALANCE

Divisions of interest and outside pressures have had a devastating effect on the operation of the Community institutions themselves. Some observers argue that the failure in 1965 to extend the Commission's financial resources and the power of the European Parliament was the turning point for the common institutions of the Community. It can be argued from the experience of the Association that the decline began much earlier.

The divisions among the Six over the Association made it hard for the Commission to foster the process of political integration. From the very start the Commission's neutrality was suspect. The first Commissioner responsible for Association policy was a Frenchman, as was most of the initial staff. This was to be expected, since most of the countries concerned were French colonies. But as a result, France's partners distrusted the operations of the French African system even more. They suspected that Paris would make all the policy decisions for the Africans and make it impossible for France's partners to sell or invest in French Africa. Once the AAMS became independent, other well-entrenched mechanisms would force the Association to serve French interests: the franc zone would make payments from Africa in currencies other than the franc difficult, if not impossible; the policy choices of the Africans would now be determined by key French advisers and technical assistance personnel. It is certainly true that the French have an enormous advantage over the other five in these countries, having been there so exclusively for so long. Moreover, there is very little doubt that even after independence, the former French colonies among the AAMS remain largely dependent on the French for their economic andsocial development. The fears of France's partners are not unfounded.

More important here, however, is the impact of this mistrust on the attitudes of France's partners toward the Commission. The Commission has always been seen as an advocate of French interests and more recently of the AAMS themselves, rather than a neutral spokesman for the Community interest. This makes it nearly impossible for the Commission to play the role of "motor of integration" and make proposals that foster further integration among the Six in all areas of policy. Whereas in other policy areas the Commission can sometimes count on Dutch and German support for enlarging its scope and powers (though this support has declined of late), these governments distrusted the Commission in the area of Association policy. Its strongest supporter for a common policy, France, was its weakest ally in general institutional terms.

The absence of allies for the Commission has had a major role in its inability to develop a common Association policy. In renewal negotiations and in the common institutions with the AAMS, for example, the Six have insisted that the Community viewpoint be presented by the President of the Council of Ministers, rather than by the Commission, as in the East African and Nigerian negotiations. The Commission has continually sought and been refused the role of negotiator for the renewal talks. This has considerably reduced the ability of the Commission to find compromise positions among the Six and to make concessions for the Community with the AAMS as it was able to do in the Kennedy Round. The Commission's role has been reduced to that of technical secretary for lower levels of the talks.

In reaction, the Commission has had to fight for a common policy in the preparatory talks among the Six in the Council of Ministers. Here too, the Commission has been put on the defensive. Having no authority to make proposals to the Council on the Association (except for trade and agricultural questions), the Commission has tried to gather together a consensus among the Six through "communications" to the Council. Although these have been important in defining the frame of reference for future commitments, the Commission has not been able to play a continuing role in the elaboration of a Community position. For serious definitions of the Community view, the Six have preferred to use those forums in which they control the flow of decisions: the AAMS Group and the Committee of Permanent Representatives. During the past ten years, these organs have begun to occupy the central position in the definition of a Community position for this as well as other areas of Community policy. What this means in practice is that the Commission's suggestions are usually changed beyond recognition as the deputies compromise national interests, ultimately up to the level of the President of the Council.

As a corollary, the Commission's role as technical adviser to the Six has been increasingly threatened by the unofficial but important Secretariat of the Council of Ministers. The vital task of setting viewpoints down on paper and seeking compromise proposals has begun to shift to the Council Secretariat, away from the Commission. More than one Commission official has expressed private concern about this trend, which tends to erode the Commission's standing as advocate for the common interest.

The member states have pushed beyond the question of negotiating forums in their effort to keep the Commission from violating important interests. An obvious example in the case of the Association has been the growth of the EDF Committee, which brings together representatives of the member states and the Commission in order to review all AAMS requests for EDF assistance. The EDF Committee had no formal standing until 1964, but since that time has given the member states a regular opportunity to pressure the Commission in its supposedly independent administration of the EDF. This is hardly surprising, given the size of the Fund, and the Commission has cooperated in the work of the Committee, which it chairs, in order to try to build a community of interest around the EDF. The Commission has been unable, however, to push common interests in the area of general development aid policy.

One final example of the institutional struggle involves the issue of direct representation of the EDF in the AAMS. The Commission has made frequent efforts to expand its role as spokesman for the Six by gaining the approval of the member states for quasi-diplomatic representation of the EDF in Africa. None of the Six, however, will allow a common voice to speak for all of them in the associates. The Commission has been forced to make do with the less politically significant, more technical solution described below.

The Commission's various efforts to expand its authority over development aid policy with limited support from the Six have been made more difficult by the existence of splits within its own ranks over the direction of Community policy. The General Directorate for Development Aid, responsible for the Association, favors policies that guarantee an exclusive commitment to the AAMS. The General Directorate for External Relations, on the other hand, which is responsible for all other Community ties with the developing countries, favors a silution of the exclusive commitment to the AAMS. The General Directorate for Agriculture has also been reluctant to approve regulations for the AAMS which might threaten Community protection for farmers in the Six. It has, for example, resisted the idea of duty-free imports of competing products from the AAMS, such as sugar and vegetable oils, or of processed agricultural products such as pineapple juice.

Under pressure from the Six, the Commission has reacted in ways that further obstruct political integration. Once the Commission defines a coherent viewpoint, it then has to define a strategy for dealing with the Council. The most natural choice, under pressure, is to emphasize its technical expertise, rather than its political position, since technical proposals are less open to political challenge.

In taking this apolitical stand, the Commission has moved in an even less integrative direction in dealing with the Six, trying to carve out a role for itself as their *equal*, rather than their spokesman. This attempt to become a seventh Community actor is particularly apparent with regard to the EDF. When the Six resisted Commission efforts to establish an EDF presence in the AAMS, for example, the Commission created a separate agency under private Belgian law, the Association Européene pour la Coopération, staffed, financed, and controlled by the EDF. The objective, beyond short-term technical assistance contracts (impossible inside the Commission) was to finance the establishment of EDF missions in the AAMS. This was done, however, by formally emphasizing the technical role of the missions, and avoiding any implication that they might speak for anyone other than the EDF.

Through choices of this kind, the Commission has been able to win acceptance from the Six and from outside countries, as an actor with regard to development aid in the international system. But this is not a step in an integrative direction; it means the Commission is accepted alongside the member states, rather than as their spokesman and eventual replacement.

The emergence of the Commission as a seventh actor has had considerable importance for the activity of the interest groups and elites which theorists expect to provide functional support for political integration. According to the theory, the emerging Community actor should draw an increasing flow of interest group and elite activity to itself away from national centers of power. The Commission has worked hard to build up a community of interest groups and elite support for the Association policy. Initially the only interest groups involved were of French or African nationality. The Commission used the EDF to widen this circle, awarding a good proportion of technical assistance contracts to non-French firms, and promoting construction contract awards that grouped French firms with partners from the other member states. The result has indeed been an increase in interest group activity in Brussels. But this has not occurred at the expense of interest group activity in the member states. For the interest groups, the EDF represents new, rather than replacement, business. Their Brussels activity reinforces the character of the Commission, a seventh actor in the Community sphere.

The same pattern exists with regard to elites in the member states. Here too the Commission has worked long hours to bring development aid officials in the Six together with Commission officials and with their counterparts in other countries. National ministries have usually responded by creating a special section for relations with the Community (often a part of a general coordinating body for relations with the Community). But in no case do ministry officials feel that they are redirecting their activity toward a new center of power. Rather they are coordinating their work with that of yet another international aid donor. This too reinforces the seventh actor nature of the Commission's program. Moreover, contacts (except in the case of France) between the EDF and national aid officials do not cut very deeply into national elites. In Germany for example, officials of the Kreditanstalt für Wiederaufbau, which handles most German aid programs, report almost no contacts with the EDF.

Another possible source of functional and political support for common aid policy is the European Parliament. As with other areas of Community policy, there is an active parliamentary lobby in behalf of the Association. The parliamentarians face three obstacles, however, in providing meaningful support for political integration. Their views on the Association are closest to the African/French/Commission pole, which reduces their influence with the other member states. The Parliament has, moreover, no significant statutory powers with regard to the Association. Finally, few parliamentarians carry back to their national parliaments strong policy statements or legislative proposals on the Association, as is true of parliamentary behavior in almost all areas of Community activity.

The experience of the Association indicates that functional support for political integration will be difficult to come by, especially with regard to foreign policy questions. Only if governments actively encouraged functional interests to redirect their activity to the Community level might such support develop. So many vital interests are protected by bilateral development aid policies that such a move is unlikely.

CONCLUSION

The history of the Association of the Community with the AAMS suggests some of the enormous difficulties the former faces in trying to carve out a common external policy. Existing theories of integration have suggested a gradual coalescing of points of view, following an internal functional logic in response to pressures from the outside, and with coaxing from the central mediating organ and changes in the activities of elites and interest groups. This is clearly far too simple a blueprint to explain and predict developments in the Community.

At the center of the Community operation, in practice, is a more traditional diplomatic process. National interests, separately defined, are the critical if not the only building blocks in a Community position. If a common policy is to exist at all these interests need to coincide, which is hardly likely to be the case on any specific policy. If national interests diverge, any common point of view, however limited, depends on a perceived equality of costs and advantages. A precarious consensus on policy can, moreover, be easily disturbed by pressures on one or another member from outside the Community.

This diplomatic process places severe limits on the ability of the central organ to mediate conflicts and emerge as spokesman for the member states. The reaction of the Commission, under pressure, is to seek independence by establishing itself as a separate, acceptable, but unthreatening partner for the member states. The potential integrator becomes simply a seventh actor in the Community.

This development, in turn, reduces the integrative impact of the actions of national elites and interest groups. Without a commitment by member governments to a community process, elites and interests look to the center only for additional business, thus reinforcing its separate, almost equal character.

This is a discouraging profile of the Community process for those who hope for a common Community foreign policy in the near future. Nor will the picture change in an enlarged Community. The lesson of the Association seems to be that the revolution in the international system that regional political integration is meant to represent is still more a figment of the theorist's imagination than a reality.

ABOUT THE EDITOR AND THE CONTRIBUTORS

STEVEN J. WARNECKE is Executive Secretary of City University of New York's Graduate Division European Studies Committee and also teaches at CUNY-Richmond. His articles on European politics and integration have appeared in American and European journals. He has lectured at several European universities.

GORDON M. ADAMS is an Assistant Professor of Political Science at Columbia University. He has published work on European political integration and various articles in *agenor: european review*, and is working on a study of technology and politics in the United Kingdom.

RALF DAHRENDORF is a Member of the Commission of the European Communities.

WILLIAM DIEBOLD, JR., presently a senior research fellow, has been on the staff of the Council on Foreign Relations since 1939. He has concentrated on U.S. foreign economic policy, Western European integration, and international economic relations. Among his books are *Trade and Payments in Western Europe, The Schuman Plan*, and *The U.S. and the Industrial World*, which will appear in 1972.

HEINZ HARTMANN, who received his Ph.D. from Princeton, is Professor of Sociology at Muenster University, West Germany. He has been a Visiting Professor at the University of Hamburg, Columbia University, and the Institute of Higher Studies in Vienna. He is editor of the social science quarterly, *Soziale Welt*.

LOUIS G. M. JAQUET is Director General of the Netherlands Society for International Affairs and editor of the *Internationale Spectator*.

UWE KITZINGER is Fellow and Investment Bursar of Nuffield College, Oxford, Visiting Professor at the University of Paris VIII, and a former Visiting Professor at Harvard. He is editor of the *Journal of Common Market Studies* and author, *inter alia*, of *German Electoral Politics, Britain, Europe and Beyond*, and *The Second Try*.

HARALD B. MALMGREN is a consulting economist and professorial lecturer at John Hopkins University. He was formerly assistant special representative for trade negotiations in the White House.

ANDREW J. PIERRE is on the studies staff of the Council on Foreign Relations where he is presently writing a book on European security and American policy. Previously he was at the Hudson Institute and the Brookings Institution, and has also taught at Columbia. His book *Nuclear Politics: The British Experience with an Independent Strategic Force 1939-1970* was published in 1972.

CHRISTOPHER WRIGHT is Director of the Institute for the Study of Science in Human Affairs at Columbia University and member of the Faculty of the School of International Affairs. His teaching has been in the areas of comparative government and science and of world politics.